Branding You Mastery

Crafting a Unique Personal Brand for Success

Moe Nawaz

Roy Smoothe

THE DUKE

Publishers details

Duke Brothers Ltd
30th Floor
Leadenhall Building
122 Leadenhall Street
London. EC3V 4AB
United Kingdom
Tel. 0207 5161 001
www.moenawaz.com

Legal Notice

This Book Is Not Legal Advice

Although we are going to give you a lot of valuable information in this book, you must understand that this book is not legal or business advice. Moreover, reading this book will not establish a consultant–client relationship between us. The only way that we can give you legal or business advice is if you engage one of us. To engage Roy Smoothe or Moe Nawaz, you must sign a written agreement, called an engagement letter, which sets forth the terms of my representation of you and the details of our consultant–client relationship, including the cost.

Only after you have engaged one or both of us as your Consultant by signing an engagement letter, We will be able to give you advice. Until that time, however, we can only help you educate yourself by providing you with some useful information about branding yourself and growing your business.

About the Author: Moe Nawaz

Visionary Mentor and Strategic Advisor to Industry Leaders

Moe Nawaz, the author of "Scaling Success: The Leader's Playbook for Sustainable Business Growth," brings over four decades of unparalleled experience in business growth and leadership development to this comprehensive guide. As a trusted mentor and strategic advisor to Fortune 500 and FTSE 100 leaders, Moe has been at the forefront of empowering visionary leaders and transforming organisations on a global scale.

Moe's journey began in the trenches of entrepreneurship, where he founded and scaled several successful companies. These firsthand experiences taught him the raw, unvarnished truth about growth—the sleepless nights, the weight of critical decisions, and the thrill of breakthrough success. Most importantly, they instilled in him the understanding that sustainable growth isn't just about inflating numbers; it's about building something enduring and meaningful.

Over the decades, Moe has guided CEOs and executive teams through complex challenges including market expansion, operational optimization, leadership development, and cultural transformation. His expertise extends to navigating mergers and acquisitions, helping startups secure funding and scale operations, and revitalizing the growth trajectories of established corporations.

As the author of several influential leadership books on Amazon including "The Leadership Mindset," and "7 Habits of Highly Successful Leaders,", "Mentored To Lead," and "Scaling Succes" Moe draws upon extensive research, insights, and firsthand experiences to provide a comprehensive exploration of the qualities and strategies that define truly great visionary leadership.

Despite not having formal education qualifications, Moe is widely recognized as an expert in strategic planning, change management, and leadership development. His practical wisdom and innovative strategies have made him a sought-after speaker, executive mentor, and thought leader, sharing his expertise at prestigious conferences, universities, and corporate events worldwide.

Specializing in working with 8 and 9-figure business leaders, Moe's methodology and systems are designed to add tens of millions, if not hundreds of millions, to the organisations he partners with. While individual business owners and CEOs may know 99% more about their industries inside out, it's Moe's 1% of specialized knowledge that consistently adds substantial value to their bottom lines.

Moe's unwavering commitment to empowering visionary leaders and catalyzing large-scale positive impact has cemented his reputation as a trailblazing authority in transformative business leadership. Through "Scaling Success" and his broader body of work, he continues to inspire a new generation of leaders to embrace the qualities required to forge their own industry-defining legacies.

Moe's and Roy's successes, challenges, and insights have been invaluable in refining and expanding the strategies presented here in this book.

To find out more about working with Moe Nawaz, visit his website www.moenawaz.com

About the Author: Roy Smoothe

Author, Presenter, Producer, Publisher, Speaker, and Branding Genius Roy Smoothe is affectionately known as 'The Cool Branding Guy' He is the renowned founder of 'Smoothe Mixx' the World's #1 Motivation & Music Label with over 400 million Streams across global music and social media platforms.

His cool, unique, and distinctive company combines fashion, music, branding, and cutting-edge audio production to create world-class projects and high-impact initiatives that improve the way people live, learn, work, and do business.

He is admired for providing only the very best service to his clients. Roy travels internationally as a branding mentor, advisor, and strategist who looks at a client's objectives and the results they are trying to achieve to construct a tailored and measurable branding strategy to reach them.

To stand out of the crowd you need to be different and that's what Roy does best. Many high-profile, successful individuals and businesses recognize the value of his Cool Branding Concepts with which he has helped individuals and businesses around the world, to increase brand awareness, generate new business leads & increase sales through referrals & recommendations.

Roy's kind heart, determined spirit, and bold mindset are focused on ensuring his clients grab all attention within their space to keep them ahead of their competitors. He focuses on making real connections, demonstrating integrity in all communications, and building long-standing relationships that last.

When you see him in person, you'll know...Roy's speeches, workshops, and seminars are immensely interactive, fun, and packed with wisdom, insights, and golden nuggets that will take you to the next level in your personal or business life.

Find out more about working with Roy at www.smoothemixx.com

Contents

Chapter 1

Understanding the Personal Branding Landscape

1. Introduction to Personal Branding

In a interconnected and highly competitive professional world, personal branding has become more than just a buzzword—it's a necessity for career success and business growth. Whether you're a consultant, accountant, lawyer, mentor, coach, trainer, or solopreneur, your personal brand is the unique combination of skills, experiences, and personality that you want the world to see. It's the telling of your story, and the impression people gain from your online and offline presence.

Personal branding is not about creating a false image or pretending to be someone you're not. Instead, it's about strategically and accurately communicating your value to those who are most interested in your services. It's about standing out from the crowd, being known for your expertise, and creating a lasting impression that opens doors to new opportunities.

The concept of personal branding has evolved significantly over the past few decades. What began as a tool primarily used by celebrities and high-profile executives has now become essential for professionals at all levels. The digital age has democratized personal branding, giving everyone the tools to build and manage their professional reputation online.

For consultants, a strong personal brand can attract high-value clients and speaking engagements. Accountants and lawyers can use personal branding to establish trust and credibility in a field where reputation is paramount. Mentors and coaches can leverage their personal brand to showcase their expertise and attract mentees or clients. Trainers can use it to fill their workshops and courses. Solopreneurs, operating in an increasingly crowded marketplace, can utilize personal branding to differentiate themselves and carve out a unique niche.

The benefits of a well-crafted personal brand are numerous:

1. Increased visibility and recognition in your industry
2. Enhanced credibility and perceived expertise
3. Higher-quality professional opportunities
4. The ability to command premium prices for your services
5. A stronger network of professional contacts
6. Greater career resilience and adaptability

However, building a personal brand requires more than just setting up a LinkedIn profile or starting a blog. It demands a strategic approach, consistency, authenticity, and a deep understanding of your target audience. It also requires staying abreast of the latest trends and technologies that shape how we communicate and connect professionally.

In this chapter, we'll explore the evolution of personal branding, examine how it has been transformed by the digital age, and look at current trends shaping the personal branding landscape. We'll also delve into industry-specific considerations, helping you understand how to tailor your personal branding efforts to your unique professional context.

By the end of this chapter, you'll have a comprehensive understanding of what personal branding means in today's professional world, why it's crucial for your success, and how you can start thinking strategically about your own personal brand. Let's begin this journey by looking at how the concept of personal branding has developed over time, starting with the groundbreaking work of management guru Tom Peters.

2. The Development of Personal Branding Concept

The concept of personal branding, while seemingly modern, has roots that stretch back decades. However, it was Tom Peters who truly brought the idea into the mainstream business consciousness with his 1997 article in Fast Company magazine, titled "The Brand Called You."

Case Study: Tom Peters - "The Brand Called You"

Tom Peters, already a respected management guru, revolutionized how professionals think about their careers with his seminal article. Peters argued that in an increasingly competitive job market, individuals needed to think of themselves as brands, much like companies do. He wrote, "We are CEOs of our own companies: Me Inc. To be in business today, our most important job is to be head marketer for the brand called You."

Peters' article came at a pivotal time. The rise of the internet was beginning to transform how people communicated and did business. The traditional notion of a "job for life" was fading, and professionals were increasingly moving between companies and even careers. In this context, Peters' ideas about personal branding struck a chord.

Key points from Peters' concept include:

1. Differentiation: Just as companies strive to differentiate their products, individuals need to identify and promote their unique value proposition.

2. Visibility: Peters emphasized the importance of making your work visible within your organization and industry.

3. Project-based thinking: He encouraged professionals to think of their careers as a series of projects rather than a linear progression.

4. Network building: Peters stressed the importance of building a strong professional network, which he saw as crucial for personal brand development.

5. Continuous learning: He advocated for constant skill development to stay relevant and valuable in a changing job market.

The impact of Peters' work was profound. It sparked a new way of thinking about career development and professional identity. In the years following the article's publication, personal branding became a topic of discussion in business schools, career counseling sessions, and boardrooms around the world.

Historical Perspective on Personal Branding

While Peters popularized the term, the concept of personal branding has deeper roots:

1. Early 20th Century: Dale Carnegie's 1936 book "How to Win Friends and Influence People" can be seen as an early precursor to personal branding, focusing on personal development and relationship building.

2. 1950s-1960s: The rise of television brought the power of personal image into sharp focus, with politicians and business leaders becoming increasingly aware of how they presented themselves to the public.

3. 1980s: With the publication of "Positioning: The Battle for Your Mind" by Al Ries and Jack Trout, the idea of positioning oneself in the marketplace gained traction.

4. 1990s: The dot-com boom saw the rise of high-profile tech entrepreneurs, who often became brands in their own right.

Key Milestones in Personal Branding Development

1. 1997: Tom Peters' "The Brand Called You" article is published.

2. Early 2000s: The launch of social media platforms like LinkedIn (2003) and Facebook (2004) provides new tools for personal brand building.

3. 2005: The term "social media" gains widespread use, marking the beginning of a new era in personal branding.

4. 2006: Twitter launches, offering a platform for real-time personal brand management.

5. 2010s: The rise of influencer marketing further blurs the lines between personal and corporate branding.

6. 2020: The COVID-19 pandemic accelerates the importance of digital personal branding as remote work becomes widespread.

The Evolution of Personal Branding in the Digital Age

The digital revolution has dramatically changed how personal branding is approached:

1. Democratization: Digital platforms have made personal branding accessible to everyone, not just high-profile individuals.

2. Increased Visibility: Online presence means personal brands are always "on," requiring careful management.

3. Data-Driven Approach: Analytics tools allow for more strategic and measurable personal branding efforts.

4. Multi-Platform Presence: Professionals now need to manage their brand across various digital platforms.

5. Content Creation: The ability to create and share content has become a key component of personal branding.

6. Global Reach: Digital platforms allow personal brands to reach a global audience, transcending geographical boundaries.

As we move forward in this chapter, we'll explore how these developments have shaped the current personal branding landscape, and how professionals like you can leverage these changes to build a powerful personal brand. Next, we'll look at how personal branding has evolved in the media industry, using Oprah Winfrey's remarkable career as a case study.

3. Personal Branding in the Media Industry

The media industry has long been at the forefront of personal branding, with personalities often becoming as famous as the content they produce. To understand the power and evolution of personal branding in media, let's examine the career of one of the most successful personal brands in the industry: Oprah Winfrey.

Case Study: Oprah Winfrey's Brand Evolution

Oprah Winfrey's journey from local TV journalist to global media mogul is a masterclass in personal brand building and evolution. Her career spans over four decades, during which she has consistently adapted her brand to changing media landscapes while maintaining her core identity.

Early Career and Brand Foundations:

Oprah began her career as a news anchor in Nashville in 1971. Even in these early days, her empathetic interview style and ability to connect with people set her apart. These qualities would become cornerstone elements of her personal brand.

The Oprah Winfrey Show (1986-2011):

Launching her talk show in 1986, Oprah revolutionized the format. She brought a level of intimacy and authenticity to daytime television that was unprecedented. Her brand became synonymous with emotional honesty, personal growth, and the power of conversation.

Key brand elements during this phase:

1. Authenticity: Oprah shared her own struggles, making her relatable to her audience.

2. Trust: She became a trusted confidante for celebrities and everyday people alike.

3. Empowerment: Her show often focused on self-improvement and overcoming adversity.

Expanding the Brand:

As her popularity grew, Oprah strategically expanded her brand:

1. Harpo Productions (1986): By forming her own production company, Oprah gained control over her content and brand.

2. O, The Oprah Magazine (2000): This publication extended her brand into print media, reaching audiences beyond her TV show.

3. Oprah's Book Club (1996): This segment of her show dramatically impacted the publishing industry and cemented her influence on American culture.

4. philanthropic efforts: Oprah's charitable work, including The Oprah Winfrey Leadership Academy for Girls, added depth to her brand and showcased her commitment to giving back.

OWN: Oprah Winfrey Network (2011-present):

After ending her talk show, Oprah launched her own TV network. This move represented a significant evolution of her brand, transitioning from a personality to a media owner.

Digital Adaptation:

Recognizing the shift towards digital media, Oprah has maintained her brand's relevance through:

1. Social media presence: Active engagement on platforms like Twitter and Instagram.

2. Oprah.com: A digital hub for her brand, offering articles, videos, and resources.

3. Podcasts: Leveraging audio content to reach audiences in new ways.

Core Brand Attributes:

Throughout her career, certain elements of Oprah's brand have remained consistent:

1. Emotional connection: An ability to relate to and move her audience.

2. Aspiration: Encouraging personal growth and self-improvement.

3. Quality: Associated with high-quality, meaningful content.

4. Trustworthiness: Maintaining credibility and integrity.

Lessons from Oprah's Brand Evolution:

1. Consistency is key: While Oprah's brand has evolved, her core values and attributes have remained consistent.

2. Adapt to changing media landscapes: Oprah has successfully transitioned from traditional TV to cable network ownership to digital platforms.

3. Diversification: By expanding into various media forms, Oprah has created multiple touchpoints for her audience.

4. Authenticity builds trust: Oprah's willingness to share personal struggles has created a strong bond with her audience.

5. Use your platform responsibly: Oprah's philanthropic efforts have added depth and purpose to her brand.

The Impact of Media Platforms on Personal Branding

Oprah's journey illustrates how media platforms have shaped personal branding:

1. Television: Allowed for visual and emotional connection with audiences on a mass scale.

2. Print Media: Offered a way to provide more in-depth content and reach audiences in a different context.

3. Digital Platforms: Enabled direct communication with audiences and provided new ways to share content.

4. Social Media: Allowed for real-time interaction and more personal glimpses into a brand.

5. Podcasts and Streaming: Offered new ways to reach audiences on-demand and in more intimate settings.

Lessons for Other Professionals:

While few will achieve Oprah's level of fame, her branding strategies offer valuable lessons for consultants, coaches, and other professionals:

1. Identify your unique strengths and consistently showcase them.

2. Be willing to evolve your brand as your industry changes.

3. Maintain authenticity to build trust with your audience.

4. Diversify your brand across different platforms to reach a wider audience.

5. Use your expertise and influence to make a positive impact, which in turn strengthens your brand.

As we move forward, we'll explore how the digital transformation has further revolutionized personal branding, opening up new possibilities for professionals in all industries.

4. Digital Transformation of Personal Branding

The digital revolution has fundamentally transformed the landscape of personal branding, democratizing the ability to build and maintain a professional image. To illustrate this transformation, let's examine the career of Gary Vaynerchuk, a pioneering figure in leveraging digital platforms for personal branding.

Case Study: Gary Vaynerchuk's Transition to Digital Marketing

Gary Vaynerchuk's journey from wine retailer to digital marketing mogul exemplifies the power of digital platforms in personal branding.

Early Career:

Vaynerchuk began his career working in his family's wine store. In 2006, he launched "Wine Library TV," a daily webcast about wine. This move marked his first step into digital content creation and personal branding.

Key Elements of Vaynerchuk's Digital Branding Strategy:

1. Content Creation: Vaynerchuk produces a vast amount of content across multiple platforms, including YouTube videos, podcasts, and social media posts.

2. Platform Diversification: He maintains a presence on nearly every major social media platform, tailoring his content to each one's unique characteristics.

3. Authenticity: Vaynerchuk is known for his unfiltered, direct communication style, which resonates with his audience and sets him apart.

4. Adaptability: He quickly adopts new platforms and technologies, often being an early user of emerging social media tools.

5. Value-First Approach: Much of Vaynerchuk's content provides actionable advice and insights, establishing him as a thought leader.

6. Personal-Professional Blend: He skillfully mixes personal anecdotes with professional advice, creating a multi-dimensional brand.

Evolution of Vaynerchuk's Brand:

1. Wine Expert to Digital Guru: Vaynerchuk transitioned from a niche wine expert to a broadly recognized digital marketing authority.

2. Entrepreneur to Influencer: He leveraged his business success to become a influential figure in entrepreneurship and marketing circles.

3. Speaker and Author: His digital presence led to opportunities in traditional media, including bestselling books and high-profile speaking engagements.

4. Agency Founder: Vaynerchuk's personal brand became the foundation for VaynerMedia, his digital agency.

Lessons from Vaynerchuk's Digital Branding Success:

1. Embrace new platforms early

2. Consistently deliver valuable content

3. Be authentic and transparent

4. Adapt your message to different platforms while maintaining a consistent core brand

5. Use your personal brand to drive business growth

The Role of Social Media and Online Platforms

Social media and online platforms have revolutionized personal branding in several key ways:

1. Accessibility: Anyone with internet access can now build a personal brand, leveling the playing field for professionals across industries.

2. Direct Communication: Platforms allow for direct interaction with audiences, bypassing traditional gatekeepers.

3. Real-Time Engagement: Brands can be built and managed in real-time, allowing for immediate responses to trends or feedback.

4. Data-Driven Insights: Analytics tools provide detailed information about audience engagement, allowing for more targeted branding efforts.

5. Multimedia Expression: Various content formats (text, images, video, audio) enable multifaceted brand expression.

6. Global Reach: Digital platforms allow personal brands to reach a global audience, transcending geographical boundaries.

7. Niche Specialization: Online platforms make it easier to find and connect with niche audiences.

Adapting Personal Brands to the Digital Landscape

For consultants, accountants, lawyers, mentors, coaches, trainers, and solopreneurs, adapting to the digital landscape is crucial. Here are key strategies:

1. Develop a Strong Online Presence:

- Create a professional website that showcases your expertise
- Maintain active, professional profiles on relevant social media platforms
- Regularly update your LinkedIn profile with achievements and skills

2. Content Marketing:

- Share valuable, industry-specific content through blogs, videos, or podcasts
- Use SEO strategies to increase visibility in search results
- Engage with your audience through comments and discussions

3. Network Digitally:

- Participate in online professional groups and forums
- Attend and host virtual events or webinars
- Collaborate with other professionals for cross-promotion

4. Showcase Expertise:

- Publish articles on platforms like Medium or LinkedIn
- Offer free resources or tools related to your expertise
- Participate in or host Twitter chats or LinkedIn Live sessions

5. Personalize Your Brand:

- Share behind-the-scenes glimpses of your work life
- Tell your professional story through various digital mediums
- Use consistent branding elements across all platforms

6. Leverage Video:

- Create short, informative videos for platforms like YouTube or TikTok
- Use live video features on social media for real-time engagement
- Incorporate video into your website or email marketing

7. Monitor and Manage Your Online Reputation:

- Set up Google Alerts for your name and brand
- Regularly review and respond to online reviews or mentions
- Address negative feedback professionally and constructively

8. Continuous Learning:

- Stay updated on digital marketing trends and platform changes
- Experiment with new features and platforms as they emerge
- Invest in digital skills training to enhance your online presence

By embracing these digital strategies, professionals can significantly expand their reach, enhance their credibility, and build stronger connections with their target audience. The digital transformation of personal branding has opened up unprecedented opportunities for individuals to showcase their expertise and build influential personal brands, regardless of their industry or background.

5. Current Trends in Personal Branding

As the digital landscape continues to evolve, so do the trends in personal branding. Staying abreast of these trends is crucial for professionals looking to maintain a relevant and impactful personal brand. Let's explore some of the most significant current trends in personal branding:

1. Authenticity and Transparency

In an era of carefully curated online personas, authenticity has become a prized attribute. Audiences are increasingly drawn to personal brands that showcase genuine personalities, including vulnerabilities and failures alongside successes.

Key aspects:

- Sharing behind-the-scenes content
- Discussing professional challenges openly
- Admitting mistakes and sharing lessons learned

Example: Brené Brown, a research professor and author, has built her personal brand around vulnerability and authenticity, resonating deeply with her audience.

2. Niche Specialization

As the online space becomes more crowded, carving out a specific niche has become essential for standing out. Professionals are finding success by becoming recognized experts in highly specialized areas.

Key aspects:

- Focusing on a specific subset of your industry
- Becoming the go-to expert for a particular problem or solution
- Creating content that caters to a well-defined audience

Example: Marie Forleo has carved out a niche as a business and life coach for entrepreneurs, particularly focusing on women and creative professionals.

3. Video Content Dominance

Video has become the preferred medium for content consumption across various platforms. Personal brands that effectively leverage video are seeing significant growth in engagement and reach.

Key aspects:

- Short-form videos (TikTok, Instagram Reels, YouTube Shorts)
- Live streaming (Facebook Live, Instagram Live, LinkedIn Live)
- Long-form video content (YouTube, Vimeo)

Example: Gary Vaynerchuk's extensive use of video content across multiple platforms has been a key factor in his brand's growth and engagement.

4. Personal Storytelling

Narrative-driven personal branding is gaining traction. Professionals are using storytelling techniques to make their brands more relatable and memorable.

Key aspects:

- Sharing personal journey and experiences
- Using anecdotes to illustrate professional insights
- Crafting a compelling brand narrative

Example: Oprah Winfrey's personal story of overcoming adversity has been central to her brand and her ability to connect with her audience.

5. Social Responsibility and Advocacy

Personal brands are increasingly expected to stand for something beyond professional success. Many professionals are incorporating social causes and advocacy into their personal branding efforts.

Key aspects:

- Aligning with relevant social causes
- Using platform to raise awareness about important issues
- Demonstrating corporate social responsibility

Example: Blake Mycoskie, founder of TOMS, has made social responsibility a core part of his personal brand, aligning it closely with his company's mission.

6. Personal Newsletters and Podcasts

Direct communication channels like newsletters and podcasts are becoming increasingly popular for personal branding. These mediums allow for deeper engagement with audiences.

Key aspects:

- Regular, value-driven newsletters
- Podcasts focusing on industry insights or personal development
- Building a loyal, engaged subscriber base

Example: Tim Ferriss's podcast and newsletter have become central to his personal brand, allowing him to deeply engage with his audience.

7. Emphasis on Personal Well-being

There's a growing trend of incorporating personal well-being into professional brands. This includes discussions about work-life balance, mental health, and holistic success.

Key aspects:

- Sharing personal wellness practices
- Discussing the importance of work-life balance
- Advocating for mental health awareness in professional contexts

Example: Arianna Huffington has repositioned her personal brand to focus on well-being and productivity, founding Thrive Global after leaving The Huffington Post.

8. AI and Personal Branding

Artificial Intelligence is starting to play a role in personal branding, from content creation to audience analysis.

Key aspects:

- Using AI tools for content optimization
- Leveraging AI for personalized audience engagement
- AI-driven analytics for brand performance

Example: While not tied to a specific individual, many personal brands are beginning to use AI tools like ChatGPT for content ideation and creation.

By understanding and selectively incorporating these trends, professionals can ensure their personal brands remain relevant and impactful. However, it's crucial to remember that trends should be adopted authentically and in alignment with your core brand identity and values.

6. THE PERSONAL BRANDING ECOSYSTEM

Understanding the personal branding ecosystem is crucial for developing a comprehensive and effective personal brand strategy. This ecosystem encompasses various interconnected components that work together to create and maintain your professional image. Let's explore the key elements of this ecosystem:

1. Core Identity

At the heart of your personal brand is your core identity. This includes:

- Your values and beliefs
- Your unique skills and expertise
- Your personality traits
- Your professional goals and vision

Your core identity should remain consistent across all aspects of your brand, serving as the foundation for all your branding efforts.

2. Online Presence

In today's digital age, your online presence is a critical component of your personal brand:

a) Website/Blog: A professional website or blog serves as your digital home base. It should clearly communicate your expertise, showcase your work, and provide valuable content to your audience.

b) Social Media Profiles: Platforms like LinkedIn, Twitter, Instagram, and Facebook allow you to engage with your audience, share content, and build your network.

c) Content Creation: Regular creation of valuable content (articles, videos, podcasts) helps establish your expertise and keeps your audience engaged.

d) Search Engine Optimization (SEO): Ensuring your online content is optimized for search engines increases your visibility to potential clients or employers.

3. Offline Presence

While digital branding is crucial, your offline presence remains important:

a) Networking: Attending industry events, conferences, and meetups helps build face-to-face connections.

b) Public Speaking: Presenting at conferences or workshops enhances your credibility and expands your reach.

c) Published Work: Books, articles in print publications, or research papers can significantly boost your authority in your field.

d) Personal Appearance: Your style, grooming, and body language contribute to your overall brand image in personal interactions.

4. Professional Reputation

Your reputation in your industry is a key part of your personal brand:

a) Work Quality: Consistently delivering high-quality work reinforces your brand's credibility.

b) Client/Colleague Relationships: Positive relationships with clients, colleagues, and peers contribute to a strong professional reputation.

c) Testimonials and Recommendations: Endorsements from others in your field can significantly enhance your brand's credibility.

5. Brand Messaging

How you communicate about yourself and your work is crucial:

a) Elevator Pitch: A concise, compelling description of who you are and what you do.

b) Brand Story: The narrative that explains your professional journey and what sets you apart.

c) Visual Branding: Consistent use of logos, colors, and design elements across all platforms.

6. Continuous Learning and Development

Staying current in your field is essential for maintaining a strong personal brand:

a) Skill Development: Regularly updating and expanding your skill set.

b) Industry Knowledge: Staying informed about the latest trends and developments in your field.

c) Adaptability: Being able to evolve your brand as your industry changes.

7. Network and Collaborations

Your professional network is an integral part of your personal brand ecosystem:

a) Mentors and Advisors: People who guide your professional development.

b) Peers and Colleagues: Your professional community that supports and challenges you.

c) Collaborators: Partners for joint projects that can expand your brand's reach.

8. Measurement and Feedback

Regularly assessing your brand's performance helps you refine and improve:

a) Analytics: Using data from your website and social media to understand your audience and engagement.

b) Feedback: Actively seeking and responding to feedback from clients, colleagues, and mentors.

c) Self-reflection: Continually evaluating how well your brand aligns with your goals and values.

By understanding and nurturing each component of this ecosystem, you can create a robust and authentic personal brand that effectively communicates your value to your target audience.

7. Challenges in the Current Personal Branding Landscape

While personal branding offers numerous opportunities, it also presents several challenges in today's dynamic professional environment. Understanding these challenges is crucial for developing effective strategies to overcome them.

1. Oversaturation and Standing Out

Challenge: With the democratization of personal branding tools, many professionals are actively building their brands, leading to a crowded marketplace.

Impact:

- Increased difficulty in capturing audience attention
- Risk of message dilution in a sea of similar voices

Strategies to overcome:

- Develop a truly unique value proposition
- Focus on niche specialization
- Consistently produce high-quality, valuable content
- Leverage emerging platforms or underutilized features of existing platforms

2. Balancing Personal and Professional Personas

Challenge: The line between personal and professional lives is increasingly blurred in the digital age.

Impact:

- Risk of oversharing personal information
- Potential for personal views to impact professional opportunities

Strategies to overcome:

- Establish clear boundaries for what you share publicly
- Develop a consistent brand voice that authentically represents both personal and professional aspects
- Use platform-specific strategies (e.g., professional content on LinkedIn, more personal on Instagram)

3. Keeping Up with Rapidly Changing Digital Trends

Challenge: The digital landscape is constantly evolving, with new platforms and features emerging regularly.

Impact:

- Risk of brand obsolescence if not adapting to new trends
- Time and resource investment required to stay current

Strategies to overcome:

- Prioritize platforms most relevant to your target audience
- Stay informed through industry news and professional development
- Experiment with new platforms, but focus on those that align with your brand goals

4. Maintaining Authenticity While Strategically Building a Brand

Challenge: Balancing the need for strategic brand building with the desire for authenticity.

Impact:

- Risk of coming across as inauthentic or overly curated

- Potential disconnect between online persona and real-life interactions

Strategies to overcome:

- Share both successes and challenges
- Use storytelling to convey authentic experiences
- Ensure your online brand aligns with your offline behavior

5. Measuring ROI and Effectiveness

Challenge: Quantifying the return on investment for personal branding efforts can be difficult.

Impact:

- Uncertainty about which branding activities are most effective
- Difficulty in justifying time and resources spent on branding

Strategies to overcome:

- Set clear, measurable goals for your personal branding efforts
- Use analytics tools to track engagement and growth
- Regularly assess and adjust your branding strategy based on data

6. Managing Online Reputation and Crisis Response

Challenge: Negative feedback or crises can quickly escalate in the digital space.

Impact:

- Potential long-term damage to personal and professional reputation
- Need for quick and effective crisis management

Strategies to overcome:

- Develop a crisis management plan in advance
- Monitor your online presence regularly
- Respond to criticism professionally and constructively

- Be transparent and accountable when mistakes occur

7. Consistency Across Multiple Platforms

Challenge: Maintaining a consistent brand image and message across various online and offline channels.

Impact:

- Risk of confusing or alienating your audience
- Dilution of brand strength

Strategies to overcome:

- Develop a clear brand style guide
- Plan content strategically across all platforms
- Use tools to manage and schedule content consistently

8. Privacy Concerns and Data Management

Challenge: Balancing the need for online visibility with personal privacy and data security.

Impact:

- Risk of personal information misuse
- Potential for cybersecurity threats

Strategies to overcome:

- Educate yourself on privacy settings across different platforms
- Be strategic about what personal information you share online
- Regularly audit and update your online security measures

By acknowledging these challenges and developing strategies to address them, professionals can build more resilient and effective personal brands. The key is to remain adaptable, authentic, and strategic in your approach to personal branding.

8. Industry-Specific Considerations for Personal Branding

While the core principles of personal branding apply across professions, each industry has its unique considerations. Understanding these nuances is crucial for tailoring your personal brand effectively. Let's explore some industry-specific considerations for the target audience of this book: consultants, accountants, lawyers, mentors, coaches, trainers, and solopreneurs.

Consultants:

- Emphasize expertise and problem-solving skills
- Showcase successful case studies and client testimonials
- Develop thought leadership through articles, whitepapers, or speaking engagements
- Balance confidentiality with the need to demonstrate results
- Consider specializing in a particular niche or industry

Key focus: Demonstrating tangible value and expertise

Accountants:

- Highlight trustworthiness and attention to detail
- Stay updated on financial regulations and share insights
- Use clear, jargon-free communication to explain complex concepts
- Showcase any specialized certifications or expertise
- Consider developing a personal brand around financial education or specific accounting niches

Key focus: Building trust and demonstrating accuracy

Lawyers:

- Balance professionalism with approachability
- Adhere to ethical guidelines and confidentiality requirements
- Showcase expertise through legal publications or commentary on relevant cases
- Develop a personal brand that aligns with your area of practice
- Consider the impact of social media on potential cases or clients

Key focus: Establishing credibility while maintaining ethical standards

Mentors:

- Emphasize experience and the ability to guide others
- Share success stories of mentees (with permission)
- Develop strong interpersonal skills and emotional intelligence
- Create content that provides valuable advice and insights
- Build a network of both mentees and fellow mentors

Key focus: Demonstrating the ability to foster growth in others

Coaches:

- Clearly define your coaching niche and methodology
- Showcase your own personal development journey
- Use various content formats to demonstrate your coaching style
- Obtain and prominently display relevant certifications
- Develop a strong testimonial strategy from successful clients

Key focus: Proving your ability to facilitate positive change

Trainers:

- Demonstrate expertise in your training area
- Showcase your teaching methodology and style
- Develop a portfolio of training materials or sample sessions
- Highlight any industry-specific certifications or experiences
- Use video content to give potential clients a taste of your training style

Key focus: Illustrating your ability to effectively transfer knowledge and skills

Solopreneurs:

- Emphasize your unique selling proposition
- Showcase your versatility and ability to wear multiple hats
- Develop a strong personal story that aligns with your business
- Leverage your personal network for business growth

- Be transparent about being a one-person operation while emphasizing its benefits

Key focus: Differentiating yourself in a competitive market

General Considerations Across Industries:

1. Professional Associations: Engage with and leverage industry-specific associations for networking and credibility.

2. Regulatory Compliance: Be aware of any industry regulations that may impact your personal branding efforts.

3. Continuing Education: Regularly update your skills and knowledge, and make this a part of your brand narrative.

4. Client Confidentiality: Balance the need to showcase your work with respecting client privacy.

5. Digital Presence: Tailor your online presence to platforms most relevant to your industry and target audience.

6. Networking: Focus on building relationships within your industry, both online and offline.

7. Thought Leadership: Develop and share insights specific to your industry to establish authority.

8. Personal vs. Professional Balance: Find the right balance between personal authenticity and professional demeanor for your specific field.

By considering these industry-specific factors, you can create a personal brand that not only stands out but also resonates with your target audience and adheres to the norms and expectations of your profession. Remember, the most effective personal brands are those that authentically represent your unique value proposition while aligning with the needs and expectations of your industry.

9. The Future of Personal Branding

As we look towards the future, personal branding is set to evolve in response to technological advancements, changing social norms, and shifts in the professional landscape. Understanding these potential changes can help professionals stay ahead of the curve and adapt their personal branding strategies accordingly.

Predictions for the next 5-10 years:

1. Increased Integration of AI and Machine Learning:

- AI-powered personal brand management tools will become more sophisticated, helping professionals optimize their online presence.
- Personalized content creation assisted by AI will become more common, allowing for more efficient and targeted messaging.
- Predictive analytics will play a larger role in personal branding strategy, helping individuals anticipate trends and audience preferences.

2. Virtual and Augmented Reality Experiences:

- Personal brands may extend into virtual spaces, with professionals creating immersive VR portfolios or hosting AR-enhanced networking events.
- Virtual avatars could become an extension of personal brands, representing individuals in digital spaces.

3. Hyper-Personalization:

- Advanced data analytics will enable ultra-targeted personal branding efforts, allowing professionals to tailor their message to specific audience segments with unprecedented precision.
- Real-time brand adjustments based on audience interaction and feedback will become more common.

4. Emphasis on Digital Ethics and Privacy:

- As concerns about data privacy grow, personal brands that prioritize ethical data use and transparency will gain favor.
- Blockchain technology might be used to verify credentials and experiences, adding a new layer of trust to personal branding.

5. Integration of Personal and Professional Lives:

- The line between personal and professional brands may blur further, with authenticity and holistic self-representation becoming increasingly important.

- Work-life integration, rather than work-life balance, may become a key aspect of personal branding.

6. Rise of Micro and Nano Influencers:

- Personal branding will become increasingly important for professionals at all levels, not just high-profile individuals.
- Niche expertise and small, highly engaged followings may be valued over large, less engaged audiences.

7. Sustainability and Social Responsibility:

- Personal brands will likely need to demonstrate a commitment to sustainability and social responsibility to remain relevant and appealing.
- Transparency about one's impact on society and the environment may become a standard expectation.

8. Continuous Learning and Adaptation:

- The ability to quickly learn and adapt to new technologies and trends will become a crucial part of maintaining a relevant personal brand.
- Lifelong learning and skill development will be increasingly integrated into personal brand narratives.

9. Multi-Modal Content:

- Personal branding will likely require proficiency in multiple content formats, including text, audio, video, and potentially VR/AR.
- The ability to adapt one's brand across various platforms and mediums will be crucial.

10. Global and Cross-Cultural Branding:

- As remote work and global collaborations increase, personal brands may need to resonate across cultural boundaries.
- Cultural intelligence and adaptability will become valuable personal brand attributes.

By staying aware of these potential future trends, professionals can position themselves to evolve their personal brands proactively, ensuring continued relevance and impact in an ever-changing professional landscape.

Decision Tree Overview

At the end of each chapter, you'll find a decision tree designed to help you apply the concepts we've discussed. A decision tree is a visual tool that guides you through a series of questions and choices, leading to specific outcomes or actions.

Purpose of Decision Trees in This Book:

1. Practical Application: These trees help you translate the chapter's concepts into actionable steps for your personal branding journey.

2. Personalized Guidance: By following the branches that apply to your situation, you'll receive tailored advice based on your current position and goals.

3. Quick Reference: Use these trees as a quick refresher on key decision points and strategies covered in each chapter.

4. Progress Tracking: As you revisit these trees over time, you can see how your personal branding journey progresses.

5. Complexity Simplification: These trees break down complex branding decisions into manageable steps.

How to Use the Decision Trees:

1. Start at the top with the first question.

2. Follow the branch that best fits your answer.

3. Continue through the tree, answering each question honestly.

4. When you reach an endpoint, you'll have a clear next step or action to take.

Remember, personal branding is an ongoing process. You may find yourself returning to these decision trees at different stages of your career, potentially taking different paths as your brand evolves.

By consistently using these decision trees, you'll be able to methodically build and refine your personal brand, ensuring it always aligns with your current goals and circumstances.

Decision Tree

Start: Do you understand what personal branding is?

• **Yes** → Proceed to **assessing your current brand**

• **No** → **Learn basics of personal branding**

- **Understand key components:**
- Unique skills & experiences
- Professional identity
- Online presence
- Reputation management

Next: Have you assessed your current personal brand?

• **Yes** → Proceed to **identifying brand goals**

• **No** → **Conduct a personal brand audit**

- **Steps to conduct the audit:**
- Review online presence
- Gather feedback from colleagues/clients
- Analyze professional reputation

Next: Do you have clear personal brand goals?

• **Yes** → Proceed to **identifying target audience**

• **No** → **Define your brand goals**

- **Consider the following:**
- Career aspirations
- Desired professional image
- Specific, measurable objectives

Next: Have you identified your target audience?

• **Yes** → Proceed to **analyzing industry trends**

• **No** → **Define your target audience**

- **Focus on:**
- Ideal clients/employers
- Demographics and psychographics
- Audience pain points and needs

Next: Are you aware of current industry trends affecting personal branding?

• **Yes** → Proceed to **developing brand strategy**

• **No → Research industry trends**

- **Key research areas:**
- Competitors' branding strategies
- Successful personal brands in your field
- Emerging platforms and technologies

Next: Do you have a personal branding strategy?

• **Yes → Implement and monitor your strategy**

• **No → Develop your personal branding strategy**

- **Steps to develop your strategy:**
- Choose appropriate platforms
- Create a content plan
- Set a timeline for brand development activities

Final: Implement your personal branding strategy and regularly reassess

Conclusion

Chapter 1 has laid the foundation for understanding the critical importance of personal branding in today's interconnected and competitive professional landscape. We've explored how personal branding has evolved from a tool used primarily by high-profile figures to an essential strategy for professionals across all industries, thanks to the democratization brought about by the digital age.

Through this chapter, you have gained insight into the origins and development of personal branding, from the pioneering concepts introduced by Tom Peters to the contemporary approaches shaped by digital platforms and social media. We also examined industry-specific considerations, recognizing that the impact of personal branding varies across different fields such as consulting, law, accounting, and coaching.

Key takeaways include the realization that a strong personal brand is more than just an online presence—it is a strategic and authentic communication of your unique skills, experiences, and personality that resonates with your target audience. This chapter also highlighted the importance of consistency, authenticity, and adaptability in building a brand that not only stands out but also endures the test of time.

As you move forward, use the principles and insights from this chapter as a compass for your personal branding journey. Reflect on your current brand, assess your goals, and start crafting a brand that truly represents who you are and what you stand for. Remember, in an era where your professional reputation can be as influential as your expertise, investing in your personal brand is not just a career strategy—it is a career necessity.

Chapter 2

Ethical Considerations in Personal Branding

1. Introduction: The Importance of Ethics in Personal Branding

In the pursuit of building a strong personal brand, it's crucial to recognize that ethics play a pivotal role. Ethics in personal branding isn't just about avoiding misconduct; it's about building a sustainable, trustworthy, and authentic professional identity that stands the test of time and scrutiny.

As consultants, accountants, lawyers, mentors, coaches, trainers, and solopreneurs, your personal brand is often synonymous with your professional reputation. In many cases, you are your brand. This reality places an even greater emphasis on ethical considerations, as your actions and public persona directly impact your credibility and the trust others place in you.

Ethical personal branding involves several key principles:

1. Authenticity: Presenting a genuine version of yourself and your capabilities.

2. Transparency: Being open about your qualifications, experiences, and potential conflicts of interest.

3. Responsibility: Using your platform and influence responsibly.

4. Respect: Respecting others' privacy, intellectual property, and professional boundaries.

5. Integrity: Maintaining consistency between your brand promises and your actions.

In today's digital age, where information is readily accessible and easily shared, unethical practices in personal branding can be quickly exposed, leading to severe reputational damage. Conversely, a consistently ethical approach to personal branding can significantly enhance your credibility, foster trust with clients and colleagues, and contribute to long-term professional success.

This chapter will explore various ethical considerations in personal branding, examining real-world examples and providing guidance on navigating complex ethical situations. We'll discuss the challenges of maintaining authenticity in a curated digital world, the importance of transparency in an era of influencer marketing, and the delicate balance between personal and professional life in branding efforts.

By the end of this chapter, you'll have a comprehensive understanding of the ethical landscape in personal branding and be equipped with strategies to build an ethical, powerful, and sustainable personal brand.

2. Authenticity and Transparency in Personal Branding

In the realm of personal branding, authenticity and transparency are not just buzzwords; they are fundamental principles that can make or break your professional reputation. To illustrate the importance and challenges of these concepts, let's examine the case of Rachel Hollis, an author and motivational speaker who faced significant backlash due to issues surrounding authenticity and transparency.

Case Study: Rachel Hollis - Authenticity and Handling Criticism

Rachel Hollis rose to fame with her 2018 self-help book "Girl, Wash Your Face," which propelled her into the spotlight as a motivational speaker and lifestyle guru. Her brand was built on relatability and authenticity, often sharing personal stories of overcoming challenges.

Key aspects of Hollis's initial brand success:

1. Sharing personal struggles and vulnerabilities

2. Offering practical advice based on her experiences

3. Cultivating a sense of friendship and connection with her audience

4. Leveraging social media to create an intimate, behind-the-scenes look at her life

However, Hollis faced significant criticism in 2021 when she made comments that were perceived as privileged and out of touch. In a TikTok video, she compared herself to other "unrelatable" women like Harriet Tubman and Ruth Bader Ginsburg, which many viewed as inappropriate and tone-deaf.

The backlash highlighted several ethical issues in personal branding:

1. Authenticity vs. Performance: Critics argued that Hollis's relatable persona was more performance than genuine authenticity.

2. Responsibility of Influence: As her platform grew, the impact of her words and actions increased, requiring greater responsibility.

3. Handling Criticism: Hollis's initial responses to criticism were perceived as defensive, further damaging her brand.

4. Consistency in Messaging: The incident revealed potential inconsistencies between her brand's message of empowerment and her actual views.

Lessons from the Rachel Hollis case:

1. True Authenticity Requires Consistency: Your brand should reflect your genuine self, values, and beliefs consistently across all platforms and over time.

2. Transparency in Growth and Change: As you evolve personally and professionally, be open with your audience about these changes.

3. Responsible Influence: Recognize the impact of your words and actions on your audience, especially as your influence grows.

4. Graceful Handling of Criticism: Be prepared to address criticism thoughtfully and humbly, viewing it as an opportunity for growth and connection with your audience.

5. Cultural Sensitivity: Be aware of the broader context in which your brand operates, including social and cultural sensitivities.

Balancing Authenticity with Strategic Self-Presentation

While authenticity is crucial, it doesn't mean sharing every aspect of your life or personality. Strategic authenticity in personal branding involves:

1. Selective Sharing: Choose to share aspects of yourself that are genuine and relevant to your professional brand.

2. Consistent Core Values: Ensure that the values you present align with your actual beliefs and actions.

3. Acknowledging Limitations: Be honest about your expertise and experiences. It's okay to not know everything.

4. Genuine Growth: Share your learning journey, including mistakes and lessons learned.

5. Appropriate Vulnerability: Share challenges in a way that adds value to your audience without oversharing.

Transparency in the Age of Influencer Marketing

As personal branding often intersects with influencer marketing, transparency becomes even more critical:

1. Disclosure of Partnerships: Clearly disclose any sponsored content or affiliate relationships.

2. Honest Reviews and Endorsements: Only endorse products or services you genuinely believe in and have experience with.

3. Clear Qualifications: Be upfront about your qualifications, experiences, and any relevant certifications.

4. Transparent Metrics: If you share success metrics, ensure they are accurate and contextually relevant.

5. Behind-the-Scenes Insights: Offer glimpses into your work process to build trust and connection.

Practical Steps for Maintaining Authenticity and Transparency:

1. Regular Self-Reflection: Periodically assess whether your brand truly reflects your current self and values.

2. Seek Feedback: Ask trusted colleagues or mentors if your brand comes across as authentic and transparent.

3. Consistent Messaging: Ensure your message is consistent across all platforms and in-person interactions.

4. Address Mistakes Promptly: If you make a mistake, acknowledge it quickly and sincerely.

5. Ongoing Education: Stay informed about ethics in your industry and in personal branding generally.

6. Clear Communication: Be clear about what your audience can expect from you and deliver on those promises.

By prioritizing authenticity and transparency in your personal branding efforts, you build a foundation of trust with your audience. This trust is invaluable in developing long-term professional relationships and establishing yourself as a credible expert in your field. Remember, in the digital age, inconsistencies or lack of transparency can be quickly exposed, potentially causing significant damage to your brand. On the other hand, a consistently authentic and transparent approach can help you weather challenges and build a resilient, respected personal brand.

3. Social Responsibility and Personal Branding

In today's interconnected world, personal brands are increasingly expected to demonstrate social responsibility. This expectation extends beyond mere lip service to actual engagement with social issues and ethical business practices. To illustrate this concept, let's examine the case of Elon Musk, a figure who has both benefited from and been challenged by his approach to social responsibility in personal branding.

Case Study: Elon Musk - Transparency and Social Responsibility

Elon Musk, the entrepreneur behind Tesla, SpaceX, and now Twitter, has built a personal brand that is intrinsically linked with innovation, sustainability, and pushing the boundaries of technology. His brand exemplifies both the opportunities and challenges of incorporating social responsibility into personal branding.

Key aspects of Musk's brand related to social responsibility:

1. Environmental Focus: Through Tesla, Musk has positioned himself as a champion for sustainable energy and transportation.

2. Space Exploration: With SpaceX, he's framed space exploration as crucial for humanity's long-term survival.

3. Transparency in Communication: Musk is known for his direct communication style, often using Twitter to share company updates and personal views.

4. Technological Innovation: His brand is associated with pushing technological boundaries to solve global problems.

However, Musk's approach to social responsibility has also faced criticism:

1. Worker Rights: Tesla has faced allegations of poor working conditions and anti-union practices.

2. Market Manipulation: Musk's tweets have sometimes led to significant market movements, raising questions about responsible communication.

3. Public Health: During the COVID-19 pandemic, Musk's statements sometimes contradicted public health advice.

4. Free Speech vs. Moderation: His acquisition of Twitter and subsequent policy changes have sparked debates about the balance between free speech and responsible content moderation.

Lessons from Elon Musk's approach to social responsibility:

1. Align Actions with Brand Values: Ensure that your business practices and personal actions align with the social values your brand promotes.

2. Responsible Communication: Recognize the impact of your statements, especially when you have a large platform.

3. Balance Innovation and Responsibility: While pushing boundaries can drive progress, it's crucial to consider the ethical implications of your work.

4. Transparency in Challenges: Be open about the challenges in achieving your social responsibility goals.

5. Stakeholder Consideration: Consider the impact of your actions on all stakeholders, including employees, customers, and the broader community.

Incorporating Social Causes into Personal Brands

For consultants, accountants, lawyers, mentors, coaches, trainers, and solopreneurs, incorporating social responsibility into your personal brand can be powerful but should be done thoughtfully:

1. Authentic Alignment: Choose causes that genuinely align with your values and expertise.

2. Education and Advocacy: Use your platform to educate others about important issues in your field.

3. Pro Bono Work: Offer your services to non-profits or underserved communities.

4. Sustainable Practices: Implement and promote sustainable business practices.

5. Partnerships: Collaborate with organizations that share your values.

6. Transparency in Efforts: Be open about your social responsibility initiatives, including both successes and challenges.

Balancing Profit and Purpose

One of the key challenges in socially responsible personal branding is balancing profit motives with social purpose:

1. Integrated Approach: Rather than treating social responsibility as separate from your core work, integrate it into your overall brand strategy.

2. Long-term Perspective: Recognize that investments in social responsibility can lead to long-term brand value and customer loyalty.

3. Measurable Impact: Set clear, measurable goals for your social impact initiatives.

4. Honest Communication: Be transparent about how you balance profit and purpose. It's okay to acknowledge that you're running a business while also trying to make a positive impact.

5. Continuous Improvement: Regularly assess and improve your social responsibility efforts.

Practical Steps for Incorporating Social Responsibility into Your Personal Brand:

1. Define Your Values: Clearly articulate the social values that are important to you and relevant to your work.

2. Assess Your Impact: Conduct an audit of your current practices to identify areas where you can improve your social impact.

3. Set Clear Goals: Establish specific, measurable objectives for your social responsibility efforts.

4. Communicate Consistently: Regularly share updates on your social responsibility initiatives across your platforms.

5. Collaborate and Learn: Engage with others in your industry who are leading in social responsibility.

6. Be Prepared for Scrutiny: As you promote your social responsibility efforts, be prepared for increased scrutiny and have systems in place to address concerns or criticisms.

7. Continuous Education: Stay informed about social issues relevant to your field and be willing to evolve your approach as new information emerges.

By thoughtfully incorporating social responsibility into your personal brand, you can create a more meaningful and impactful professional presence. This approach not only contributes to positive change but can also enhance your brand's reputation, attract like-minded clients or employers, and provide a sense of purpose in your work. Remember, in the age of conscious consumerism and corporate social responsibility, professionals who demonstrate a genuine commitment to social good often find themselves with a competitive advantage and a more loyal audience.

4. Balancing Personal and Professional Life in Branding

In the digital age, the line between personal and professional life has become increasingly blurred, particularly when it comes to personal branding. This blurring presents both opportunities and challenges for professionals. To illustrate these complexities, let's examine the case of Kim Kardashian, a figure who has masterfully navigated the integration of personal and professional life in her branding efforts.

Case Study: Kim Kardashian - Navigating Personal and Professional Boundaries

Kim Kardashian has built an empire by effectively blending her personal life with her professional endeavors. Her journey from reality TV star to successful entrepreneur and aspiring lawyer offers valuable insights into the delicate balance of personal and professional branding.

Key aspects of Kardashian's personal-professional brand integration:

1. Reality TV Foundation: Kardashian's initial fame came from sharing her personal life on "Keeping Up with the Kardashians," which served as a launchpad for her brand.

2. Social Media Mastery: She uses platforms like Instagram to share both personal moments and promote her businesses, creating a seamless blend of the personal and professional.

3. Family Brand: Kardashian has incorporated her family relationships into her brand, making them a central part of her public image.

4. Business Ventures: Her businesses, such as KKW Beauty and SKIMS, often tie directly into her personal image and lifestyle.

5. Personal Growth Narrative: Kardashian has shared her journey of personal growth, including her pursuit of a legal career, integrating it into her evolving brand.

Challenges and Criticisms:

1. Privacy Concerns: The extensive sharing of personal life has led to issues with privacy and security.

2. Authenticity Questions: The highly curated nature of her personal sharing has sometimes led to accusations of inauthenticity.

3. Controversy Management: Personal actions or statements have sometimes negatively impacted her professional brand.

4. Balancing Serious Pursuits: As Kardashian ventures into more serious professional areas like law, she faces the challenge of balancing this with her existing celebrity image.

Lessons from Kim Kardashian's approach:

1. Strategic Sharing: Be intentional about what aspects of your personal life you share professionally.

2. Consistent Narrative: Ensure that your personal story aligns with and enhances your professional goals.

3. Adaptability: Be willing to evolve your brand as your personal and professional life changes.

4. Boundary Setting: Establish clear boundaries to protect your privacy and mental health.

5. Authenticity in Growth: Share personal growth in a way that adds value to your professional brand.

Balancing Personal and Professional in Your Brand

For consultants, accountants, lawyers, mentors, coaches, trainers, and solopreneurs, finding the right balance between personal and professional branding is crucial:

1. Determine Your Comfort Level: Decide how much of your personal life you're comfortable sharing professionally.

2. Relevance is Key: Share personal aspects that are relevant to your professional brand and add value to your audience.

3. Maintain Professionalism: Ensure that personal sharing doesn't undermine your professional credibility.

4. Use Personal Experiences Strategically: Share personal anecdotes or experiences that illustrate professional points or showcase relevant skills.

5. Be Mindful of Your Industry: Consider industry norms and client expectations when deciding how to blend personal and professional.

6. Consistency Across Platforms: Maintain a consistent persona across different social media platforms, adjusting the tone as appropriate for each.

7. Privacy Protection: Be cautious about sharing information that could compromise your or others' privacy.

Strategies for Effective Personal-Professional Integration:

1. Define Your Brand Personality: Develop a clear brand personality that authentically represents both your personal and professional self.

2. Create Content Buckets: Categorize your content into professional, personal-professional blend, and strictly personal. Use these categories to guide your sharing decisions.

3. Use Storytelling: Frame your personal experiences as stories that reinforce your professional expertise or values.

4. Behind-the-Scenes Glimpses: Offer controlled glimpses into your

personal life that humanize your professional brand without oversharing.

5. Personal Passion Projects: Share personal interests or side projects that complement your professional brand.

6. Family and Relationship Boundaries: Decide how much, if any, of your family life or relationships to incorporate into your brand.

7. Crisis Management Plan: Develop a plan for handling situations where personal issues might impact your professional brand.

Navigating Challenges:

1. Online Harassment: Be prepared to deal with potential negative comments or online harassment that can come with increased personal sharing.

2. Separation Anxiety: Create clear mental and physical boundaries between work and personal life to avoid burnout.

3. Evolving Boundaries: Regularly reassess and adjust your boundaries as your career and personal life evolve.

4. Professional Relationships: Be mindful of how personal sharing might affect relationships with clients, colleagues, or employers.

5. Digital Footprint: Remember that anything shared online can potentially become permanent. Think carefully before posting.

By thoughtfully integrating elements of your personal life into your professional brand, you can create a more relatable and engaging presence. This integration can help build stronger connections with your audience, showcase your authenticity, and differentiate you in your field. However, it's crucial to approach this integration strategically, always keeping in mind your long-term professional goals and personal comfort levels. The key is to find a balance that feels authentic to you, adds value to your professional brand, and respects the boundaries you need for a healthy personal life.

5. Cultural Sensitivity and Inclusivity

In our increasingly globalized and diverse professional landscape, cultural sensitivity and inclusivity have become crucial aspects of ethical personal branding. A brand that demonstrates awareness and respect for diverse cultures and promotes inclusivity can significantly enhance its appeal and impact. Conversely, cultural insensitivity can lead to severe reputational damage and loss of trust.

Key Aspects of Cultural Sensitivity in Personal Branding:

1. Awareness of Cultural Differences: Recognize that your audience may come from diverse cultural backgrounds with different values, norms, and expectations.

2. Respectful Communication: Use language and imagery that is respectful and inclusive of various cultures.

3. Avoiding Stereotypes: Be cautious of perpetuating cultural stereotypes, even unintentionally.

4. Openness to Learning: Demonstrate a willingness to learn about and from different cultures.

5. Inclusive Representation: Ensure that your brand imagery and content represent diverse groups.

Strategies for Building a Culturally Sensitive Personal Brand:

1. Educate Yourself: Continuously learn about different cultures, especially those relevant to your field or target audience.

2. Seek Diverse Perspectives: Engage with people from various cultural backgrounds to broaden your understanding.

3. Cultural Competence Training: Consider undergoing formal training in cultural competence and sensitivity.

4. Inclusive Language: Use language that is inclusive and avoids cultural biases or assumptions.

5. Celebrate Diversity: Highlight the value of diversity in your work and communications.

6. Be Mindful of Cultural Contexts: Consider how your message might be perceived in different cultural contexts.

7. Address Mistakes Promptly: If you make a cultural misstep, acknowledge it quickly and sincerely, and take steps to learn from it.

Avoiding Cultural Appropriation:

Cultural appropriation in personal branding can be particularly damaging. It occurs when elements of a minority or disadvantaged culture are adopted by members of a dominant culture without understanding or respect for their original meaning. To avoid this:

1. Give Credit: If you're inspired by or using elements from another culture, acknowledge the source.

2. Understand Context: Ensure you understand the cultural significance of any elements you incorporate into your brand.

3. Collaborate Respectfully: If incorporating elements from another culture, consider collaborating with members of that culture.

4. Avoid Sacred Elements: Be particularly cautious about using elements that have sacred or deep cultural significance.

Creating an Inclusive Personal Brand:

Inclusivity goes beyond avoiding offense; it actively welcomes and values diversity. To create an inclusive personal brand:

1. Diverse Representation: Ensure your brand visuals and content represent a diverse range of people.

2. Accessible Content: Make your content accessible to people with disabilities (e.g., using alt text for images, providing transcripts for audio content).

3. Inclusive Language: Use gender-neutral language and avoid assumptions about your audience's background or experiences.

4. Highlight Diverse Voices: Feature or collaborate with diverse voices in your field.

5. Address Systemic Issues: Be willing to acknowledge and discuss systemic inequalities in your industry.

Navigating Global Markets:

For professionals working across different countries or cultures:

1. Localization: Adapt your brand message and content for different cultural contexts.

2. Cultural Research: Conduct thorough research on cultural norms and business practices in target markets.

3. Local Partnerships: Consider partnering with local professionals or organizations to enhance cultural authenticity.

4. Flexibility: Be prepared to adjust your branding approach based on cultural feedback.

Case Study: A management consultant expanding their practice internationally might:

- Research business etiquette in target countries
- Adapt their communication style for different cultural contexts (e.g., more formal in some cultures, more relationship-focused in others)
- Ensure their branding materials are culturally appropriate and accurately translated
- Seek feedback from local professionals to refine their approach

By prioritizing cultural sensitivity and inclusivity in your personal brand, you not only avoid potential pitfalls but also create a brand that resonates with a broader audience. This approach demonstrates respect, opens up new opportunities, and contributes to a more inclusive professional environment. Remember, cultural sensitivity is an ongoing process of learning and adaptation, requiring continuous effort and openness to feedback.

6. Intellectual Property and Attribution

In the realm of personal branding, respecting intellectual property rights and properly attributing sources are crucial ethical considerations. As professionals build their brands through content creation, sharing insights, and developing unique methodologies, it's essential to understand and adhere to intellectual property laws and best practices.

Key Aspects of Intellectual Property in Personal Branding:

1. Copyright: Protects original works of authorship, including written content, images, and videos.

2. Trademarks: Safeguard brand names, logos, and slogans that distinguish your services.

3. Patents: While less common in personal branding, they may be relevant for innovative methodologies or tools you develop.

4. Trade Secrets: Confidential business information that provides a competitive edge.

Respecting Others' Intellectual Property:

1. Proper Attribution: Always credit the original creators when using or referencing their work.

2. Fair Use: Understand the limits of fair use when incorporating others' content for commentary, criticism, or educational purposes.

3. Obtaining Permissions: Seek explicit permission when using copyrighted material beyond fair use.

4. Avoiding Plagiarism: Never present others' ideas or work as your own.

Example: A business coach sharing insights from a book in their social media content should clearly attribute quotes, mention the author and book title, and encourage followers to read the full work.

Protecting Your Own Intellectual Property:

1. Copyright Notices: Include copyright notices on your original content.

2. Trademark Registration: Consider registering trademarks for key elements of your brand.

3. Confidentiality Agreements: Use these when sharing sensitive information with collaborators or employees.

4. Monitoring: Regularly check for unauthorized use of your content or brand elements.

Case Study: Gary Vaynerchuk and Content Creation

Gary Vaynerchuk, a prominent entrepreneur and social media personality, is known for his prolific content creation. His approach to intellectual property and attribution offers valuable lessons:

1. Original Content Focus: Vaynerchuk emphasizes creating original content, reducing reliance on others' intellectual property.

2. Transparent Attribution: When referencing others' ideas, he clearly credits the source, often tagging or mentioning them directly on social media.

3. Encouraging Sharing: He openly allows and encourages sharing of his content, with proper attribution, expanding his reach.

4. Brand Protection: Vaynerchuk has trademarked key phrases and logos associated with his brand.

Lessons from Vaynerchuk's approach:

- Prioritize creating original content to build your unique brand voice.
- Be generous in crediting others, which can also help build relationships in your industry.
- Clearly communicate your policies on content sharing and attribution.
- Protect key elements of your brand through appropriate legal measures.

Best Practices for Intellectual Property and Attribution:

1. Develop an Attribution Policy: Create clear guidelines for how you'll credit sources in your content.

2. Educate Yourself: Stay informed about intellectual property laws relevant to your field.

3. Use Content Management Systems: Implement systems to track and manage the use of others' content in your work.

4. Seek Legal Advice: Consult with an intellectual property lawyer for complex situations or when developing unique methodologies.

5. Be Transparent About Collaborations: Clearly communicate the nature of collaborations and joint work.

6. Create an Intellectual Property Strategy: Develop a plan for protecting and leveraging your own intellectual property.

7. Use Creative Commons Licenses: Consider using these licenses to clearly communicate how others can use your work.

8. Document Your Process: Keep records of your creative process to demonstrate the originality of your work if questioned.

Navigating Grey Areas:

1. Inspiration vs. Copying: There's a fine line between being inspired by others' work and copying it. Always strive to add your unique perspective or value.

2. Evolving Ideas: Ideas often build upon each other. Be clear about your contributions to evolving concepts in your field.

3. Common Knowledge: Determine what constitutes common knowledge in your industry versus proprietary information.

4. Cultural References: Be cautious when using cultural references, ensuring you're not appropriating protected cultural elements.

By respecting intellectual property rights and maintaining ethical attribution practices, you not only protect yourself legally but also build a reputation for integrity and professionalism. This approach fosters trust with your audience and peers, enhancing the credibility of your personal brand. Remember, in the interconnected world of personal branding, how you handle intellectual property and attribution can significantly impact your relationships within your industry and your overall brand perception.

7. Data Privacy and Protection

In the digital age, data privacy and protection have become critical ethical considerations in personal branding. As professionals collect, use, and store data about their clients, followers, or audience, they must navigate complex legal requirements and ethical responsibilities. Proper handling of data not only ensures legal compliance but also builds trust and credibility with your audience.

Key Aspects of Data Privacy in Personal Branding:

1. Data Collection: Understanding what personal data you're collecting and why.

2. Data Storage: Securely storing collected data to prevent breaches.

3. Data Usage: Using personal data ethically and transparently.

4. User Consent: Obtaining clear consent for data collection and usage.

5. Data Access and Control: Allowing individuals to access, correct, or delete their data.

Legal Compliance:

Different regions have varying data protection laws. Some key regulations to be aware of include:

1. General Data Protection Regulation (GDPR): Applies to the European Union and has global implications.

2. California Consumer Privacy Act (CCPA): Applies to businesses serving California residents.

3. Personal Information Protection and Electronic Documents Act (PIPEDA): Applies in Canada.

Familiarize yourself with the regulations applicable to your location and audience.

Ethical Handling of Audience Data:

1. Transparency: Clearly communicate what data you collect and how you use it.

2. Minimization: Collect only the data you genuinely need.

3. Purpose Limitation: Use data only for the purposes you've communicated.

4. Security: Implement strong security measures to protect stored data.

5. Retention: Keep data only for as long as necessary.

Case Study: Ethical Data Handling in Email Marketing

Consider a business coach who uses email marketing to grow their personal brand. Here's how they might approach data privacy ethically:

1. Consent: Use double opt-in for newsletter subscriptions to ensure clear consent.

2. Transparency: Provide a clear privacy policy explaining how email addresses will be used.

3. Data Minimization: Collect only necessary information (e.g., name and email) unless there's a clear need for more.

4. Security: Use a reputable email marketing platform with strong security measures.

5. User Control: Include an easy unsubscribe option in every email.

6. Regular Audits: Periodically review the email list, removing inactive subscribers.

This approach not only complies with regulations but also builds trust with the audience, enhancing the coach's personal brand.

Best Practices for Data Privacy and Protection:

1. Conduct a Data Audit: Regularly review what data you collect, how it's stored, and how it's used.

2. Implement a Privacy Policy: Clearly communicate your data practices on your website or in your communications.

3. Use Secure Systems: Invest in secure platforms for data storage and communication.

4. Educate Yourself and Your Team: Stay informed about data protection laws and best practices.

5. Obtain Explicit Consent: Use clear, specific language when asking for consent to collect or use data.

6. Provide Control: Give your audience easy ways to update their preferences or delete their data.

7. Be Prepared for Breaches: Have a plan in place for quickly addressing and communicating any data breaches.

8. Limit Access: Restrict access to personal data to only those who need it for specific purposes.

9. Use Encryption: Encrypt sensitive data, especially when transferring it.

10. Regular Updates: Keep all software and systems up-to-date to protect against vulnerabilities.

Balancing Personalization with Privacy:

Personal branding often involves personalized communication, which requires data. Strike a balance by:

1. Being transparent about how personalization works.

2. Allowing users to opt-out of personalized content if they prefer.

3. Using anonymized data for broader insights when possible.

Handling Sensitive Information:

If your personal brand involves dealing with sensitive information (e.g., as a consultant or coach):

1. Implement strict confidentiality policies.

2. Use secure communication channels for sensitive discussions.

3. Be clear about what information you keep on record and why.

4. Consider professional liability insurance for added protection.

By prioritizing data privacy and protection in your personal branding efforts, you demonstrate respect for your audience and commitment to ethical practices. This not only helps you comply with legal requirements but also builds a foundation of trust that is crucial for long-term success. Remember, in an era where data breaches and privacy concerns are common, a strong stance on data protection can significantly differentiate your personal brand and attract privacy-conscious clients or followers.

8. Dealing with Mistakes and Brand Crises

In the journey of building and maintaining a personal brand, mistakes and crises are almost inevitable. How you handle these situations can significantly impact your brand's integrity and longevity. Ethical approaches to admitting and correcting mistakes, along with effective crisis management strategies, are crucial skills for any professional focused on personal branding.

Ethical Approaches to Admitting and Correcting Mistakes:

1. Quick Acknowledgment: Address the mistake promptly. Delays can exacerbate the situation and erode trust.

2. Take Responsibility: Avoid shifting blame. Own your mistakes directly and sincerely.

3. Transparent Communication: Clearly explain what happened, without making excuses.

4. Genuine Apology: Offer a sincere apology to those affected by your mistake.

5. Corrective Action: Outline the steps you're taking to rectify the situation and prevent future occurrences.

6. Learn and Grow: Use the experience as a learning opportunity and share those lessons if appropriate.

Case Study: Brené Brown's Approach to Mistakes

Brené Brown, a research professor and author known for her work on vulnerability and leadership, provides an excellent example of handling mistakes ethically:

In 2020, Brown launched a podcast that initially lacked proper attribution for some of the music used. When this was brought to her attention, she:

1. Immediately acknowledged the mistake publicly.

2. Took full responsibility, not blaming her team or pleading ignorance.

3. Explained clearly what happened and why it was wrong.

4. Apologized sincerely to the artists and her audience.

5. Outlined steps to correct the issue, including proper licensing and attribution.

6. Shared the experience as a learning moment about the importance of crediting creative work.

Brown's handling of this situation aligned with her brand values of authenticity and vulnerability, ultimately reinforcing her credibility.

Crisis Management Strategies for Personal Brands:

1. Preparation:

- Identify potential crisis scenarios relevant to your brand.
- Develop a crisis communication plan in advance.
- Designate a spokesperson (often yourself in personal branding).

- 2. Immediate Response:
- Assess the situation quickly but thoroughly.
- Respond promptly, even if it's just to acknowledge you're aware and investigating.
- Be present and accessible.

3. Honest and Transparent Communication:

- Provide accurate information about the situation.
- If you don't have all the facts, say so, but commit to finding out.
- Avoid speculation or making promises you can't keep.

4. Empathy and Accountability:

- Show genuine concern for those affected.
- Take responsibility for your part in the situation.
- Avoid defensive or dismissive language.

5. Action Plan:

- Clearly communicate the steps you're taking to address the issue.
- Follow through on your commitments.

6. Continuous Updates:

- Keep your audience informed as the situation evolves.
- Be consistent in your messaging across all platforms.

7. Learn and Adapt:

- After the crisis, conduct a thorough review.
- Implement changes to prevent similar issues in the future.
- Share the lessons learned if appropriate.

8. Rebuild Trust:

- Be patient in rebuilding relationships and trust.
- Demonstrate through actions that you've learned and improved.

Remember, how you handle mistakes and crises can actually strengthen your personal brand if done ethically and effectively. It demonstrates integrity, resilience, and a commitment to growth – all valuable traits in a personal brand.

By approaching mistakes and crises with honesty, accountability, and a willingness to learn, you can turn potentially damaging situations into opportunities to reinforce your brand values and deepen your audience's trust in you.

CHAPTER 2 DECISION TREE: NAVIGATING ETHICAL PERSONAL BRANDING

This decision tree guides you through the ethical considerations of personal branding, helping you assess authenticity, transparency, social responsibility, and more.

Start: Is your personal brand an authentic representation of you?

• Yes → Proceed to assessing transparency.

• No → Identify areas of inauthenticity.

- Revise brand elements to align with your true self.
- Consider seeking feedback from trusted colleagues.

Next: Are you transparent about your qualifications and experiences?

• Yes → Proceed to evaluating social responsibility.

• No → Improve transparency.

- Clearly state your qualifications.
- Be honest about your experience level.
- Disclose any potential conflicts of interest.

Next: Does your brand demonstrate social responsibility?

• Yes → Proceed to assessing privacy considerations.

• No → Incorporate social responsibility.

- Identify causes aligned with your values.
- Integrate social responsibility into your brand messaging.
- Ensure actions match your stated values.

Next: Are you respecting others' privacy in your branding efforts?

• Yes → Proceed to evaluating professional ethics.

• No → Adjust your approach.

- Review and revise content for privacy concerns.
- Obtain necessary permissions before sharing others' information.
- Develop clear guidelines for maintaining privacy.

Next: Does your personal brand align with the ethical standards of your profession?

• Yes → Proceed to balancing personal and professional aspects.

• No → Align with professional ethics.

- Review your industry's ethical guidelines.
- Adjust your brand to comply with these standards.
- Consider consulting with an ethics professional in your field.

Next: Have you found a balance between personal and professional in your brand?

• Yes → Proceed to social media ethics.

• No → Adjust the balance.

- Define boundaries for personal sharing.
- Ensure personal content aligns with your professional image.
- Consider creating separate personal and professional profiles if necessary.

Next: Are your social media practices ethical and responsible?

• Yes → Your brand demonstrates strong ethical considerations.

• No → Improve social media ethics.

- Develop a personal social media policy.
- Be mindful of the impact of your posts.
- Fact-check before sharing information.

Final: Regularly review and update your ethical branding practices

Conclusion

Chapter 2 has delved into the crucial role of ethics in personal branding, emphasizing that building a strong and sustainable brand goes beyond visibility and recognition—it requires a firm commitment to authenticity, transparency, and integrity. In this chapter, we've explored how ethical considerations influence every aspect of your brand, from how you present yourself to how you interact with your audience and handle challenges.

We discussed the importance of maintaining authenticity in a world where curated online personas can easily lead to perceptions of inauthenticity. Through the lens of case studies, we saw the consequences of failing to uphold ethical standards, such as the backlash faced by public figures when their actions didn't align with their brand promises. The chapter also highlighted the delicate balance between personal and professional lives in branding, the need for cultural sensitivity, and the importance of respecting intellectual property and data privacy.

Moreover, we examined the significance of social responsibility in personal branding, stressing that today's audiences expect more than just professional expertise—they want to support brands that stand for something meaningful and contribute positively to society. Handling mistakes and crises was also covered, underscoring the importance of quick, transparent, and responsible responses to maintain trust and credibility.

As you continue to develop and refine your personal brand, keep these ethical considerations at the forefront of your strategy. An ethical brand not only protects you from potential pitfalls but also builds a foundation of trust that is invaluable in today's professional environment. By integrating authenticity, transparency, cultural sensitivity, and social responsibility into your brand, you will create a reputation that is not only respected but also resilient in the face of challenges.

In moving forward, remember that ethical personal branding is an ongoing process. Regularly assess and update your practices to ensure they align with both your professional goals and the evolving expectations of your audience. By doing so, you will not only strengthen your personal brand but also contribute positively to your industry and society at large.

Chapter 3

Discovering Your Unique Value Proposition (UVP)

1. Introduction: The Importance of a Unique Value Proposition

In the crowded marketplace of ideas and services, standing out is not just an advantage—it's a necessity. This is where your Unique Value Proposition (UVP) comes into play. Your UVP is the cornerstone of your personal brand, the clear message that states why you are the best choice for your target audience. It's what sets you apart from others in your field and communicates the distinct value you bring to the table.

For consultants, accountants, lawyers, mentors, coaches, trainers, and solopreneurs, a well-crafted UVP is particularly crucial. In fields where services can often seem similar on the surface, your UVP is what will make potential clients choose you over your competitors. It's not just about what you do, but how you do it, why you do it, and the unique combination of skills, experiences, and perspectives you bring to your work.

Your UVP should succinctly answer these questions:

- What specific problem do you solve?
- How do you solve it differently or better than others?
- Why are you particularly suited to address this problem?

A strong UVP goes beyond listing your qualifications or services. It communicates the unique benefit you provide, the distinctive way you provide it, and the particular audience you serve. It's the promise of value to be delivered and the belief from the client about how value will be experienced.

Throughout this chapter, we'll explore various approaches to discovering and articulating your UVP. We'll examine case studies, provide practical exercises, and offer strategies to help you uncover what truly makes you unique in your field. By the end of this chapter, you'll have the tools to craft a compelling UVP that resonates with your target audience and forms the foundation of a powerful personal brand.

Let's begin this journey by exploring a fundamental concept in understanding your unique value: the "Start with Why" approach popularized by Simon Sinek.

2. The "Start with Why" Approach

At the heart of every compelling Unique Value Proposition is a clear understanding of your fundamental purpose—your "why." To explore this concept, let's delve into the groundbreaking work of Simon Sinek and his Golden Circle theory.

Case Study: Simon Sinek - The Golden Circle Concept

Simon Sinek, an author and motivational speaker, introduced the concept of the Golden Circle in his book "Start with Why" and his immensely popular TED Talk. This simple but powerful idea has revolutionized how many people think about personal branding and business strategy.

The Golden Circle consists of three concentric circles:

1. Why (the innermost circle): Your purpose, cause, or belief. Why does your organization exist?

2. How: The methods or processes you use to realize that purpose.

3. What: The products or services you offer.

Sinek argues that most organizations and individuals communicate from the outside in—they start with what they do, sometimes address how they do it, but rarely articulate why they do what they do. However, the most influential leaders and brands, according to Sinek, communicate from the inside out. They start with why.

Examples Sinek uses include Apple and Martin Luther King Jr. Apple's why isn't to make computers (that's what they do); it's to challenge the status quo and think differently. This why permeates everything they do and how they do it, making their brand message consistent and compelling.

Key Takeaways from Sinek's Approach:

1. People don't buy what you do; they buy why you do it.

2. The why taps into the part of the brain that influences behavior and decision-making.

3. When you communicate your why, you attract people who believe what you believe.

Identifying Your Core Purpose and Values

To apply Sinek's approach to your personal brand and UVP, start by identifying your core purpose and values. Here are some steps to help you uncover your why:

1. Reflect on Your Motivations:

- What drives you in your work beyond making money?
- What impact do you want to have on your clients or the world?
- What would you do even if you weren't paid for it?

2. Examine Your Past:

- Look for patterns in the types of problems you've enjoyed solving.
- Identify moments when you felt most fulfilled in your work.
- Consider feedback you've received about when you're at your best.

3. Define Your Values:

- What principles guide your decision-making?
- What do you stand for, and what do you stand against?
- What values do you never want to compromise, even for success?

4. Envision Your Ideal Future:

- If you could change one thing about your industry, what would it be?
- What legacy do you want to leave?
- How do you want to be remembered professionally?

5. Ask for External Input:

- Ask colleagues or clients why they enjoy working with you.
- Seek feedback on what others see as your unique strengths.

Exercise: Write Your Why Statement

Craft a simple statement that captures your why. It should be:

- Action-oriented
- Focused on the contribution you make or the impact you have
- Free from any mentions of specific products or services

Example: "To empower individuals to reach their full potential by challenging limiting beliefs and fostering self-discovery."

Aligning Your UVP with Your "Why"

Once you've identified your why, the next step is to align your Unique Value Proposition with this core purpose. Your UVP should be a natural extension of your why, demonstrating how your purpose translates into tangible value for your clients.

Steps to Align Your UVP with Your Why:

1. Connect Purpose to Problem-Solving:

Show how your why drives you to solve specific problems for your clients.

2. Highlight Unique Approaches:

Explain how your why influences your methods or approach, setting you apart from others.

3. Define Your Ideal Client:

Identify the type of client who would resonate most with your why.

4. Articulate Outcomes:

Describe the results clients can expect, framed within the context of your why.

5. Use Emotive Language:

Choose words that reflect the passion behind your why.

Example UVP Aligned with a Why:

Why: "To empower individuals to reach their full potential by challenging limiting beliefs and fostering self-discovery."

UVP: "I help ambitious professionals break through self-imposed barriers and discover hidden strengths, leading to unprecedented career growth and personal fulfillment. Through a unique blend of cognitive coaching and practical strategy, I guide clients to not just set higher goals, but to fundamentally shift how they see themselves and their possibilities."

By starting with why, you create a UVP that goes beyond features and benefits. It communicates a purpose that can inspire and attract clients who share your values and vision. This approach not only differentiates you in the market but also ensures that your personal brand is built on a foundation of authentic purpose and passion.

3. Leveraging Vulnerability and Authenticity

In the realm of personal branding, vulnerability and authenticity have emerged as powerful tools for building genuine connections and establishing trust with your audience. To understand how these elements can be effectively incorporated into your Unique Value Proposition, let's examine the work of Dr. Brené Brown, a renowned researcher and author who has revolutionized our understanding of vulnerability in professional contexts.

Case Study: Brené Brown - The Power of Vulnerability in Branding

Dr. Brené Brown's journey to becoming a globally recognized thought leader on vulnerability and courage offers valuable insights into the power of authenticity in personal branding.

Brown's breakthrough moment came with her 2010 TEDx Houston talk, "The Power of Vulnerability." In this talk, she shared not only her research findings but also her personal struggles with vulnerability. The talk went viral, amassing millions of views and catapulting Brown into the spotlight.

Key aspects of Brown's approach:

1. Sharing Personal Struggles: Brown openly discussed her own "breakdown" or "spiritual awakening" that occurred during her research, demonstrating the very vulnerability she studied.

2. Balancing Expertise and Humanity: While establishing her credentials as a researcher, Brown also presented herself as a relatable individual grappling with the same issues she studied.

3. Consistent Message Across Platforms: Whether in her books, talks, or interviews, Brown maintains a consistent message about the importance of embracing vulnerability.

4. Practical Application: Brown translates her research into actionable insights, making her work valuable for both personal and professional development.

5. Authenticity in Growth: As her brand has evolved, Brown has been open about her learning process and the challenges of living up to her own teachings.

The impact of Brown's vulnerable and authentic approach:

- Built a loyal and engaged audience across various demographics
- Established trust and credibility in both academic and popular circles
- Created a distinctive brand in the crowded self-help and leadership development space

Incorporating Personal Experiences into Your Brand

Drawing from Brown's example, here are strategies for incorporating personal experiences into your brand:

1. Identify Relevant Experiences:

- Reflect on personal or professional challenges you've overcome
- Consider moments of growth or insight that shaped your approach

- Look for experiences that connect directly to the value you offer clients

2. Frame Experiences as Learning Opportunities:

- Focus on the lessons learned rather than dwelling on difficulties
- Show how these experiences inform your current expertise

3. Be Selective:

- Share experiences that are relevant to your brand and audience
- Maintain appropriate professional boundaries

4. Use Storytelling Techniques:

- Craft narratives that illustrate key points in your professional philosophy
- Use vivid details to make your stories memorable and relatable

5. Connect Personal Stories to Client Benefits:

- Clearly articulate how your experiences translate into value for clients
- Use personal anecdotes to illustrate your unique approach or methodology

Building Trust Through Authentic Self-Expression

Authenticity in personal branding goes beyond sharing personal stories. It involves consistently presenting a genuine version of yourself across all brand touchpoints. Here's how to build trust through authentic self-expression:

1. Develop a Consistent Voice:

- Identify your natural communication style
- Use language that feels true to you, avoiding jargon or forced formality
- Maintain this voice across all platforms (social media, website, presentations)

2. Acknowledge Limitations:

- Be honest about what you do and don't know
- Frame limitations as opportunities for growth or collaboration

3. Show Your Process:

- Share behind-the-scenes glimpses of your work
- Discuss your approach to problem-solving, including challenges

4. Express Genuine Emotions:

- Allow appropriate emotional expression in your brand communications
- Share your passion for your work and your excitement about client successes

5. Stand for Something:

- Clearly articulate your values and beliefs
- Take stands on issues relevant to your field, even if they're controversial

6. Admit and Learn from Mistakes:

- When you make errors, acknowledge them openly
- Share how you've grown from these experiences

7. Engage Authentically with Your Audience:

- Respond to comments and messages in a personal, non-scripted manner
- Show genuine interest in your audience's thoughts and experiences

Balancing Vulnerability and Professionalism

While vulnerability can be a powerful tool in personal branding, it's important to strike a balance with professionalism:

1. Set Clear Boundaries:

   - Decide in advance what aspects of your life you're comfortable sharing
   - Maintain a distinction between personal vulnerability and oversharing

2. Focus on Relevant Vulnerability:

   - Share experiences and emotions that relate to your professional value
   - Avoid sharing vulnerabilities that might undermine client confidence

3. Frame Vulnerability as Strength:

   - Present your willingness to be vulnerable as a asset in your work
   - Show how your openness contributes to better outcomes for clients

4. Timing and Context:

   - Choose appropriate moments for vulnerable sharing
   - Consider the readiness of your audience to receive vulnerable content

By incorporating vulnerability and authenticity into your personal brand, you create a UVP that goes beyond skills and services. You offer clients a genuine human connection, building trust and fostering deeper engagement. Remember, the goal is not to expose every aspect of your life, but to strategically share experiences and emotions that reinforce your brand's value and resonate with your target audience.

4. Blending Business Expertise with Personal Development

In today's competitive market, professionals who can seamlessly blend business acumen with personal development often create the most compelling and unique value propositions. This combination allows for a holistic approach to problem-solving and client service. To illustrate this concept, let's examine the case of Marie Forleo, a prominent entrepreneur who has successfully merged business expertise with personal growth strategies.

Case Study: Marie Forleo - Combining Business Acumen with Personal Growth

Marie Forleo has built a powerful personal brand by integrating her business knowledge with a focus on personal development. Her approach offers valuable insights into creating a multifaceted brand that appeals to both the professional and personal aspirations of her audience.

Key aspects of Forleo's approach:

1. Diverse Background: Forleo leverages her varied experiences, including work in finance, publishing, and choreography, to offer a unique perspective on business and life.

2. B-School Program: Her signature online business program combines practical business strategies with personal development concepts, addressing both the tactical and mindset aspects of entrepreneurship.

3. MarieTV: Through her web television show, Forleo tackles a wide range of topics, from marketing strategies to overcoming self-doubt, demonstrating how personal growth and business success are inter-connected.

4. "Everything is Figureoutable" Philosophy: This core belief, which became the title of her book, encapsulates her approach of applying a growth mindset to both business challenges and personal obstacles.

5. Engagement Across Platforms: Forleo maintains a consistent message of empowerment and practical advice across her website, social media, podcasts, and live events.

The impact of Forleo's blended approach:

- Appeals to a broad audience of entrepreneurs and individuals seeking both professional success and personal fulfillment
- Positions her as a versatile expert capable of addressing various aspects of her clients' lives
- Creates multiple revenue streams through different products and services catering to both business and personal development needs

Identifying Your Unique Skill Set and Experiences

To create a UVP that blends business expertise with personal development, start by identifying your unique combination of skills and experiences:

1. Professional Skills Inventory:

   - List your core business skills (e.g., financial analysis, marketing strategy, legal expertise)
   - Identify specialized knowledge or certifications you possess

2. Personal Development Journey:

   - Reflect on personal growth experiences that have shaped your approach
   - Consider challenges you've overcome and how they've influenced your professional perspective

3. Transferable Skills:

   - Identify skills from other areas of your life that apply to your professional work
   - Consider how hobbies or personal interests might inform your business approach

4. Unique Combinations:

   - Look for unexpected connections between different areas of expertise
   - Consider how your diverse experiences create a unique lens for problem-solving

5. Client Feedback:

   - Review client testimonials or feedback for insights into what others value about your approach
   - Identify recurring themes in how clients describe working with you

Exercise: Create a Venn Diagram

Draw three overlapping circles representing:

1. Business Expertise

2. Personal Development Skills

3. Unique Life Experiences

In the overlapping areas, identify how these elements combine to create your unique offering.

Creating a Multifaceted Personal Brand

Once you've identified your unique blend of skills and experiences, the next step is to create a personal brand that effectively communicates this multifaceted value:

1. Develop a Holistic Brand Statement:

- Craft a statement that encapsulates both your business expertise and personal development focus

Example: "I help tech entrepreneurs scale their businesses while maintaining work-life balance through data-driven strategies and mindfulness practices."

2. Create Content That Bridges Business and Personal Growth:

- Develop blog posts, videos, or podcasts that show the intersection of professional skills and personal development
- Share case studies that demonstrate how personal growth strategies enhance business outcomes

3. Offer Diverse Services or Products:

- Design a range of offerings that cater to both business needs and personal development
- Consider how your services can address the whole person, not just their professional challenges

4. Use Storytelling to Illustrate Your Approach:

- Share personal anecdotes that demonstrate how you've applied personal growth principles to business challenges
- Use client success stories that highlight both professional achievements and personal transformations

5. Develop a Unique Methodology:

- Create a signature process or framework that integrates business strategies with personal development techniques
- Give your methodology a memorable name that reflects its dual focus

6. Cultivate a Well-Rounded Online Presence:

- Ensure your website and social media profiles reflect both your business expertise and personal development focus
- Use varied content formats (e.g., infographics for business data, inspirational quotes for personal growth) to appeal to different aspects of your audience's needs

7. Network Across Diverse Fields:

- Engage with professionals in both business and personal development circles
- Seek speaking opportunities or collaborations that allow you to showcase your multifaceted approach

8. Continuous Learning and Growth:

- Regularly update your skills in both business and personal development areas
- Share your learning journey with your audience, demonstrating your commitment to ongoing growth

By blending your business expertise with personal development insights, you create a UVP that addresses the whole person. This approach allows you to differentiate yourself in the market by offering a more comprehensive solution to your clients' challenges. It also positions you as a well-rounded expert capable of guiding clients through both the practical and personal aspects of their professional journeys.

Remember, the key is to find authentic connections between your business knowledge and personal growth experiences. This genuine integration will resonate with your audience and create a truly unique and valuable brand proposition.

5. Self-Assessment Techniques

Understanding yourself thoroughly is crucial in developing a compelling Unique Value Proposition. Self-assessment techniques provide valuable insights into your strengths, weaknesses, personality traits, and potential areas for growth. These insights form the foundation of an authentic and powerful personal brand. Let's explore two key self-assessment techniques: SWOT analysis and personality assessments.

SWOT Analysis for Personal Branding

SWOT analysis, traditionally used in business strategy, can be an effective tool for personal branding. It helps you identify your Strengths, Weaknesses, Opportunities, and Threats.

How to Conduct a Personal SWOT Analysis:

1. Strengths:

- List your key skills, qualifications, and positive attributes
- Include unique experiences or knowledge that set you apart
- Consider feedback from colleagues, clients, or mentors

Example: "Deep expertise in data analytics, strong communication skills, ability to simplify complex concepts"

2. Weaknesses:

- Identify areas where you lack experience or skills
- Be honest about personal traits that might hinder your professional growth
- Consider skills gaps in your field

Example: "Limited experience with public speaking, tendency to overcommit, need to improve networking skills"

3. Opportunities:

- Look for trends in your industry that align with your strengths
- Identify unmet needs in the market that you could potentially fill
- Consider emerging technologies or methodologies you could leverage

Example: "Growing demand for data privacy experts, increasing interest in ethical AI practices"

4. Threats:

- Recognize external factors that could challenge your position
- Identify competitors or changing market conditions
- Consider personal circumstances that might impact your professional growth

Example: "Rapid technological changes in the field, increasing competition from AI-driven analytics tools"

Applying SWOT to Your UVP:

- Focus on leveraging your strengths to address market opportunities
- Develop strategies to mitigate weaknesses and threats
- Use insights to craft a UVP that highlights your unique strengths in relation to market needs

Personality Assessments and Their Role in UVP Development

Personality assessments can provide deep insights into your natural tendencies, working style, and interpersonal dynamics. These insights can help you articulate your unique approach and value more effectively.

Popular Personality Assessments:

1. Myers-Briggs Type Indicator (MBTI):

- Provides insights into how you perceive the world and make decisions
- Can help identify natural strengths and potential growth areas

2. Big Five (OCEAN):

- Measures Openness, Conscientiousness, Extraversion, Agreeableness, and Neuroticism
- Offers a comprehensive view of your personality traits

3. StrengthsFinder:

- Identifies your top natural talents
- Helps focus on developing and leveraging your strengths

4. DISC Assessment:

Categorizes behavioral styles (Dominance, Influence, Steadiness, Conscientiousness)

- Useful for understanding your communication and work style

Using Personality Assessment Results in UVP Development:

1. Identify Natural Strengths:

- Highlight personality traits that contribute to your professional effectiveness

Example: If you score high on "Openness," emphasize your innovative thinking in your UVP

2. Understand Your Work Style:

- Articulate how your personality enhances your approach to tasks and problem-solving

Example: An MBTI "INTJ" might emphasize their strategic planning and analytical skills

3. Improve Self-Awareness:

- Recognize potential blind spots or areas for growth
- Demonstrate self-awareness by acknowledging these in your professional development

4. Tailor Your Communication:

- Use insights to craft messages that resonate with your natural style
- Adapt your UVP presentation to different personality types in your audience

5. Find Your Niche:

- Identify roles or industries where your personality traits are particularly valuable

Example: High "Agreeableness" might be especially valuable in customer service or team leadership roles

6. Enhance Team Dynamics:

- If relevant, highlight how your personality complements team dynamics

Example: "As an 'Influencer' in the DISC model, I excel at motivating teams and building consensus"

Integrating SWOT and Personality Insights:

Combine insights from both SWOT analysis and personality assessments to create a comprehensive view of your professional self. Look for patterns and connections:

- How do your personality strengths align with your professional strengths?
- Can your personality traits help address some of your weaknesses?
- How can you leverage your personality to capitalize on opportunities?

Example UVP Incorporating Self-Assessment Insights:

"As a data analyst with a naturally strategic mindset (INTJ), I excel at turning complex data into actionable business strategies. My strength in pattern recognition, combined with strong communication skills, allows me to bridge the gap between technical insights and practical business applications. I thrive in dynamic environments where I can leverage my adaptability and innovative thinking to stay ahead of rapid technological changes in data analytics."

Remember, while these assessments provide valuable insights, they are tools for self-reflection, not definitive labels. Use them as a starting point for deeper self-understanding and as a guide in crafting a UVP that authentically represents your unique combination of skills, experiences, and personal qualities.

6. Identifying Your Strengths and Passions

Discovering and leveraging your unique strengths and aligning them with your passions is crucial in developing a compelling Unique Value Proposition. This alignment not only makes your work more fulfilling but also enhances your authenticity and effectiveness in your chosen field. Let's explore techniques for uncovering hidden strengths and ways to align your passions with your professional goals.

Techniques for Uncovering Hidden Strengths

1. Reflect on Past Successes:

- List your significant achievements, both personal and professional.
- Analyze what skills or qualities contributed to each success.
- Look for patterns in these successes to identify recurring strengths.

2. Seek Feedback:

- Ask colleagues, mentors, friends, and family what they see as your strengths.
- Pay attention to compliments you frequently receive.
- Consider using a 360-degree feedback tool for a comprehensive view.

3. Energy Mapping:

- Track your activities for a week, noting which tasks energize you and which drain you.
- The tasks that energize you often align with your natural strengths.

4. Challenge Analysis:

- Reflect on challenges you've overcome.
- Identify the skills or qualities that helped you navigate these difficulties.

5. The 'Flow State' Technique:

- Identify moments when you lose track of time while working.
- These 'flow state' activities often indicate natural strengths.

6. Skill Inventory:

- Create a comprehensive list of your skills, including those from hobbies and volunteer work.
- Rate your proficiency and enjoyment level for each skill.
- Skills you excel at and enjoy are likely your strengths.

7. Strengths-Based Assessments:

- Take formal strengths assessments like CliftonStrengths or VIA Character Strengths.
- These tools can reveal strengths you might not have recognized.

Exercise: Strength Story Analysis

Write about three instances where you felt particularly successful or proud. Analyze these stories to identify the strengths that contributed to these outcomes. Look for commonalities across these experiences.

Aligning Passions with Professional Goals

1. Identify Your Core Passions:

- List activities or causes that excite you, both within and outside of work.
- Consider what you loved doing as a child or what you'd do if money wasn't a concern.
- Reflect on topics that consistently capture your interest.

2. Find Intersections:

- Create a Venn diagram with your strengths, passions, and market needs.
- Look for overlaps that could inform your professional direction.

3. Conduct Informational Interviews:

- Speak with professionals in fields that interest you.
- Learn how they incorporate their passions into their work.

4. Experiment with Side Projects:

- Start small projects or volunteer work related to your passions.
- Use these experiences to test potential career directions.

5. Reframe Current Work:

- Identify aspects of your current role that align with your passions.
- Look for ways to incorporate more of these elements into your daily work.

6. Set Passion-Aligned Goals:

- Create professional goals that incorporate your passions.
- Break these down into actionable steps.

7. Continuous Learning:

- Pursue education or training in areas that excite you.
- This can open new opportunities that align with your passions.

Exercise: Passion-Profession Integration Map

Create a mind map starting with your core passions. Branch out to list related skills, potential roles, industries, or projects that could incorporate these passions professionally.

Bringing It All Together in Your UVP

Once you've identified your strengths and aligned them with your passions, you can craft a UVP that authentically represents your unique offering:

1. Highlight Unique Combinations:

- Emphasize how your particular mix of strengths and passions sets you apart.

Example: "I combine my passion for environmental sustainability with my strength in data analysis to help companies implement eco-friendly practices that also improve their bottom line."

2. Show Authenticity:

- Let your genuine enthusiasm for your work shine through in your UVP.

Example: "My lifelong fascination with human behavior fuels my innovative approach to marketing strategy, allowing me to create campaigns that deeply resonate with target audiences."

3. Demonstrate Value:

- Clearly articulate how your strengths and passions benefit clients or employers.

Example: "By merging my technical expertise in software development with my passion for user experience design, I create intuitive, efficient applications that users love and businesses rely on."

4. Evolve Over Time:

- Regularly reassess your strengths and passions as they develop.
- Update your UVP to reflect your growth and changing interests.

Remember, the most compelling UVPs are those that genuinely reflect who you are and what you care about. By aligning your strengths with your passions, you create a personal brand that not only stands out in the market but also provides you with a sense of purpose and fulfillment in your professional life. This authentic alignment will naturally attract opportunities and clients that are the best fit for your unique offerings.

7. Crafting Your Unique Value Proposition

A well-crafted Unique Value Proposition (UVP) is the cornerstone of your personal brand. It succinctly communicates what makes you valuable and different from others in your field. Let's explore the key components of a strong UVP and provide a step-by-step guide to creating your own.

Components of a Strong UVP:

1. Target Audience: Clearly identifies who you serve.

2. Problem Solved: Articulates the specific issue or need you address.

3. Unique Solution: Describes how you solve the problem differently or better than others.

4. Key Benefit: Highlights the primary advantage of working with you.

5. Proof: Includes evidence or a reason to believe your claim.

Step-by-Step Guide to Creating Your UVP:

Step 1: Identify Your Target Audience

- Define your ideal client or employer.
- Consider demographics, psychographics, and specific needs.

Step 2: Pinpoint the Problem You Solve

- What pain points or challenges does your audience face?
- How do these problems impact their life or business?

Step 3: Articulate Your Unique Solution

- How do you address the identified problem?
- What makes your approach different or better?

Step 4: Highlight Key Benefits

- What are the tangible and intangible benefits of your solution?
- How do these benefits improve your audience's situation?

Step 5: Provide Proof

- What evidence supports your claims?
- Consider certifications, testimonials, or specific results.

Step 6: Craft Your UVP Statement

- Combine the above elements into a concise, compelling statement.
- Aim for clarity, specificity, and authenticity.

Step 7: Refine and Polish

- Edit for brevity and impact.
- Ensure every word adds value.

UVP Formula:

I help [target audience] to [solve problem] by [unique solution], resulting in [key benefit]. [Proof]

Example UVPs:

For a Financial Advisor:

"I help tech entrepreneurs navigate complex financial decisions by combining cutting-edge investment strategies with personalized wealth management, resulting in optimized financial growth and security. With a track record of helping clients increase their net worth by an average of 30% in three years."

For a Leadership Coach:

"I empower emerging female leaders in STEM fields to break through glass ceilings by leveraging emotional intelligence and strategic communication skills, resulting in accelerated career advancement. My clients report a 40% increase in successful leadership role acquisitions within 12 months."

For a Digital Marketing Consultant:

"I assist small e-commerce businesses in boosting their online presence through tailored, data-driven digital marketing strategies, resulting in increased traffic and sales. My approach has helped clients achieve an average 50% increase in online revenue within six months."

Remember, your UVP should be:

- Clear and concise
- Focused on client benefits
- Differentiating
- Authentic to your brand
- Easy to understand and remember

8. Testing and Refining Your UVP

Creating your UVP is an iterative process. Once you've crafted an initial version, it's crucial to test and refine it based on feedback and real-world application.

Gathering Feedback on Your UVP:

1. Peer Review:

- Share your UVP with colleagues or mentors in your industry.
- Ask for honest feedback on clarity, impact, and differentiation.

2. Client Feedback:

- Present your UVP to current or potential clients.
- Gauge their reaction and ask if it resonates with their needs.

3. A/B Testing:

- Create two versions of your UVP and test them in different contexts (e.g., website, networking events).
- Compare which version generates more interest or engagement.

4. Online Surveys:

- Use tools like SurveyMonkey or Google Forms to gather feedback from a larger audience.
- Include questions about clarity, appeal, and believability.

5. Social Media Testing:

- Share different versions of your UVP on professional social media platforms.
- Analyze engagement metrics to see which version performs better.

6. Elevator Pitch Practice:

- Use your UVP as an elevator pitch in networking situations.
- Note the responses and questions you receive.

7. Professional Associations:

- Present your UVP at industry events or association meetings.
- Collect feedback from peers and potential clients in your field.

Iterative Process of UVP Refinement:

1. Collect and Analyze Feedback:

- Gather all feedback received through various channels.
- Look for patterns or common themes in the responses.

2. Identify Areas for Improvement:

- Is your UVP clear to your target audience?
- Does it effectively communicate your unique value?
- Are there any parts that consistently confuse or fail to resonate?

3. Refine Your Language:

- Adjust wording to address any clarity issues.
- Strengthen phrases that highlight your unique value.

4. Enhance Specificity:

- Add more concrete details or examples if feedback suggests vagueness.

- Ensure your UVP speaks directly to your target audience's needs.

5. Align with Market Needs:

- If feedback reveals misalignment with market demands, reassess and adjust your value offering.

6. Simplify:

- If your UVP feels too complex, streamline it without losing essential elements.

7. Re-test:

- After making adjustments, go through another round of testing.
- This could be a smaller scale test focusing on the elements you've changed.

8. Continuous Improvement:

- View your UVP as a living statement that evolves with your skills and market needs.
- Schedule regular reviews (e.g., every 6-12 months) to ensure it remains relevant and impactful.

Example of UVP Refinement:

Original UVP:

"I help businesses improve their online presence through digital marketing strategies."

Feedback: Too vague, doesn't specify target audience or unique approach.

Refined UVP:

"I empower small e-commerce businesses to double their online sales within 6 months through customized, data-driven digital marketing strategies and AI-powered customer insights."

This refined version addresses the initial feedback by specifying the target audience (small e-commerce businesses), quantifying the benefit (double online sales), providing a timeframe (within 6 months), and highlighting the unique approach (customized, data-driven strategies with AI insights).

Remember, refining your UVP is an ongoing process. As you grow professionally and as market needs evolve, your UVP should adapt to reflect your current value offering. Regular testing and refinement ensure that your UVP remains a powerful tool in your personal branding arsenal.

CHAPTER 3 DECISION TREE: CRAFTING YOUR UNIQUE VALUE PROPOSITION

Start: Have you identified your core strengths and skills?

• **Yes** → Proceed to **Identifying Passions**

• **No** → Conduct a **Self-Assessment**:

- Take a skills inventory
- Seek feedback from colleagues/mentors
- Consider professional assessment tools

Next: Have you identified your passions and values?

• **Yes** → Proceed to **Market Research**

• **No** → Explore your **Passions and Values**:

- Reflect on what energizes you
- Identify causes you care about
- Consider your long-term goals

Next: Have you researched market needs in your industry?

• **Yes** → Proceed to **Aligning Skills with Market Needs**

• **No** → Conduct **Market Research**:

- Analyze industry trends
- Identify common pain points in your field
- Research competitor offerings

Next: Can you align your skills and passions with market needs?

• **Yes** → Proceed to **Developing Your Personal Narrative**

• **No** → Reassess or Consider **Pivoting**:

- Identify transferable skills
- Explore adjacent markets
- Consider additional training or education

Next: Have you developed a compelling personal narrative?

• **Yes** → Proceed to **Crafting UVP Statement**

• **No** → Create Your **Personal Story**:

- Identify key moments in your journey
- Highlight challenges overcome
- Show how your experiences shaped your expertise

Next: Have you crafted a clear UVP statement?

• **Yes** → Proceed to **Testing Your UVP**

• **No** → Develop Your **UVP Statement**:

- Clearly state who you help
- Articulate the specific problem you solve
- Explain your unique approach or solution

Next: Have you tested your UVP with your target audience?

• **Yes** → Implement Your **UVP in Your Branding**

• **No** → **Test and Refine** Your UVP:

- Seek feedback from trusted peers
- Test different versions with your audience
- Refine based on feedback

Final: Regularly review and update your UVP as you grow and market needs change

CONCLUSION

Chapter 3 has taken you on a journey to uncover and define your Unique Value Proposition (UVP), a critical element that sets you apart in a crowded marketplace. Your UVP is not just a statement of what you do, but a clear articulation of how you uniquely solve problems for your target audience, why you are the best at what you do, and what makes your approach distinctive.

By exploring the "Start with Why" approach and understanding the importance of aligning your UVP with your core purpose and values, you have gained the tools to communicate your brand's essence effectively. The exercises and strategies discussed in this chapter are designed to help you pinpoint the intersection of your skills, passions, and the needs of your audience, ultimately crafting a UVP that resonates deeply with those you seek to serve.

Remember, a compelling UVP is the foundation of a strong personal brand. It is the promise you make to your audience and the reason they will choose you over others. As you continue to refine your UVP, ensure it remains authentic, clear, and aligned with your long-term goals. This clarity will not only attract the right opportunities but will also reinforce your brand's credibility and influence in your field.

Moving forward, let your UVP guide your branding efforts, from your messaging and content creation to your interactions with clients and peers. By staying true to your unique value and consistently communicating it, you will build a powerful, sustainable personal brand that stands out and makes a lasting impact.

Chapter 4

Defining and Understanding Your Target Audience

1. Introduction: The Importance of Audience in Personal Branding

In the realm of personal branding, understanding your target audience is not just important—it's essential. Your personal brand doesn't exist in a vacuum; it thrives on the connection and value it provides to a specific group of people. Whether you're a consultant, accountant, lawyer, mentor, coach, trainer, or solopreneur, knowing exactly who you're trying to reach and serve is fundamental to your success.

Defining and understanding your target audience allows you to:

1. Tailor Your Message: When you know who you're speaking to, you can craft your message in a way that resonates deeply with their needs, aspirations, and pain points.

2. Focus Your Efforts: Instead of trying to appeal to everyone, you can concentrate your time and resources on the individuals most likely to benefit from your expertise.

3. Stand Out from Competitors: By addressing the specific needs of your target audience, you differentiate yourself from others who may be taking a more generalized approach.

4. Create Relevant Content: Understanding your audience helps you

produce content that they find valuable, increasing engagement and building trust.

5. Develop Targeted Services: Knowing your audience's needs allows you to create or refine services that directly address their challenges.

6. Build Stronger Connections: When you truly understand your audience, you can form more meaningful and lasting professional relationships.

7. Increase ROI: By focusing on the right audience, you can improve the return on investment for your branding and marketing efforts.

Throughout this chapter, we'll explore various strategies for defining and understanding your target audience. We'll examine case studies, discuss segmentation techniques, and provide practical tools for audience analysis. By the end, you'll have a clear framework for identifying and connecting with the individuals who are most likely to value and benefit from your unique offerings.

Let's begin by exploring marketing and audience segmentation strategies, starting with insights from Seth Godin's concept of "Tribes" and its application to personal branding.

2. Marketing and Audience Segmentation Strategies

In the world of marketing and personal branding, few voices are as influential as Seth Godin. His concept of "Tribes" has revolutionized how we think about audience segmentation and niche marketing. Let's explore Godin's ideas and how they apply to personal branding, along with broader strategies for market segmentation.

Case Study: Seth Godin - Tribes and Niche Marketing

Seth Godin introduced the concept of "Tribes" in his 2008 book of the same name. According to Godin, a tribe is a group of people connected to one another, a leader, and an idea. In the context of marketing and personal branding, tribes represent niche audiences united by shared interests, values, or goals.

Key principles of Godin's Tribes concept:

1. Leadership: Tribes need leadership. In personal branding, you position yourself as a leader or expert for your specific tribe.

2. Communication: Tribes thrive on communication, both between members and with the leader. Facilitating and engaging in this communication is crucial.

3. Shared Interest: A tribe rallies around a common interest or goal. Your personal brand should align with and support this shared interest.

4. Action: Tribes are about more than just shared interest; they're about making things happen. Your brand should inspire and facilitate action.

5. Connection: Tribes provide a sense of belonging. Your brand can create a community around your expertise and values.

Application to Personal Branding:

1. Identify Your Tribe: Define the specific group of people who share the problems you solve or the aspirations you help fulfill.

2. Speak Their Language: Use terminology, references, and communication styles that resonate with your tribe.

3. Provide Value: Offer insights, solutions, or resources that are specifically valuable to your tribe.

4. Foster Community: Create opportunities for your tribe members to connect with each other, not just with you.

5. Lead with Purpose: Clearly articulate the mission or goal that unites your tribe, and show how your brand supports it.

Example: A financial advisor specializing in sustainable investing might identify their tribe as environmentally conscious professionals seeking to align their investments with their values. Their brand communication would focus on the intersection of financial growth and environmental impact, using language and concepts that resonate with this specific group.

Understanding Market Segmentation

Market segmentation is the process of dividing a broad market into subgroups based on shared characteristics. This approach allows for more targeted and effective marketing efforts. There are several types of market segmentation:

1. Demographic Segmentation: Based on factors like age, gender, income, education, and occupation.

2. Psychographic Segmentation: Focuses on personality traits, values, attitudes, interests, and lifestyles.

3. Behavioral Segmentation: Divides the market based on consumer behaviors, such as purchasing habits, brand interactions, or product usage.

4. Geographic Segmentation: Considers location-based factors, from broad (country, region) to specific (city, neighborhood).

5. Technographic Segmentation: Segments based on technology adoption and usage patterns.

6. Firmographic Segmentation: Used in B2B contexts, focusing on company characteristics like size, industry, and revenue.

Applying Segmentation to Personal Branding

To effectively apply segmentation to your personal brand, follow these steps:

1. Identify Potential Segments:

- List all possible ways to divide your potential audience.
- Consider which segments are most relevant to your expertise and offerings.

2. Research Your Segments:

- Gather data on each potential segment's needs, preferences, and behaviors.
- Use surveys, interviews, and market research tools to deepen your understanding.

3. Evaluate Segment Viability:

- Assess each segment's size, accessibility, and potential for growth.
- Consider how well your skills and offerings align with each segment's needs.

4. Select Target Segments:

- Choose one or more segments that offer the best opportunity for your personal brand.
- Ensure the selected segments are distinct enough to warrant specialized attention.

5. Develop Segment Profiles:

- Create detailed personas for each chosen segment.
- Include demographic information, psychographic characteristics, and behavioral patterns.

6. Tailor Your Brand Message:

- Craft your UVP and brand messaging to speak directly to your chosen segments.
- Ensure your communication channels and style align with your audience's preferences.

7. Test and Refine:

- Implement your segmented branding strategy.
- Monitor results and gather feedback to refine your approach.

Example Application:

A leadership coach might segment their audience as follows:

1. Emerging Tech Leaders: Young professionals in tech companies aspiring to leadership roles.

2. Women in STEM Executive Track: Mid-career women in STEM fields aiming for C-suite positions.

3. Non-Profit Visionaries: Leaders in non-profit organizations seeking to scale their impact.

For each segment, the coach would tailor their messaging, content, and services to address the specific challenges and aspirations of that group.

By applying these segmentation strategies to your personal brand, you can create a more focused, resonant, and effective brand presence.

Remember, the goal is not to exclude potential clients or opportunities, but to concentrate your efforts where they'll have the most impact. In the next section, we'll explore how to target niche audiences with specific needs, drawing insights from Tim Ferriss's approach to audience engagement.

3. Targeting Niche Audiences with Specific Needs

In the world of personal branding, the ability to target and serve a niche audience effectively can be a game-changer. One of the most influential concepts in this area is the "1,000 True Fans" theory, popularized by Tim Ferriss but originally conceived by Kevin Kelly. This approach emphasizes the power of a dedicated niche following over a larger, less engaged audience.

Case Study: Tim Ferriss - The "1,000 True Fans" Concept

Tim Ferriss, author of "The 4-Hour Work Week" and host of "The Tim Ferriss Show" podcast, has been a strong advocate of the "1,000 True Fans" concept. This theory suggests that to make a living as a creator, you don't need millions of casual fans. Instead, you need about 1,000 true fans who will purchase anything you produce.

Key aspects of Ferriss's application of this concept:

1. Focus on Quality Over Quantity: Ferriss emphasizes building deep connections with a smaller, more dedicated audience.

2. Diverse Content Offerings: He provides various ways for his true fans to engage, from books and podcasts to online courses and speaking engagements.

3. Consistent Value Delivery: Ferriss consistently delivers high-quality, actionable content that resonates deeply with his niche audience.

4. Engagement and Accessibility: He maintains a connection with his audience through social media, email newsletters, and occasional direct interactions.

5. Leveraging the Audience for Growth: Ferriss often involves his audience in his projects, from book titles to podcast questions, fostering a sense of community and loyalty.

Applying the "1,000 True Fans" concept to your personal brand:

1. Identify Your Niche: Define the specific group of people who would benefit most from your unique skills and perspective.

2. Create Superfan-Worthy Content: Develop content and offerings that deeply resonate with your niche audience's needs and interests.

3. Build Multiple Touchpoints: Offer various ways for your true fans to engage with and support your brand.

4. Foster Direct Connections: Create opportunities for more personal interactions with your most dedicated followers.

5. Continually Deliver Value: Consistently provide high-quality content and services that keep your true fans engaged and loyal.

Identifying and Defining Your Niche

To effectively target a niche audience, you need to clearly define who they are and what they need. Here's how to approach this:

1. Analyze Your Expertise:

- List your unique skills, experiences, and knowledge.
- Identify the specific problems you're best equipped to solve.

2. Research Potential Niches:

- Look for underserved markets within your broader field.
- Identify groups with specific, urgent needs that align with your expertise.

3. Assess Market Viability:

- Evaluate the size and accessibility of potential niches.
- Consider the purchasing power and willingness to invest in solutions.

4. Define Niche Characteristics:

- Create detailed profiles of your ideal clients within the niche.
- Include demographics, psychographics, and behavioral traits.

5. Validate Your Niche:

- Conduct surveys or interviews with potential niche members.
- Test your offerings on a small scale to gauge interest and effectiveness.

Tailoring Your Brand to Meet Specific Audience Needs

Once you've identified your niche, tailor your personal brand to meet their specific needs:

1. Craft a Niche-Focused UVP:

- Refine your Unique Value Proposition to speak directly to your niche audience's pain points and aspirations.

2. Develop Specialized Offerings:

- Create products, services, or content that address the unique challenges of your niche.

3. Speak Their Language:

- Use terminology, examples, and references that resonate specifically with your niche audience.

4. Choose Appropriate Channels:

- Identify and focus on the communication channels most used and valued by your niche.

5. Showcase Relevant Expertise:

- Highlight case studies, testimonials, and results that are most relevant to your niche audience.

6. Address Specific Pain Points:

- Create content and offerings that directly tackle the most pressing issues faced by your niche.

7. Build Niche Authority:

- Position yourself as the go-to expert for your specific niche through targeted thought leadership.

Example:

A marketing consultant might identify their niche as "eco-friendly startups seeking sustainable growth." They would then tailor their brand by:

- Focusing on green marketing strategies
- Using case studies from successful eco-friendly businesses
- Creating content about balancing growth with sustainability
- Offering specialized services like "Green Brand Development"
- Engaging with the audience through sustainability-focused platforms and events

By targeting a niche audience and tailoring your brand to their specific needs, you can create a more impactful and memorable personal brand. This focused approach allows you to become the go-to expert in your niche, fostering deeper connections and loyalty among your audience.

4. Building and Leveraging Online Communities

In the digital age, building and nurturing online communities has become a crucial aspect of personal branding. One individual who has mastered this art is Pat Flynn, the entrepreneur behind Smart Passive Income. His approach to community building offers valuable lessons for personal brand development.

Case Study: Pat Flynn - Creating Engaged Online Communities

Pat Flynn has built a thriving online community around his personal brand, focusing on passive income strategies and online entrepreneurship. His success in community building stems from several key strategies:

1. Transparency and Authenticity: Flynn is known for his honesty about his successes and failures, which builds trust with his audience.

2. Consistent Value Delivery: He regularly provides high-quality, actionable content through his blog, podcast, and YouTube channel.

3. Engagement and Accessibility: Flynn actively engages with his community through social media, comments, and live Q&A sessions.

4. Community-Centric Approach: He often involves his audience in his business decisions and content creation process.

5. Multiple Platforms: Flynn uses various platforms to reach and engage different segments of his community.

6. Focus on Relationships: He emphasizes building genuine relationships with his audience members, not just treating them as customers.

Strategies for Community Building

Building a strong online community around your personal brand involves several key strategies:

1. Define Your Community's Purpose:

- Clearly articulate what brings your community together.
- Identify the shared interests, goals, or challenges of your audience.

2. Choose the Right Platforms:

- Select platforms where your target audience is most active.
- Consider a mix of social media, forums, and owned platforms (like a website with comments or a private community platform).

3. Create Valuable Content:

- Regularly share content that addresses your community's needs and interests.
- Encourage discussion and interaction around your content.

4. Foster Engagement:

- Ask questions and encourage community members to share their thoughts and experiences.
- Respond promptly to comments and messages.
- Create opportunities for members to interact with each other, not just with you.

5. Establish Community Guidelines:

- Set clear rules for interaction to maintain a positive and supportive environment.
- Moderate discussions to ensure they remain constructive and on-topic.

6. Recognize and Reward Participation:

- Highlight active community members.
- Create special roles or privileges for highly engaged members.

7. Host Virtual Events:

- Organize webinars, live Q&A sessions, or virtual meetups to strengthen community bonds.

8. Encourage User-Generated Content:

- Prompt community members to share their own stories, tips, or achievements.
- Feature standout contributions from community members.

9. Provide Exclusive Value:

- Offer special content, discounts, or early access to new offerings for community members.

10. Continuously Gather Feedback:

- Regularly ask for input on how to improve the community experience.
- Be responsive to the evolving needs of your community.

Leveraging Community for Brand Growth

A strong online community can significantly enhance your personal brand. Here's how to leverage your community for brand growth:

1. Market Research:

    - Use your community as a sounding board for new ideas or offerings.
    - Gather insights about your audience's evolving needs and preferences.

2. Content Creation:

    - Draw inspiration for content topics from community discussions.
    - Create collaborative content featuring community members.

3. Social Proof:

    - Showcase testimonials and success stories from community members.
    - Highlight the size and engagement of your community to establish credibility.

4. Word-of-Mouth Marketing:

    - Encourage community members to share your content and offerings with their networks.
    - Create referral programs to incentivize community-driven growth.

5. Product Development:

    - Involve your community in the development process of new offerings.
    - Use community feedback to refine and improve your products or services.

6. Partnerships and Collaborations:

    - Identify potential partners or collaborators from within your community.
    - Leverage community connections to access new opportunities.

7. Brand Advocacy:

- Nurture your most engaged community members into brand advocates.
- Provide them with tools and incentives to promote your brand.

8. Continuous Learning:

- Use community interactions to stay updated on industry trends and challenges.
- Adapt your brand messaging and offerings based on community insights.

9. Crisis Management:

- In times of controversy or challenge, a loyal community can provide support and defend your brand.

10. Monetization Opportunities:

- Develop premium community features or exclusive offerings for dedicated members.
- Create community-driven events or products.

Example Application:

A personal fitness trainer might build a community around sustainable weight loss and healthy living. They could:

- Create a Facebook group for daily motivation and support
- Host weekly live workout sessions on Instagram
- Encourage members to share their progress and tips
- Feature success stories in their content
- Develop a premium membership with exclusive workouts and nutrition plans
- Use community feedback to create new fitness programs

By building and nurturing an engaged online community, you create a powerful ecosystem around your personal brand. This community not only provides ongoing support and validation for your brand but also becomes a valuable asset for growth, innovation, and resilience in your professional journey.

5. Market Research Techniques for Personal Branding

Effective personal branding relies on a deep understanding of your target audience. Market research techniques can provide valuable insights into your audience's needs, preferences, and behaviors. Let's explore both quantitative and qualitative research methods, as well as the use of social media listening and analytics.

Quantitative vs. Qualitative Research Methods

Quantitative Research:

Quantitative research focuses on collecting numerical data that can be analyzed statistically. It's useful for understanding trends, patterns, and generalizations about your audience.

Key quantitative methods for personal branding:

1. Surveys: Use online tools like SurveyMonkey or Google Forms to gather large-scale data.

2. Analytics: Analyze website traffic, social media engagement rates, and other measurable metrics.

3. A/B Testing: Compare different versions of your content or offerings to see which performs better.

Advantages:

- Provides concrete, measurable data
- Can reach a large sample size
- Useful for identifying trends and patterns

Limitations:

- May miss nuanced insights
- Can be impersonal
- Might not capture the 'why' behind responses

Qualitative Research:

Qualitative research focuses on in-depth, descriptive information. It's valuable for understanding motivations, opinions, and underlying reasons for behavior.

Key qualitative methods for personal branding:

1. Interviews: Conduct one-on-one conversations with members of your target audience.

2. Focus Groups: Gather small groups for guided discussions about your brand or offerings.

3. Open-ended Surveys: Use questions that allow for detailed, free-form responses.

4. Social Media Engagement: Analyze comments, messages, and discussions related to your brand.

Advantages:

- Provides rich, detailed insights
- Helps understand motivations and opinions
- Allows for unexpected discoveries

Limitations:

- Time-consuming
- Smaller sample sizes
- Can be subjective in interpretation

Using Social Media Listening and Analytics

Social media platforms offer powerful tools for understanding your audience:

1. Social Listening:

- Monitor mentions of your brand, industry keywords, and competitors.
- Analyze sentiment and themes in discussions related to your field.
- Use tools like Hootsuite, Brandwatch, or Mention for comprehensive listening.

2. Analytics:

- Utilize built-in analytics tools on platforms like Facebook Insights, Twitter Analytics, and LinkedIn Analytics.
- Track engagement rates, follower growth, and popular content topics.
- Analyze demographic data of your followers and engaged audience.

3. Hashtag Analysis:

- Identify popular hashtags in your niche.
- Analyze the content and engagement associated with these hashtags.

4. Competitor Analysis:

- Study the social media presence of competitors or industry leaders.
- Identify gaps or opportunities in their content strategy.

5. Audience Surveys:

- Use social media polls or questions to gather quick insights from your followers.

6. Content Performance:

- Analyze which types of content (e.g., videos, infographics, text posts) perform best with your audience.
- Identify optimal posting times and frequencies.

Implementing Market Research for Personal Branding:

1. Define Clear Objectives: Determine what specific insights you need about your audience.

2. Choose Appropriate Methods: Select research techniques that align with your objectives and resources.

3. Develop Research Tools: Create surveys, interview questions, or social media monitoring plans.

4. Collect Data: Implement your chosen research methods.

5. Analyze Results: Look for patterns, trends, and insights in the data collected.

6. Apply Findings: Use the insights to refine your personal brand strategy, content, and offerings.

7. Continual Monitoring: Regularly update your research to stay aligned with your audience's evolving needs.

By combining quantitative and qualitative research methods with social media insights, you can gain a comprehensive understanding of your target audience. This knowledge will enable you to tailor your personal brand more effectively, creating content and offerings that truly resonate with your audience.

6. Creating Detailed Audience Personas

Audience personas are fictional, generalized representations of your ideal audience members. They help you visualize and understand your target audience, making it easier to tailor your personal brand and content to their specific needs and preferences.

Key Components of an Effective Persona

1. Demographics:

- Age range
- Gender
- Location
- Education level
- Income bracket
- Occupation or industry

2. Psychographics:

- Values and beliefs
- Lifestyle choices
- Interests and hobbies
- Personality traits

3. Goals and Challenges:

- Professional aspirations
- Personal goals
- Key challenges or pain points
- Obstacles to achieving goals

4. Information Sources:

- Preferred social media platforms
- Favorite websites or blogs
- Trusted information sources
- Influential figures they follow

5. Buying Behavior:

- Decision-making process
- Factors influencing purchases
- Preferred communication channels
- Budget considerations

6. Brand Interactions:

- How they might discover your brand
- What they seek from your content or services
- Potential objections or hesitations

7. Quote:

- A fictional quote that captures the persona's voice and primary concern

8. Name and Image:

- Give your persona a name and add a stock photo to make them feel more real

Tools and Templates for Persona Development

1. HubSpot's Make My Persona:

   - Free online tool that guides you through creating detailed buyer personas
   - Provides a downloadable, visual representation of your persona

2. Xtensio User Persona Creator:

   - Customizable template for creating detailed, visually appealing personas
   - Allows for easy sharing and collaboration

3. Up Close & Persona:

   - Mobile app that helps you create and store multiple personas
   - Includes prompts to help you think through various aspects of your persona

4. Personapp:

   - Simple, web-based tool for creating basic personas quickly
   - Good for initial brainstorming and concept development

5. Userforge:

   - Offers templates and a user-friendly interface for creating detailed personas
   - Allows for team collaboration and persona sharing

6. DIY Spreadsheet Template:

   - Create your own template in Excel or Google Sheets
   - Customize categories to fit your specific needs

Steps to Create Effective Personas:

1. Gather Data:

- Use your market research findings, including both quantitative and qualitative data.
- Analyze your current audience or client base for common characteristics.

2. Identify Patterns:

- Look for recurring themes or characteristics in your data.
- Group similar traits to form the basis of distinct personas.

3. Create Multiple Personas:

- Develop 2-4 personas to represent different segments of your audience.
- Ensure each persona is distinct and represents a significant portion of your audience.

4. Add Detail:

- Flesh out each persona with specific details that make them feel like real individuals.
- Include a mix of professional and personal characteristics.

5. Validate Your Personas:

- Cross-check your personas with real audience members or clients.
- Adjust based on feedback and additional insights.

6. Use Your Personas:

- Reference your personas when creating content, developing offerings, or making branding decisions.
- Regularly update your personas as you gain new insights about your audience.

Example Persona for a Leadership Coach:

Name: Ambitious Anna

Demographics: Female, 32, Urban, MBA, $80,000/year, Marketing Manager

Psychographics: Ambitious, values work-life balance, interested in personal development

Goals: Advance to a director-level position within 2 years, improve team management skills

Challenges: Imposter syndrome, difficulty delegating, work-stress management

Information Sources: LinkedIn, Harvard Business Review, TED Talks

Buying Behavior: Researches thoroughly, values social proof, willing to invest in career development

Quote: "I know I have the potential to lead, but I need guidance on how to step into a leadership role confidently."

By creating detailed audience personas, you can better tailor your personal brand messaging, content, and offerings to meet the specific needs and preferences of your target audience. This personalized approach can lead to stronger connections, increased engagement, and more effective personal branding overall.

7. Psychographics in Personal Branding

While demographics provide important factual information about your audience, psychographics delve deeper into the psychological aspects that influence behavior, preferences, and decision-making. Understanding psychographic factors can significantly enhance your personal branding efforts by allowing you to connect with your audience on a more meaningful level.

Understanding Psychographic Factors

Psychographic factors include:

1. Values: Core beliefs that guide decisions and behavior.

2. Attitudes: Opinions and feelings about various topics or issues.

3. Interests: Activities, topics, or ideas that capture attention and engagement.

4. Lifestyle: Daily routines, habits, and choices that reflect overall way of life.

5. Personality Traits: Characteristic patterns of thinking, feeling, and behaving.

6. Motivations: Underlying reasons for actions and decisions.

7. Aspirations: Goals, ambitions, and desired future states.

Gathering Psychographic Data:

1. Surveys and Questionnaires: Use open-ended questions to explore attitudes and motivations.

2. Social Media Analysis: Examine content preferences, interactions, and shared interests.

3. In-Depth Interviews: Conduct one-on-one conversations to uncover deeper insights.

4. Observational Research: Study behavior patterns in relevant contexts.

5. Psychographic Segmentation Tools: Utilize specialized tools like VALS (Values and Lifestyles) or PRIZM.

Applying Psychographic Data to Brand Messaging

Once you've gathered psychographic data, here's how to apply it to your personal brand messaging:

1. Tailor Your Language:

- Use words and phrases that resonate with your audience's values and attitudes.
- Example: For an environmentally conscious audience, emphasize sustainability in your messaging.

2. Address Motivations:

- Craft your UVP to speak directly to your audience's underlying motivations.
- Example: If your audience is motivated by career advancement, highlight how your services can accelerate professional growth.

3. Align with Lifestyle:

- Present your brand in a way that fits seamlessly into your audience's lifestyle.
- Example: For a busy, on-the-go audience, emphasize convenience and efficiency in your offerings.

4. Appeal to Aspirations:

- Connect your brand with your audience's goals and ambitions.
- Example: If your audience aspires to be thought leaders, show how your brand can help them achieve that status.

5. Match Personality Traits:

- Adjust your brand voice to complement your audience's dominant personality traits.
- Example: For an audience that values innovation, adopt a forward-thinking, creative tone in your communications.

6. Create Relatable Content:

- Develop content that reflects your audience's interests and concerns.
- Example: If your audience is interested in work-life balance, create content addressing this topic.

7. Choose Appropriate Channels:

- Select communication channels that align with your audience's preferences and habits.
- Example: If your audience values personal connections, prioritize one-on-one interactions or small group settings.

8. Develop Targeted Offerings:

- Create products or services that cater to specific psychographic segments.
- Example: Offer different coaching packages tailored to various personality types or career stages.

By incorporating psychographic insights into your personal branding strategy, you can create a more nuanced, relatable, and impactful brand presence. This deeper level of understanding allows you to connect with your audience on an emotional and psychological level, fostering stronger relationships and brand loyalty.

8. Aligning Your Brand with Your Audience's Needs

To create a truly effective personal brand, it's crucial to align your brand closely with your audience's needs, pain points, and desires. This alignment ensures that your brand not only attracts your target audience but also provides genuine value, fostering long-term engagement and loyalty.

Identifying Audience Pain Points and Desires

1. Direct Feedback:

- Conduct surveys or interviews with your current audience or clients.
- Ask open-ended questions about their challenges and aspirations.

2. Social Listening:

- Monitor social media discussions, forums, and comments related to your field.
- Look for recurring themes or complaints.

3. Competitor Analysis:

- Examine reviews of competitors or similar services.
- Identify unmet needs or common criticisms.

4. Industry Research:

- Stay updated on industry reports and trends.
- Identify emerging challenges or opportunities in your field.

5. Behavior Analysis:

- Analyze your audience's interaction with your content or services.
- Identify which topics or offerings generate the most engagement.

6. Empathy Mapping:

- Create empathy maps to visualize what your audience thinks, feels, says, and does.
- Use this to uncover underlying needs and motivations.

7. Customer Journey Mapping:

- Map out your audience's journey in solving the problem you address.
- Identify pain points at each stage of this journey.

Common Categories of Pain Points:

1. Financial: Cost-related issues or desire for better value.

2. Productivity: Inefficiencies or time management challenges.

3. Process: Difficulties with specific procedures or systems.

4. Support: Lack of guidance or assistance in achieving goals.

5. Technological: Struggles with adopting or using technology effectively.

6. Communication: Challenges in conveying or receiving information.

7. Emotional: Stress, frustration, or lack of confidence in certain areas.

Mapping Your UVP to Audience Needs

Once you've identified your audience's pain points and desires, the next step is to align your Unique Value Proposition (UVP) with these needs. Here's how to create this alignment:

1. Create a Needs-Solution Matrix:

- List identified audience needs in one column.

- In the adjacent column, detail how your skills, experience, or offerings address each need.

2. Prioritize Key Pain Points:

- Focus on the most pressing or common needs.
- Ensure your UVP directly addresses these primary concerns.

3. Highlight Unique Approaches:

- Emphasize how your approach to solving problems is different or more effective than alternatives.

4. Use Audience Language:

- Incorporate terms and phrases your audience uses to describe their challenges in your UVP.

5. Quantify Benefits:

- Where possible, include specific, measurable benefits your audience can expect.

6. Address Emotional and Practical Needs:

- Ensure your UVP speaks to both logical and emotional aspects of your audience's needs.

7. Create Segment-Specific UVPs:

- If you have distinct audience segments, consider crafting tailored UVPs for each.

8. Test and Refine:

- Present your UVP to members of your target audience and gather feedback.
- Iterate based on responses to ensure maximum relevance and impact.

Example of Aligning UVP with Audience Needs:

Audience: Mid-career professionals seeking career advancement

Identified Needs:

- Lack of leadership skills
- Difficulty balancing work and personal life
- Desire for industry recognition

Aligned UVP:

"I help ambitious mid-career professionals develop executive-level leadership skills and achieve work-life harmony, positioning them as recognized industry experts within 12 months. Through my unique blend of strategic coaching and personal branding techniques, clients report an average 40% increase in productivity and a 30% boost in industry visibility."

This UVP directly addresses the identified needs:

- Addresses the lack of leadership skills
- Promises work-life balance
- Offers a path to industry recognition
- Provides specific, measurable outcomes

By aligning your personal brand closely with your audience's needs, you create a powerful resonance that attracts and retains your ideal clients or followers. This alignment not only makes your brand more appealing but also ensures that you're providing genuine value, which is the foundation of a successful and sustainable personal brand.

Chapter 4 Decision Tree: Identifying and Connecting with Your Target Audience

This decision tree guides you through the process of defining, understanding, and engaging with your target audience.

Start: Have you identified your target audience segments?

• **Yes** → Proceed to **Creating Audience Personas**

• **No → Define Your Target Segments**

- Consider **Demographics** (age, location, profession)
- Analyze **Psychographics** (values, interests, lifestyle)
- Identify which segments align with your **UVP** (Unique Value Proposition)

Next: Have you created detailed audience personas?

• **Yes** → Proceed to **Understanding Audience Needs**

• **No** → **Develop Audience Personas**

- Create **2-3 Detailed Fictional Characters** representing your audience
- Include **Demographics, Goals, Challenges, and Preferences**
- Use **Market Research** and **Real-World Observations**

Next: Do you understand your audience's needs and pain points?

• **Yes** → Proceed to **Platform Selection**

• **No** → **Research Audience Needs**

- Conduct **Surveys or Interviews**
- Analyze **Industry Reports** and **Trends**
- Engage in **Social Listening**

Next: Have you identified the best platforms to reach your audience?

• **Yes** → Proceed to **Content Strategy**

• **No** → **Select Appropriate Platforms**

- Research where your audience **Spends Time Online**
- Consider which platforms **Suit Your Content Type**
- Evaluate **Platform Demographics** and **User Behavior**

Next: Have you developed a targeted content strategy?

• **Yes** → Proceed to **Engagement Measurement**

• **No** → **Create a Content Strategy**

- Align content topics with **Audience Interests and Needs**
- Choose **Content Formats** your audience prefers
- Develop a **Content Calendar**

Next: Are you measuring audience engagement?

• Yes → Analyze and Refine Your Approach

• No → Implement Engagement Metrics

- Set up **Analytics Tools**
- Track **Key Performance Indicators** (likes, shares, comments)
- Monitor **Audience Growth and Retention**

Final: Regularly reassess your audience and adjust your strategy

Conclusion

Chapter 4 has guided you through the critical process of defining and understanding your target audience, a foundational step in building a successful personal brand. In this chapter, we've explored how identifying the right audience is not just about demographics but about deeply understanding the needs, preferences, and pain points of those you seek to serve. By doing so, you can tailor your brand messaging and strategies to resonate powerfully with your audience, ensuring that your brand connects on a meaningful level.

We discussed the importance of creating detailed audience personas that go beyond basic characteristics to include behaviors, motivations, and challenges. These personas serve as a blueprint for all your branding efforts, helping you craft content and strategies that speak directly to your audience's needs and desires. Furthermore, we examined the role of empathy in personal branding, highlighting that truly understanding your audience means seeing the world from their perspective and addressing their concerns authentically.

The chapter also covered the significance of segmenting your audience, allowing you to focus your efforts more effectively and engage different segments with tailored messaging. This approach ensures that your brand remains relevant and compelling to all parts of your audience, whether you're addressing potential clients, collaborators, or industry peers.

As you move forward, use the insights and tools from this chapter to continually refine your understanding of your audience. Remember that audience preferences and behaviors can evolve, so it's essential to stay attuned to these changes and adapt your branding strategies accordingly. By keeping your audience at the center of your branding efforts, you will build a brand that not only attracts attention but also fosters loyalty and long-term engagement.

In summary, defining and understanding your target audience is an ongoing journey that requires regular reflection and adjustment. The more you align your brand with the true needs and desires of your audience, the more impactful and sustainable your personal brand will become. This audience-centric approach will not only enhance your brand's effectiveness but also position you as a trusted and valued leader in your field.

Chapter 5

Crafting Your Brand Story and Message

1. Introduction: The Power of Storytelling in Personal Branding

In the realm of personal branding, few tools are as powerful or as universally engaging as storytelling. A well-crafted brand story has the ability to captivate your audience, create emotional connections, and make your personal brand memorable and meaningful. It's not just about listing your achievements or skills; it's about weaving a narrative that resonates with your audience on a deeper level.

Storytelling in personal branding serves multiple purposes:

1. Differentiation: In a crowded marketplace, your unique story sets you apart from others in your field.

2. Emotional Connection: Stories evoke emotions, helping your audience relate to you on a personal level.

3. Memorability: People are more likely to remember a compelling story than a list of facts or accomplishments.

4. Trust Building: Sharing your journey, including struggles and successes, builds authenticity and trust with your audience.

5. Value Demonstration: Your story can illustrate the value you bring and the problems you solve in a relatable way.

6. Brand Consistency: A well-defined story provides a framework for consistent messaging across all platforms.

Throughout this chapter, we'll explore the elements of effective brand storytelling and how to craft a narrative that authentically represents your personal brand. We'll examine case studies of successful brand storytelling, provide techniques for incorporating personal experiences into your narrative, and offer strategies for adapting your story across various platforms.

By the end of this chapter, you'll have the tools to create a compelling brand story that not only captures the essence of who you are and what you offer but also resonates deeply with your target audience. Let's begin by exploring how to create a compelling personal narrative, starting with a case study of one of the most famous author success stories of our time: J.K. Rowling.

2. Creating a Compelling Personal Narrative

A compelling personal narrative is at the heart of a strong personal brand. It's the story that explains who you are, where you've come from, and why you do what you do. To understand how to craft such a narrative, let's examine the story of J.K. Rowling, whose personal journey has become almost as famous as her literary creations.

Case Study: J.K. Rowling - From Struggle to Success Story

J.K. Rowling's journey from struggling single mother to world-renowned author is a masterclass in compelling personal narrative:

1. Humble Beginnings: Rowling often speaks about her time as a single mother living on state benefits, writing in cafes while her baby daughter slept beside her.

2. The Spark of Inspiration: She shares the story of how the idea for Harry Potter came to her fully formed while on a delayed train journey.

3. Perseverance Through Rejection: Rowling's manuscript was rejected by multiple publishers before being accepted, a detail she's open about sharing.

4. Overnight Success: The meteoric rise of the Harry Potter series is contrasted with her previous struggles, creating a dramatic arc.

5. Giving Back: Her narrative includes her philanthropic efforts and how she's used her success to make a positive impact.

6. Continued Growth: Rowling's story doesn't end with Harry Potter; she talks about her continued writing under a pseudonym and her expansion into screenwriting.

Key Elements of Rowling's Narrative:

- Relatable struggle
- Moment of inspiration
- Perseverance in the face of rejection
- Dramatic transformation
- Using success for good
- Continued evolution

Elements of an Effective Brand Story

Drawing from Rowling's example and other successful personal brand narratives, we can identify key elements of an effective brand story:

1. Authenticity: Your story should be genuine and true to your experiences.

2. Vulnerability: Sharing challenges and setbacks makes your story relatable and builds trust.

3. Transformation: Highlight how you've grown or changed over time.

4. Unique Angle: Identify what makes your story different from others in your field.

5. Relevance to Your Audience: Your story should resonate with the needs and aspirations of your target audience.

6. Clear Purpose: Your narrative should illustrate why you do what you do and what drives you.

7. Conflict and Resolution: Include challenges you've faced and how you've overcome them.

8. Emotional Appeal: Incorporate elements that evoke emotional responses from your audience.

9. Consistency: Ensure your story aligns with your brand values and messaging across all platforms.

Incorporating Personal Experiences into Your Narrative

To create a compelling personal narrative, consider these strategies for incorporating your own experiences:

1. Identify Key Moments:

- List significant events or decisions that shaped your professional journey.
- Look for turning points or moments of realization.

2. Find the Universal in the Personal:

- Consider how your personal experiences relate to broader themes or common challenges.
- Frame your story in a way that others can see themselves in it.

3. Use Sensory Details:

- Include specific, vivid details that bring your story to life.
- Appeal to multiple senses to make your narrative more engaging.

4. Show Growth and Learning:

- Highlight how you've evolved through your experiences.
- Share lessons learned and how they've shaped your approach.

5. Connect Past to Present:

- Draw clear lines between your past experiences and your current expertise or offerings.
- Show how your journey has uniquely prepared you to serve your audience.

6. Be Selective:

- Choose experiences that are most relevant to your brand and audience.
- Not every detail needs to be included; focus on impactful moments.

7. Use Anecdotes:

- Incorporate short, illustrative stories within your larger narrative.
- Use these to exemplify key points or values.

8. Balance Professional and Personal:

- While your focus is professional, including relevant personal details can make your story more relatable.
- Ensure personal elements tie back to your professional brand.

Example Outline for a Personal Brand Narrative:

1. Early Inspiration: What first drew you to your field?

2. Initial Challenges: What obstacles did you face starting out?

3. Key Learning Moment: What experience significantly shaped your approach?

4. Pivotal Decision: What choice set you on your current path?

5. Breakthrough: When did you first see significant success or recognition?

6. Current Mission: What drives you now, and how does it relate to your journey?

7. Future Vision: How do you aim to grow or impact your field moving forward?

By crafting a personal narrative that incorporates these elements and your unique experiences, you create a powerful tool for connecting with your audience. Your story becomes not just a recounting of events, but a compelling reason for others to engage with your brand, trust your expertise, and believe in your mission. Remember, your narrative should evolve as you grow professionally, always reflecting the current state of your brand while honoring the journey that brought you here.

3. Inspiring Others Through Personal Transformation Stories

Personal transformation stories are powerful tools in personal branding, as they not only showcase your journey but also inspire and motivate your audience. To understand how to effectively craft and use these narratives, let's examine the case of Tony Robbins, a master of using personal growth to inspire others.

Case Study: Tony Robbins - Using Personal Growth to Inspire Others

Tony Robbins, a world-renowned life coach and motivational speaker, has built his brand around his own transformation story and his ability to help others transform their lives.

Key elements of Robbins' transformation narrative:

1. Humble Beginnings: Robbins often speaks about his challenging childhood, including poverty and an abusive household.

2. Turning Point: He describes a pivotal moment when he decided to change his life after attending a seminar by Jim Rohn.

3. Self-Education: Robbins emphasizes his voracious appetite for learning and self-improvement.

4. Early Success: He shares stories of his rapid rise as a young motivational speaker.

5. Continuous Growth: Robbins consistently highlights his ongoing journey of personal development.

6. Helping Others: His narrative always circles back to how his transformation enables him to help others change their lives.

What makes Robbins' story effective:

- Relatability: His struggles are relatable to many people.
- Hope: His transformation offers hope for others facing challenges.
- Actionability: He provides clear steps for others to achieve similar transformations.
- Authenticity: Robbins is open about his ongoing challenges and growth.

Crafting Transformation Narratives

To create your own compelling transformation narrative, consider these steps:

1. Identify Your Starting Point:

- Describe your initial state or challenge.
- Be specific about the obstacles you faced.

2. Highlight the Catalyst:

- Pinpoint the moment or realization that sparked your transformation.
- Explain what motivated you to change.

3. Detail the Journey:

- Outline the steps you took to transform.
- Include both successes and setbacks.

4. Showcase the Results:

- Describe your transformed state.
- Highlight tangible and intangible outcomes.

5. Connect to Your Audience:

- Explain how your transformation relates to what you offer your audience.
- Show how your experience can benefit others.

6. Emphasize Ongoing Growth:

- Indicate that transformation is a continuous process.
- Share your current growth goals.

Balancing Vulnerability and Expertise in Storytelling

Effective transformation stories require a delicate balance between showing vulnerability and demonstrating expertise:

1. Strategic Vulnerability:

    - Share struggles that are relevant to your brand and audience.
    - Be honest about challenges without oversharing.

2. Focus on Lessons Learned:

    - Frame difficulties as learning experiences.
    - Emphasize the skills or insights gained from challenges.

3. Demonstrate Growth:

    - Show how you've developed expertise through your experiences.
    - Use your story to establish credibility in your field.

4. Link Personal Growth to Professional Skills:

    - Connect your personal transformation to your professional offerings.
    - Show how your journey has uniquely prepared you to help others.

5. Use Vulnerability to Build Connection:

    - Share emotions and personal insights to create relatability.
    - Use vulnerable moments to demonstrate authenticity.

6. Balance with Achievements:

    - Complement vulnerable moments with stories of success and accomplishment.
    - Show how overcoming challenges led to significant achievements.

7. Maintain Professional Boundaries:

    - While being open, maintain appropriate professional distance.
    - Ensure all shared information serves a purpose in your brand narrative.

By crafting a compelling transformation narrative that balances vulnerability with expertise, you create a powerful tool for inspiring and connecting with your audience. Your story becomes not just a personal account, but a beacon of possibility for others facing similar challenges.

4. Using Personal Experiences to Drive Change

Personal experiences, when shared effectively, can be catalysts for significant change. They can inspire action, shift perspectives, and mobilize communities. To understand how to leverage personal experiences for broader impact, let's examine the case of Malala Yousafzai, who turned her personal struggle into a global advocacy movement.

Case Study: Malala Yousafzai - Turning Personal Struggle into Global Advocacy

Malala Yousafzai, the youngest Nobel Prize laureate, has used her personal story to become a powerful advocate for girls' education worldwide.

Key elements of Malala's story:

1. Context: She describes growing up in Pakistan's Swat Valley under Taliban rule.

2. Personal Passion: Malala shares her love for learning and her father's support for her education.

3. Defiance: She recounts how she continued to attend school despite Taliban threats.

4. Attack: Malala openly discusses the assassination attempt she survived.

5. Recovery and Resolve: She shares her journey of recovery and her strengthened commitment to education advocacy.

6. Global Platform: Malala explains how she uses her experiences to fight for girls' education globally.

What makes Malala's story impactful:

- Courage: Her bravery in the face of extreme adversity is inspiring.
- Resilience: Her ability to turn a traumatic experience into a force for good is powerful.

- Universal Theme: Education is a relatable and widely supported cause.
- Ongoing Commitment: She continues to work towards her goal, showing dedication beyond her personal story.

Linking Personal Stories to Broader Causes

To effectively use your personal experiences to drive change, consider these strategies:

1. Identify the Universal in Your Personal:

    - Reflect on how your experiences relate to broader social issues.
    - Find common themes that others can relate to.

2. Articulate the Broader Impact:

    - Clearly explain how your personal experience connects to a larger societal challenge.
    - Use data and research to support the wider relevance of your story.

3. Create a Call to Action:

    - Develop specific, actionable steps others can take to support your cause.
    - Make it clear how individual actions can contribute to broader change.

4. Build a Movement:

    - Use your story as a rallying point for others with similar experiences.
    - Create platforms or communities for shared advocacy.

5. Evolve Your Narrative:

    - As your cause progresses, update your story to reflect new challenges and achievements.
    - Show how individual stories, including your own, have contributed to progress.

Creating Emotional Connections Through Storytelling

Emotional connections are key to inspiring action and driving change. Here's how to create these connections through your storytelling:

1. Use Sensory Details:

- Provide vivid descriptions that allow the audience to see, hear, and feel your experience.
- Use specific, concrete language to make your story more tangible.

2. Share Authentic Emotions:

- Be honest about the feelings you experienced.
- Allow yourself to be vulnerable in sharing difficult emotions.

3. Create Relatable Moments:

- Include elements in your story that your audience can relate to their own lives.
- Use universal themes like family, hope, or perseverance.

4. Use Pacing and Structure:

- Build tension and resolution in your narrative to keep the audience engaged.
- Use pauses and emphasis to heighten emotional impact.

5. Incorporate Dialogue:

- Include conversations or quotes that bring your story to life.
- Use dialogue to show different perspectives or key moments of realization.

6. Connect Past to Present:

- Show how your past experiences influence your current actions and future goals.
- Draw clear lines between your personal journey and your advocacy work.

7. Use Metaphors and Analogies:

- Employ figurative language to make complex issues more relatable and understandable.
- Choose metaphors that resonate with your target audience.

8. End with Hope and Possibility:

- While acknowledging challenges, conclude with a message of hope.
- Inspire your audience by showing the potential for positive change.

By effectively linking your personal experiences to broader causes and creating emotional connections through your storytelling, you can inspire others to take action and drive meaningful change. Your personal brand becomes not just a professional asset, but a platform for social impact. Remember, the most powerful stories are those that not only share a personal journey but also invite others to be part of a larger narrative of change and progress.

5. Developing Your Core Brand Message

Your core brand message is the foundation of your personal brand communication. It encapsulates who you are, what you do, and why it matters. A well-crafted core message ensures consistency across all your brand touchpoints and helps your audience quickly understand your value proposition.

Defining Your Brand's Central Theme

To define your brand's central theme, consider these steps:

1. Identify Your Purpose:

- What drives you in your professional life?
- What impact do you want to make in your field or the world?

2. Articulate Your Unique Value:

- What sets you apart from others in your field?
- What unique combination of skills, experiences, and perspectives do you offer?

3. Define Your Target Audience:

- Who are you primarily trying to reach?
- What are their key needs or pain points?

4. Clarify Your Solution:

- How do you address your audience's needs?
- What specific benefits do you provide?

5. Incorporate Your Personality:

- What personal qualities define your approach?
- How can you infuse your authentic self into your brand theme?

6. Consider Your Legacy:

- What do you want to be known for in the long term?
- How does your work contribute to your field or community?

Example:

Central Theme for a Leadership Coach:

"Empowering emerging leaders to navigate complex business environments through innovative problem-solving and authentic communication strategies."

Crafting a Compelling Brand Tagline

A brand tagline is a short, memorable phrase that captures the essence of your brand. It should be concise, impactful, and reflective of your central theme. Here's how to craft an effective tagline:

1. Keep it Short:

- Aim for 37 words.
- Ensure it's easy to remember and repeat.

2. Make it Unique:

- Avoid clichés or generic phrases.

- Incorporate elements specific to your brand.

3. Focus on Benefits:

- Highlight the value you provide to your audience.
- Address a key pain point or aspiration.

4. Use Strong Language:

- Choose powerful, active verbs.
- Select words with emotional resonance.

5. Ensure Relevance:

- Align the tagline with your brand's central theme.
- Make it meaningful to your target audience.

6. Test for Versatility:

- Ensure the tagline works across various platforms and contexts.

7. Make it Timeless:

- Avoid trendy language that might quickly become outdated.
- Focus on enduring qualities or values.

Tagline Examples:

- For a Financial Advisor: "Building Wealth, Securing Futures"
- For a Wellness Coach: "Energize Your Body, Empower Your Life"
- For a Tech Consultant: "Innovating Solutions, Transforming Businesses"

Iterative Process:

Developing your core brand message and tagline is often an iterative process. Create multiple versions, test them with your target audience, and refine based on feedback. Your message should evolve as your brand grows, but the central theme should remain consistent.

Consistency Across Platforms:

Once you've defined your core message and tagline, ensure they're consistently represented across all your brand touchpoints – your website, social media profiles, marketing materials, and personal interactions.

6. Storytelling Techniques for Personal Branding

Effective storytelling is crucial for bringing your personal brand to life. By using proven narrative structures and incorporating vivid details, you can create stories that engage your audience and reinforce your brand message.

Narrative Structures and Their Application

1. The Hero's Journey:

This classic structure follows a protagonist through challenges and transformation.

Application: Use this to narrate your professional journey, highlighting obstacles overcome and lessons learned.

Example: A software engineer describing her journey from coding bootcamp to leading a major tech project, overcoming imposter syndrome along the way.

2. The Mountain:

This structure builds tension to a climax before reaching a resolution.

Application: Ideal for describing a significant project or challenge you've tackled.

Example: A marketing consultant narrating a campaign that faced initial setbacks but ultimately achieved record-breaking results.

3. Nested Loops:

This involves telling multiple stories within a larger narrative.

Application: Use this to weave together various experiences that collectively reinforce your brand message.

Example: A leadership coach sharing three client success stories within the broader narrative of developing their coaching methodology.

4. In Medias Res:

Start in the middle of the action, then backtrack to explain how you got there.

Application: Effective for grabbing attention quickly, especially in presentations or pitches.

Example: A public speaker beginning with a vivid description of standing on a TED Talk stage, then explaining the journey to that moment.

5. Sparklines:

Contrast the ordinary world with an ideal, improved world.

Application: Use this to highlight the transformation you offer to clients or in your field.

Example: A sustainability consultant contrasting current business practices with the positive impact of adopting green strategies.

Using Anecdotes and Sensory Details Effectively

Anecdotes:

Short, focused stories can powerfully illustrate your points and make your message more memorable.

1. Keep them Relevant:

Ensure each anecdote directly supports your main message or brand theme.

2. Be Concise:

Stick to the essential details that drive your point home.

3. Use Dialogue:

Include brief snippets of conversation to bring the anecdote to life.

4. Highlight the Lesson:

Clearly articulate what the anecdote demonstrates about your skills or approach.

Example Anecdote:

"During a crucial client presentation, our projector failed. Instead of panicking, I quickly sketched our key points on a whiteboard. The clients were impressed by our adaptability, and we won the contract. This experience epitomizes my approach: stay calm, think creatively, and always focus on delivering value to the client."

Sensory Details:

Incorporating sensory information makes your stories more vivid and engaging.

1. Visual Details:

Describe colors, shapes, and movements to create a clear picture.

2. Auditory Elements:

Include sounds that bring the scene to life.

3. Tactile Sensations:

Describe textures and physical feelings to make the experience tangible.

4. Emotional Atmosphere:

Convey the mood or emotional tone of the situation.

5. Use Specific Language:

Opt for precise, descriptive words over vague generalities.

Example with Sensory Details:

"As I stepped into the bustling startup incubator, the air buzzed with the energy of a dozen conversations and the rhythmic tapping of keyboards. The scent of fresh coffee mingled with the crisp smell of new electronics. My heart raced with a mix of nervousness and excitement as I clutched my pitch deck, ready to present my vision to potential investors."

By mastering these storytelling techniques, you can create narratives that not only engage your audience but also reinforce your personal brand in a memorable and impactful way. Remember, the goal is to use these techniques in service of your core brand message, ensuring that every story you tell contributes to a cohesive and compelling brand narrative.

7. Adapting Your Message for Different Platforms

In today's digital landscape, your personal brand story needs to be adaptable across various platforms while maintaining its core essence. Each platform has its unique characteristics and audience expectations, requiring you to tailor your storytelling approach accordingly.

Platform-specific Storytelling Strategies

1. LinkedIn:

- Focus on professional achievements and industry insights
- Use long-form articles to share detailed experiences and expertise
- Highlight career milestones and professional transformations

Example: Share a story about overcoming a significant workplace challenge, emphasizing the skills you developed and how they benefit your current role.

2. Instagram:

- Utilize visual storytelling through high-quality images and short videos
- Use carousel posts to tell a story in multiple parts
- Leverage Instagram Stories for behind-the-scenes glimpses and day-to-day experiences

Example: Create a series of posts showcasing your work process, from initial concept to final product, with captions explaining each stage.

3. Twitter:

- Craft concise, impactful messages that capture the essence of your story
- Use thread features for longer narratives
- Incorporate relevant hashtags to increase visibility

Example: Share a brief, powerful quote from a pivotal moment in your career, then expand on it in a thread.

4. YouTube:

- Create longer, more in-depth video content
- Use storytelling techniques like the Hero's Journey in your video narratives
- Incorporate visual aids and B-roll footage to enhance your story

Example: Produce a video series chronicling your entrepreneurial journey, with each episode focusing on a different challenge or milestone.

5. Personal Website/Blog:

- Provide comprehensive, long-form content that deeply explores your experiences and insights
- Use a mix of text, images, and embedded media to create an immersive storytelling experience
- Organize content into themed series or categories that reflect different aspects of your brand story

Example: Write a series of blog posts detailing your professional evolution, with each post focusing on a key learning experience or pivotal project.

6. Podcasts:

- Use audio storytelling techniques to create an intimate connection with listeners
- Incorporate interview formats to add diverse perspectives to your story
- Use episodic structures to explore different aspects of your brand narrative

Example: Launch a podcast where each episode explores a different aspect of your industry, weaving in personal anecdotes and lessons learned.

Maintaining Brand Consistency Across Platforms

While adapting your story for different platforms, it's crucial to maintain consistency in your overall brand message:

1. Core Message Consistency:

    - Ensure the fundamental elements of your brand story remain constant across all platforms
    - Use consistent language and key phrases that define your brand

2. Visual Branding:

    - Maintain consistent color schemes, fonts, and imagery across platforms
    - Use a recognizable profile picture or logo across all your social media accounts

3. Tone and Voice:

    - While adapting to platform-specific norms, maintain a consistent brand voice
    - Ensure your personality shines through regardless of the platform

4. Cross-Platform Storytelling:

    - Create interconnected narratives across platforms, with each platform offering a unique piece of your larger brand story
    - Use cross-platform promotions to guide your audience through your complete brand narrative

5. Unified Bio/About Sections:

    - Craft a concise brand statement that can be adapted for different platform bios while maintaining core elements

6. Content Calendar:

- Develop a content calendar that ensures a cohesive story is told across all platforms over time
- Plan how different aspects of your story will be shared across various platforms

Remember, while the format and presentation may vary, the essence of your brand story should remain consistent, providing a unified experience for your audience regardless of where they encounter your brand.

8. Measuring the Impact of Your Brand Story

To ensure your brand story is effectively reaching and resonating with your audience, it's crucial to measure its impact. By analyzing key metrics and testing different approaches, you can refine your storytelling strategy for maximum effectiveness.

Metrics for Evaluating Story Effectiveness

1. Engagement Metrics:

- Social media likes, comments, shares, and saves
- Blog post comments and shares
- Video views and watch time
- Podcast downloads and listen-through rates

What it tells you: These metrics indicate how well your story is resonating with your audience and inspiring them to interact.

2. Reach and Visibility:

- Follower growth
- Post reach and impressions
- Website traffic
- Search engine rankings for brand-related keywords

What it tells you: These metrics show how far your brand story is spreading and how discoverable it is.

3. Conversion Metrics:

- Click-through rates on calls-to-action

- Email sign-ups
- Product purchases or service inquiries
- Event registrations

What it tells you: These metrics indicate how effectively your story is driving your audience to take desired actions.

4. Qualitative Feedback:

- Direct messages and emails from your audience
- Testimonials and reviews
- Mentions and references in other media

What it tells you: This feedback provides deeper insights into how your story is impacting individuals and shaping perceptions.

5. Brand Sentiment:

- Social media sentiment analysis
- Brand mention sentiment in reviews and articles
- Changes in brand perception surveys over time

What it tells you: These metrics help you understand the emotional impact of your brand story and how it's shaping overall brand perception.

A/B Testing Different Narrative Approaches

A/B testing involves comparing two versions of your story to see which performs better. Here's how to approach it:

1. Identify Elements to Test:

- Different story structures (e.g., chronological vs. thematic)
- Varying emotional tones (e.g., inspirational vs. pragmatic)
- Different storytelling mediums (e.g., video vs. written content)

2. Create Two Versions:

- Develop two versions of your story, changing only one element at a time

3. Split Your Audience:

- Randomly divide your audience into two groups, each receiving a different version

4. Set a Timeframe:

- Run the test for a set period, ensuring it's long enough to gather significant data

5. Measure Key Metrics:

- Track relevant metrics for each version (e.g., engagement rates, conversion rates)

6. Analyze Results:

- Compare the performance of each version
- Look for statistically significant differences

7. Implement and Iterate:

- Apply the insights gained to refine your storytelling approach
- Continue testing other elements to continuously improve

Example A/B Test:

Version A: A chronological narrative of your entrepreneurial journey

Version B: A thematic narrative focusing on key lessons learned

Measure engagement rates, time spent on page, and subsequent action taken (e.g., contacting you for services). If Version B results in higher engagement and more inquiries, it suggests that your audience responds better to thematic, lesson-focused storytelling.

Remember, measuring and testing should be an ongoing process. As your brand evolves and your audience grows, continually reassess the effectiveness of your brand story and be prepared to adapt your approach based on the insights you gain.

By systematically measuring the impact of your brand story and testing different approaches, you can ensure that your narrative not only reaches your intended audience but also resonates deeply and drives the desired outcomes for your personal brand.

DECISION TREE FOR DEVELOPING YOUR COMPELLING BRAND NARRATIVE

This decision tree guides you through the process of crafting a powerful brand story and message. Follow the steps to ensure that your narrative resonates with your audience and communicates your unique value effectively.

Start: Have you identified key moments in your personal/professional journey?

• **Yes** → Proceed to developing the narrative structure

• **No** → Reflect on your journey

- **Actions:**
- List significant milestones and challenges
- Identify turning points in your career
- Consider lessons learned and skills acquired

Next: Have you developed a narrative structure for your brand story?

• **Yes** → Proceed to aligning with brand values

• **No** → Create your narrative structure

- **Actions:**
- Choose a storytelling framework (e.g., Hero's Journey)
- Identify your story's beginning, middle, and end
- Highlight conflicts and resolutions

Next: Does your story align with your brand values and goals?

• **Yes** → Proceed to crafting a core message

• **No** → Align your story with your brand

- **Actions:**
- Review your brand values and goals
- Identify elements of your story that reflect these values

- Adjust your narrative to reinforce your brand positioning

Next: Have you crafted a clear core brand message?

• **Yes** → Proceed to platform adaptation

• **No** → Develop your core message

- **Actions:**
- Summarize your value proposition in one sentence
- Ensure the message is clear, concise, and memorable
- Test the message with trusted peers or mentors

Next: Have you adapted your story for different platforms and audiences?

• **Yes** → Proceed to measuring effectiveness

• **No** → Adapt your story for platforms/audiences

- **Actions:**
- Identify key platforms for your brand
- Adjust story length and format for each platform
- Tailor language and focus for different audience segments

Next: Are you measuring the effectiveness of your brand story?

• **Yes** → Analyze and refine your narrative

• **No** → Implement measurement strategies

- **Actions:**
- Set up analytics to track engagement with your story
- Gather feedback through surveys or interviews
- Monitor how your story impacts brand perception

Final: Regularly review and update your brand story to keep it relevant and impactful

Conclusion

Chapter 5 has equipped you with the knowledge and tools to craft a compelling brand story and message, integral components of a strong personal brand. Throughout this chapter, we explored the power of storytelling in branding and how a well-crafted brand story can differentiate you from others, resonate with your audience, and leave a lasting impression.

We delved into the elements of a successful brand story, emphasizing the importance of authenticity, relatability, and clarity. Your brand story is not just about sharing your achievements; it's about connecting with your audience on a deeper level by sharing your journey, values, challenges, and triumphs. This narrative forms the emotional core of your brand, allowing your audience to see the person behind the brand and understand the passion and purpose that drive your work.

The chapter also covered the significance of aligning your brand message with your unique value proposition and target audience. By ensuring consistency between what you say and what you do, you build credibility and trust, essential components of a strong personal brand. We discussed how to articulate your brand message clearly and concisely, making it easy for your audience to understand who you are, what you stand for, and why they should engage with you.

Furthermore, we explored practical strategies for disseminating your brand story and message across different platforms and mediums. Whether through your website, social media, speaking engagements, or content marketing, your brand story should be consistently communicated, ensuring that it reaches and resonates with your target audience.

As you continue to develop your personal brand, remember that your brand story and message are dynamic—they can evolve as you grow personally and professionally. Regularly revisit and refine your narrative to ensure it remains aligned with your current goals, values, and audience needs. By staying true to your story and consistently sharing your message, you will build a brand that not only stands out but also inspires and engages your audience.

In conclusion, your brand story and message are the heart of your personal brand. They are what make your brand memorable, relatable, and influential. By crafting and sharing a story that authentically represents who you are and what you offer, you will create a powerful connection with your audience that drives long-term success and impact.

Chapter 6

Visual Branding: Creating Your Professional Image

1. Introduction: The Importance of Visual Branding

In the realm of personal branding, visual elements play a crucial role in shaping how you're perceived by your audience. Visual branding goes beyond just looking good; it's about creating a cohesive, memorable, and authentic representation of your professional identity. In today's image-driven world, where first impressions are often formed in mere seconds, a strong visual brand can be the difference between being remembered or overlooked.

Visual branding encompasses various elements, including:

- Your personal style and appearance
- Logo and color schemes
- Website and social media design
- Presentation materials
- Professional photography

When done effectively, visual branding:

1. Creates instant recognition

2. Communicates your brand values and personality

3. Establishes credibility and professionalism

4. Differentiates you from competitors

5. Ensures consistency across all platforms

6. Enhances memorability

Throughout this chapter, we'll explore how to craft a visual brand that authentically represents your professional identity and resonates with your target audience. We'll examine case studies of individuals who have mastered visual branding, discuss strategies for developing your personal style, and provide practical tips for maintaining visual consistency across various platforms.

By the end of this chapter, you'll have the tools and insights needed to create a compelling visual brand that enhances your professional image and supports your overall personal branding efforts. Let's begin by looking at one of the most iconic examples of visual branding in the business world: Steve Jobs and Apple.

2. Iconic Visual Branding and Presentation

To understand the power of consistent and minimalist visual branding, there's perhaps no better example than Steve Jobs and Apple. Jobs' approach to visual branding not only defined Apple's aesthetic but also became inextricably linked with his personal brand.

Case Study: Steve Jobs - Minimalism and Consistency in Visual Branding

Steve Jobs, co-founder of Apple, was a master of visual branding, both for his company and himself. His approach was characterized by:

1. Simplicity: Jobs embraced minimalism in design, focusing on clean lines and uncluttered aesthetics.

2. Consistency: He maintained a consistent personal uniform and ensured Apple's visual identity remained coherent across all products and communications.

3. Attention to Detail: Jobs was known for his obsession with even the smallest design elements, believing that every visual aspect contributed to the overall brand experience.

4. Emotional Appeal: Despite the minimalism, Jobs understood the importance of creating an emotional connection through visual design.

Key elements of Jobs' visual branding:

Personal Uniform:

Jobs was famous for his black turtleneck, blue jeans, and New Balance sneakers. This signature look became an integral part of his personal brand, embodying simplicity and focus.

Apple's Product Design:

Under Jobs' leadership, Apple products were characterized by sleek, minimalist designs with a focus on user-friendly interfaces.

Presentation Style:

Jobs' keynote presentations were visually simple yet impactful, often featuring large, high-quality images and minimal text.

Apple Stores:

The design of Apple stores reflected the same principles of simplicity and elegance seen in their products, creating a cohesive brand experience.

The impact of Jobs' visual branding:

- Created instant recognition for both himself and Apple
- Communicated values of innovation, simplicity, and quality
- Differentiated Apple in the tech market
- Built a cult-like following for the brand

Creating a Signature Look

Developing a signature look for your personal brand can significantly enhance your professional image. Here's how to create one:

1. Reflect Your Brand Values:

Ensure your visual elements align with your brand's core values and message.

2. Consider Your Industry:

While being distinctive is important, your look should still be appropriate for your professional context.

3. Focus on Versatility:

Choose elements that work across various settings and platforms.

4. Embrace Authenticity:

Your signature look should feel natural and true to your personality.

5. Invest in Quality:

High-quality visual elements reflect well on your brand's perceived value.

6. Seek Professional Help:

Consider working with a stylist or designer to refine your visual brand.

The Power of Consistent Visual Elements

Consistency in visual branding is crucial for building recognition and trust. Here's why it matters and how to achieve it:

1. Brand Recognition:

Consistent visuals make your brand instantly recognizable across different platforms.

2. Professionalism:

A cohesive visual identity demonstrates attention to detail and professionalism.

3. Trust Building:

Consistency in visuals helps build trust with your audience over time.

4. Memorability:

Consistent visual elements are more likely to stick in people's minds.

Strategies for maintaining visual consistency:

1. Develop Brand Guidelines:

Create a document outlining your color scheme, fonts, logo usage, and other visual elements.

2. Use Templates:

Develop templates for presentations, social media posts, and other frequently used materials.

3. Consistent Color Palette:

Choose a set of colors that represent your brand and use them consistently across all platforms.

4. Cohesive Imagery:

Ensure all imagery, including photos and graphics, adheres to a consistent style and tone.

5. Signature Design Elements:

Incorporate unique design elements (e.g., a particular graphic style or layout) that become associated with your brand.

6. Regular Audits:

Periodically review all your visual touchpoints to ensure they maintain consistency.

By creating a signature look and maintaining consistent visual elements, you can develop a powerful visual brand that enhances your professional image and makes a lasting impression on your audience. Remember, like Steve Jobs demonstrated, your visual brand should be a reflection of your core values and professional identity, communicated through every visual aspect of your personal brand.

3. Personal Style Influencing Professional Image

Your personal style is a powerful component of your visual brand, often serving as the first point of contact between you and your audience. It goes beyond mere fashion choices; it's a visual representation of your professional identity, values, and expertise. To understand the impact of personal style on professional image, let's examine the case of Anna Wintour, one of the most recognizable figures in the fashion industry.

Case Study: Anna Wintour - Distinctive Personal Style as a Brand

Anna Wintour, the Editor-in-Chief of Vogue, has cultivated a personal style so distinctive that it has become an integral part of her brand identity.

Key elements of Wintour's style:

1. Signature Bob Haircut: Her precision-cut bob has remained largely unchanged for decades, becoming instantly recognizable.

2. Sunglasses: Large, dark sunglasses are a constant presence, adding an air of mystery and authority.

3. Tailored Dresses: Wintour often opts for structured, knee-length dresses that convey professionalism and sophistication.

4. Statement Necklaces: Bold, often colorful necklaces add a touch of flair to her otherwise understated outfits.

5. High Heels: Typically Manolo Blahnik, her footwear choices reflect her connection to high fashion.

The impact of Wintour's style on her brand:

1. Instant Recognition: Her consistent look makes her immediately identifiable, even from a distance.

2. Authority: Her polished appearance reinforces her position as a fashion authority.

3. Consistency: The unchanging nature of her style over decades has made it iconic.

4. Alignment with Brand Values: Her look embodies the elegance and attention to detail associated with Vogue.

5. Memorability: The distinctiveness of her style makes her unforgettable in an industry full of striking personalities.

Developing a Personal Style that Aligns with Your Brand

Creating a personal style that enhances your professional image requires thoughtful consideration. Here's how to develop a style that aligns with your brand:

1. Identify Your Brand Attributes:

List the key characteristics of your professional brand (e.g., innovative, trustworthy, approachable).

2. Translate Attributes to Visual Elements:

Consider how these attributes can be expressed visually (e.g., innovative might translate to modern cuts or unexpected color combinations).

3. Consider Your Industry:

Ensure your style is appropriate for your professional context while still being distinctive.

4. Embrace Authenticity:

Your style should feel natural and comfortable, reflecting your true personality.

5. Find Your Signature Pieces:

Identify items that can become your trademark, like Wintour's sunglasses or Steve Jobs' black turtleneck.

6. Maintain Consistency:

Once you've established your style, maintain it consistently across various professional settings.

7. Evolve Thoughtfully:

Allow your style to evolve over time, but do so in a way that maintains your core brand identity.

8. Seek Feedback:

Ask trusted colleagues or a stylist for input on how your style is perceived.

The Impact of Appearance on Brand Perception

Your appearance significantly influences how others perceive you professionally. Here's how different aspects of your appearance can affect your brand perception:

1. Credibility:

A polished, well-put-together appearance can enhance your perceived credibility and expertise.

2. Approachability:

Your style can make you seem more or less approachable, influencing how others interact with you.

3. Innovation:

Forward-thinking style choices can reinforce a brand image of innovation and creativity.

4. Attention to Detail:

A meticulously maintained appearance suggests an eye for detail in your professional work as well.

5. Values Alignment:

Your style choices can reflect your values, such as sustainability or traditionalism.

6. Cultural Fit:

Your appearance can signal how well you understand and fit into specific professional or cultural contexts.

7. Memorability:

A distinctive style makes you more memorable in networking and professional interactions.

8. Confidence:

A style that makes you feel confident can positively impact your professional demeanor and performance.

Strategies for Leveraging Appearance in Personal Branding:

1. Dress for Your Audience:

Consider who you're trying to reach and what style will resonate with them.

2. Consistency Across Platforms:

Ensure your appearance in photos, videos, and live appearances is consistent with your brand image.

3. Adapt to Different Settings:

Develop variations of your style that work in different professional contexts while maintaining your core look.

4. Grooming and Maintenance:

Pay attention to details like grooming and clothing maintenance, as these subtleties impact overall perception.

5. Nonverbal Communication:

Remember that posture, facial expressions, and body language are also part of your visual brand.

6. Photograph Well:

Learn how to present yourself effectively in photographs, as these often form first impressions in the digital world.

7. Evolve with Your Brand:

Allow your style to evolve as your brand and career progress, ensuring it always aligns with your current professional identity.

By thoughtfully developing a personal style that aligns with your brand and understanding the impact of appearance on perception, you can create a powerful visual component of your personal brand. Like Anna Wintour, your distinctive style can become a memorable and integral part of your professional identity, enhancing your credibility, recognition, and overall brand impact.

4. Revolutionizing Personal and Professional Style

Sometimes, creating a powerful personal brand involves challenging existing norms and redefining what professional style means in your industry. Few individuals have done this as effectively as Coco Chanel, who not only revolutionized fashion but also set new standards for personal branding.

Case Study: Coco Chanel - Redefining Fashion and Personal Branding

Gabrielle "Coco" Chanel transformed women's fashion in the early 20th century and, in doing so, created an enduring personal brand that continues to influence fashion and branding today.

Key elements of Chanel's revolutionary approach:

1. Simplicity and Comfort: Chanel rejected the restrictive corsets and ornate styles of her time, introducing simpler, more comfortable designs.

2. Masculine Elements: She incorporated traditionally masculine elements into women's fashion, like trousers and suits.

3. The Little Black Dress: Chanel popularized the concept of the "little black dress," making it a staple of women's wardrobes.

4. Costume Jewelry: She made costume jewelry fashionable, challenging the notion that only fine jewelry was acceptable.

5. Personal Branding: Chanel herself became the embodiment of her brand, living the lifestyle she promoted through her designs.

Impact of Chanel's approach:

- Redefined femininity in fashion
- Challenged social norms and expectations
- Created a brand that transcended clothing to become a lifestyle
- Established a visual identity that remains instantly recognizable decades later

Breaking Conventions in Your Industry

To revolutionize your personal and professional style within your industry:

1. Identify Industry Norms:

Analyze the typical style and branding approaches in your field.

2. Find Pain Points:

Determine what aspects of current professional style in your industry are outdated or ineffective.

3. Draw Inspiration from Outside:

Look to other industries or cultures for fresh ideas that could be adapted to your field.

4. Start Small:

Introduce subtle changes to test reception before making major shifts.

5. Create a Narrative:

Develop a story around your new style choices that aligns with your brand values and goals.

6. Be Consistent:

Once you've established your new style, maintain consistency to build recognition.

7. Educate Your Audience:

Help your audience understand the rationale behind your new approach.

Balancing Innovation with Professionalism

While breaking conventions can set you apart, it's crucial to maintain an appropriate level of professionalism:

1. Understand Your Audience:

Consider how your target audience will perceive your style innovations.

2. Respect Industry Standards:

Ensure your style still adheres to necessary professional standards in your field.

3. Gradual Evolution:

Introduce changes gradually to allow your audience time to adjust.

4. Functionality First:

Ensure that any style innovations don't compromise the functionality required in your role.

5. Maintain Quality:

High-quality presentation remains crucial, even when breaking conventions.

6. Be Prepared to Explain:

Be ready to articulate how your innovative style aligns with and enhances your professional brand.

7. Adapt When Necessary:

Be willing to adjust your style for specific situations where adherence to traditional norms is crucial.

Example:

A financial advisor looking to break conventions might:

- Introduce more vibrant colors into their wardrobe to stand out in a sea of navy suits
- Create a more relaxed office environment to make clients feel at ease
- Use innovative data visualization in presentations instead of traditional charts

- Develop a unique personal logo that incorporates financial symbols in an unexpected way

By thoughtfully challenging conventions while maintaining professionalism, you can create a distinctive personal brand that stands out in your industry and resonates with your target audience.

5. Developing Your Visual Brand Identity

Your visual brand identity is the collection of all visual elements that represent your personal brand. It's crucial in creating a cohesive and memorable professional image.

Key Components of a Visual Brand Identity

1. Logo:

A personal logo can be your name in a distinctive font, an icon that represents you, or a combination of both.

2. Color Palette:

A set of 2-4 colors that represent your brand and are used consistently across all materials.

3. Typography:

The fonts you use for your brand materials, including your name, tagline, and body text.

4. Imagery Style:

The type of images, illustrations, or graphics you use in your branding materials.

5. Layout and Composition:

How you arrange visual elements in your marketing materials, website, and social media.

6. Personal Style:

Your fashion choices and overall appearance, as discussed earlier.

7. Digital Presence:

The visual design of your website, social media profiles, and email signature.

Color Psychology and Typography in Branding

Color Psychology:

Colors evoke emotional responses and can significantly impact how your brand is perceived. Here's a brief overview of common color associations:

- Red: Energy, passion, excitement
- Blue: Trust, stability, professionalism
- Green: Growth, health, nature
- Yellow: Optimism, creativity, warmth
- Purple: Luxury, creativity, wisdom
- Orange: Enthusiasm, adventure, confidence
- Black: Sophistication, luxury, power
- White: Purity, cleanliness, simplicity

When choosing your brand colors:

1. Consider the emotions and traits you want to convey

2. Look at color usage in your industry and decide whether to align or differentiate

3. Ensure your colors work well together and are versatile across different media

Typography:

The fonts you choose can communicate subtle messages about your brand's personality. Typography broadly falls into these categories:

1. Serif Fonts (e.g., Times New Roman):

Convey tradition, respectability, and formality

2. Sans-serif Fonts (e.g., Arial):

Suggest modernity, clean design, and straightforwardness

3. Script Fonts:

Can indicate creativity, elegance, or a personal touch

4. Display Fonts:

Often used for headings to create impact and personality

When selecting typography:

1. Choose fonts that reflect your brand's personality

2. Ensure readability across different sizes and media

3. Limit yourself to 2-3 fonts for consistency

4. Consider how your fonts pair together

Developing Your Visual Brand Identity:

1. Start with Brand Attributes:

List 3-5 key attributes that define your professional brand.

2. Create a Mood Board:

Collect images, colors, and fonts that resonate with your brand attributes.

3. Develop Your Color Palette:

Choose colors that align with your brand personality and work well together.

4. Select Your Typography:

Choose fonts that complement your brand style and are versatile.

5. Design Your Logo:

Create a simple, memorable logo that encapsulates your brand.

6. Establish Guidelines:

Document how your visual elements should be used to ensure consistency.

7. Apply Across Platforms:

Implement your visual identity consistently across all your professional materials and platforms.

8. Seek Feedback:

Get input from colleagues or a professional designer to refine your visual brand.

By carefully developing each component of your visual brand identity, you create a cohesive and impactful visual representation of your personal brand. This visual identity will help you stand out in your industry, create a memorable impression, and effectively communicate your brand values to your target audience.

6. Professional Photography for Personal Branding

In the digital age, high-quality images are crucial for personal branding. They often serve as the first visual representation of you and your brand, making a significant impact on how you're perceived professionally.

The Importance of High-Quality Images

1. First Impressions: Professional photos create a strong, positive first impression.

2. Credibility: High-quality images enhance your perceived professionalism and expertise.

3. Brand Consistency: Professional photos ensure visual consistency across all platforms.

4. Versatility: A range of high-quality images can be used across various marketing materials.

5. Memorability: Striking, professional images make you more memorable to your audience.

Tips for Successful Personal Branding Photoshoots

1. Choose the Right Photographer:

- Select a photographer experienced in personal branding or corporate photography.
- Review their portfolio to ensure their style aligns with your brand.

2. Plan Your Wardrobe:

- Choose outfits that align with your brand and industry.
- Bring multiple options to provide variety.
- Avoid busy patterns or logos that may distract from you.

3. Select Appropriate Locations:

- Choose settings that reflect your brand and profession.

- Consider both indoor and outdoor locations for variety.

4. Prepare a Shot List:

- Plan for a variety of shots: headshots, full-body, and action shots.
- Include images of you working or interacting with others if relevant.

5. Convey Your Brand Personality:

- Practice expressing different emotions that align with your brand (e.g., approachable, confident, thoughtful).
- Incorporate props or tools relevant to your profession if appropriate.

6. Lighting Matters:

- Opt for natural light when possible.
- If indoors, ensure the space has good lighting or that the photographer brings appropriate equipment.

7. Posing and Body Language:

- Work with your photographer on poses that feel natural and align with your brand.
- Pay attention to your posture and facial expressions.

8. Post-Production:

- Discuss retouching preferences with your photographer.
- Ensure edits enhance your images without making them look unnatural.

9. Update Regularly:

- Plan to update your professional photos every 1-2 years or when you undergo significant changes in your appearance or brand.
- 10. Rights and Usage:

- Clarify image rights and usage with your photographer to ensure you can use the photos as needed for your brand.

Remember, the goal is to create images that authentically represent you and your brand while presenting you in the best possible light.

7. Creating Brand Consistency Across Platforms)

Maintaining visual consistency across different platforms is crucial for building a strong, recognizable personal brand. It ensures that your audience has a cohesive experience regardless of where they encounter your brand.

Developing a Visual Style Guide

A visual style guide is a document that outlines the key elements of your visual brand and how they should be used. It typically includes:

1. Logo Usage:

- Different versions of your logo (full color, black and white, etc.)
- Minimum size requirements
- Clear space rules

2. Color Palette:

- Primary and secondary brand colors
- Color codes (RGB, CMYK, Pantone) for consistent reproduction

3. Typography:

- Primary and secondary fonts
- Font sizes and weights for different uses (headings, body text, etc.)

4. Imagery Style:

- Guidelines for photo styles, illustrations, or graphics
- Image treatment preferences (e.g., filters, cropping styles)

5. Layout Principles:

- How to arrange visual elements in marketing materials

6. Brand Voice:

- While not strictly visual, include guidelines on tone and messaging to ensure consistency

Creating Your Style Guide:

1. Document your current visual elements
2. Define rules for their usage
3. Include examples of correct and incorrect usage
4. Make it easily accessible to anyone working on your brand materials

Adapting Your Visual Brand for Different Media

While consistency is key, you may need to adapt your visual brand for different platforms:

1. Social Media:

- Create profile pictures and cover images that align with your brand
- Develop templates for posts that incorporate your visual style
- Adjust your color palette to work well on different platforms

2. Website:

- Ensure your website design fully embodies your visual brand
- Create a cohesive user experience that reflects your brand personality

3. Print Materials:

- Adapt your color palette for print (CMYK or Pantone)
- Ensure your design works in various print formats (business cards, brochures, etc.)

4. Video Content:

- Create branded intros and outros
- Use consistent lower thirds and graphics that align with your brand

5. Email Marketing:

- Design email templates that incorporate your visual brand elements
- Ensure your brand is recognizable even when images are blocked

6. Presentations:

- Develop slide templates that reflect your visual brand
- Use consistent formatting for charts and graphs

Tips for Maintaining Consistency:

1. Use templates whenever possible

2. Regularly audit your brand presence across platforms

3. Train anyone who creates content for your brand on your style guide

4. Be flexible within your brand guidelines to suit each platform's unique requirements

By maintaining visual consistency across platforms while adapting to each medium's specific needs, you create a strong, cohesive brand experience for your audience.

8. Evolving Your Visual Brand

As your career progresses and your personal brand develops, there may come a time when you need to refresh or evolve your visual brand. This process should be approached thoughtfully to maintain the equity you've built while allowing your brand to grow.

When to Refresh Your Visual Brand:

1. Your brand feels outdated

2. Your professional focus has shifted

3. You're targeting a new audience
4. Your current branding isn't effectively communicating your value
5. You've undergone significant personal or professional changes

How to Refresh Your Visual Brand:

1. Assess Your Current Brand:
    - Identify elements that are working well and those that need updating
    - Gather feedback from your audience and colleagues
2. Clarify Your Brand Strategy:
    - Revisit your brand values, mission, and target audience
    - Ensure your visual refresh aligns with your overall brand strategy
3. Evolve Gradually:
    - Consider a phased approach to changes, especially if you have a large following
    - Start with subtle updates before making major changes
4. Maintain Core Elements:
    - Identify key visual elements that are strongly associated with your brand
    - Find ways to evolve these elements rather than completely replacing them
5. Test Before Fully Implementing:
    - Try out new visual elements on a small scale
    - Gather feedback and make adjustments before a full rollout
6. Update All Touchpoints:
    - Once you've finalized your refreshed visual brand, update all your materials and platforms

- Ensure consistency across all brand touchpoints

Maintaining Brand Recognition During Visual Changes:

1. Communicate Changes:

- Inform your audience about the upcoming changes and the reasons behind them
- Use this as an opportunity to reinforce your brand story

2. Bridge the Old and New:

- Initially, use elements of both your old and new visual brand to ease the transition
- Gradually phase out old elements over time

3. Retain Key Brand Markers:

- Keep some recognizable elements of your original brand (e.g., a specific color or symbol)
- This helps maintain a connection with your existing audience

4. Explain the Evolution:

- Share the story behind your brand's evolution
- Connect the visual changes to your professional growth or new direction

5. Be Consistent After the Change:

- Once you've implemented changes, maintain strict consistency with your new visual brand

Evolving your visual brand is a natural part of professional growth. When done thoughtfully, it can rejuvenate your personal brand, attract new opportunities, and better reflect your current professional identity. The key is to approach the process strategically, always keeping your audience and brand equity in mind.

CHAPTER 6 DECISION TREE: DEVELOPING YOUR VISUAL BRAND IDENTITY: PURPOSE:

This decision tree will help you create a cohesive and impactful visual brand by guiding you through each essential step.

Objectives:

1. Define your visual brand elements
2. Ensure consistency across all visual touchpoints
3. Create a professional image aligned with your brand message
4. Develop guidelines for your visual brand
5. Implement your visual brand across various platforms
6. Evaluate and refine your visual branding strategy

Decision Tree

Start: Have you defined your core visual brand elements?

• Yes → Proceed to Color Palette Selection

• No → Define Core Visual Elements

- Choose a primary logo or personal mark
- Decide on typography (fonts for headings and body text)
- Select key imagery or graphic styles

Next: Have you selected a cohesive color palette?

• Yes → Proceed to Professional Image Development

• No → Develop Color Palette

- Choose 2-3 primary colors that reflect your brand personality
- Select 2-3 complementary secondary colors
- Ensure colors work well in digital and print formats

Next: Have you developed a professional image aligned with your brand?

• Yes → Proceed to Creating Brand Guidelines

• No → Create Professional Image

- Invest in professional photography
- Develop a consistent personal style
- Ensure your image aligns with industry expectations

Next: Have you created comprehensive brand guidelines?

• Yes → Proceed to Implementing Across Platforms

• No → Develop Brand Guidelines

- Document proper usage of all visual elements
- Specify color codes, font sizes, and image styles
- Include examples of correct and incorrect usage

Next: Have you implemented your visual brand across all relevant platforms?

• Yes → Proceed to Consistency Check

• No → Implement Across Platforms

- Update all social media profiles
- Redesign website to align with new visual brand
- Create templates for presentations and documents

Next: Have you checked for consistency across all brand touchpoints?

• Yes → Proceed to Gathering Feedback

• No → Conduct Consistency Audit

- Review all online and offline materials
- Ensure consistent use of visual elements
- Make necessary adjustments for uniformity

Next: Have you gathered feedback on your visual brand?

• Yes → Analyze and Refine Your Visual Brand

• No → Collect Feedback

- Ask trusted colleagues and mentors for input
- Conduct a survey with your target audience

- Monitor reactions on social media

Final Step: Regularly review and update your visual brand to keep it fresh and relevant.

Conclusion

Chapter 6 has provided a comprehensive understanding of the personal branding ecosystem, highlighting the interconnected components that contribute to a successful and sustainable personal brand. In this chapter, we explored how your brand is more than just your online presence —it is an integrated system of identity, communication, and reputation management that requires careful cultivation and continuous adaptation.

We discussed the core elements of this ecosystem, starting with your core identity, which includes your values, skills, and professional goals. Establishing a clear and consistent core identity is essential, as it serves as the foundation for all other branding efforts. From there, we examined the importance of a strong online presence, including a professional website, active social media profiles, and consistent content creation, all optimized to enhance visibility and credibility.

The chapter also emphasized the role of offline presence, professional reputation, and continuous learning in building a robust personal brand. Networking, public speaking, and published work are crucial for expanding your reach and establishing authority in your field. Additionally, we explored the importance of brand messaging and how to communicate your value proposition effectively across various platforms.

Understanding and nurturing your professional network is another critical aspect of the personal branding ecosystem. Building relationships with mentors, peers, and collaborators can significantly enhance your brand's influence and reach. We also touched on the importance of measuring your brand's performance through analytics and feedback, allowing you to refine and improve your strategies over time.

As you continue to build and maintain your personal brand, it's vital to approach it as an evolving ecosystem that requires regular attention and adaptation. By understanding and managing the various components discussed in this chapter, you can create a cohesive and impactful personal brand that resonates with your target audience and stands out in a competitive landscape.

In conclusion, the personal branding ecosystem is a dynamic and multifaceted system that, when carefully nurtured, can significantly enhance your professional reputation and opportunities. By integrating your core identity with a strategic online and offline presence, maintaining consistent and authentic communication, and continuously adapting to industry trends, you will build a personal brand that is not only successful but also resilient and enduring.

Chapter 7

Building Your Online Presence

1. Introduction: The Digital Landscape of Personal Branding

In today's interconnected world, your online presence is often the first —and sometimes the only—impression you make on potential clients, employers, or collaborators. The digital landscape offers unprecedented opportunities to showcase your expertise, connect with your audience, and build a powerful personal brand. However, it also presents challenges in standing out amidst the noise and maintaining a consistent, authentic presence across multiple platforms.

Your online presence encompasses various elements, including:

- Personal website or blog
- Social media profiles
- Professional networking platforms
- Content creation and sharing
- Online portfolios or case studies
- Digital marketing efforts

A strong online presence can:

1. Increase your visibility and reach

2. Establish your credibility and authority in your field

3. Facilitate networking and professional opportunities

4. Provide a platform for showcasing your work and ideas

5. Allow for direct engagement with your audience

6. Support your career growth and business development

Throughout this chapter, we'll explore strategies for building and optimizing your online presence. We'll examine case studies of individuals who have successfully leveraged digital platforms for personal branding, discuss key techniques for improving your online visibility, and provide practical tips for creating and managing your digital footprint.

By the end of this chapter, you'll have the knowledge and tools to create a compelling online presence that effectively communicates your personal brand and helps you achieve your professional goals. Let's begin by diving into SEO and digital marketing strategies, starting with a case study of Neil Patel, a master of online visibility.

2. SEO and Digital Marketing Strategies

In the realm of online personal branding, few have mastered the art of SEO and digital marketing as effectively as Neil Patel. His strategies for increasing online visibility and driving traffic offer valuable lessons for anyone looking to enhance their digital presence.

Case Study: Neil Patel - Mastering SEO for Personal Branding

Neil Patel is a digital marketing entrepreneur and online influencer known for his expertise in SEO, content marketing, and digital strategy.

Key aspects of Patel's approach:

1. Content Creation: Patel consistently produces high-quality, in-depth content on digital marketing topics.

2. Data-Driven Strategies: He uses analytics to inform his content and marketing decisions.

3. Personal Branding: Patel has built a strong personal brand around his expertise, becoming a go-to source for digital marketing advice.

4. Tool Development: He's created several popular marketing tools, further establishing his authority in the field.

5. Multi-Platform Presence: Patel maintains an active presence across various digital platforms, including his blog, YouTube channel, and social media accounts.

Impact of Patel's strategy:

- Established himself as a leading authority in digital marketing
- Built a massive online following across multiple platforms
- Created multiple successful businesses based on his personal brand
- Consistently ranks high in search results for digital marketing topics

Key SEO Techniques for Personal Websites and Content

Drawing from Patel's approach and broader SEO best practices, here are key techniques for optimizing your personal website and content:

1. Keyword Research:

- Identify keywords relevant to your expertise and industry
- Use tools like Google Keyword Planner or SEMrush for research
- Focus on long-tail keywords for less competition and more specificity

2. On-Page SEO:

- Optimize page titles, meta descriptions, and headers
- Use keywords naturally throughout your content
- Ensure your content is well-structured with appropriate heading tags (H1, H2, etc.)

3. Quality Content Creation:

- Produce in-depth, valuable content that addresses your audience's needs
- Aim for longer-form content (1500+ words) for comprehensive topics
- Update your content regularly to keep it fresh and relevant

4. Link Building:

- Seek opportunities for guest posting on reputable sites in your industry

- Engage in networking to earn backlinks from other professionals
- Create shareable content that naturally attracts links

5. Technical SEO:

- Ensure your website is mobile-friendly
- Improve page load speed
- Use SSL encryption (https) for security
- Create an XML sitemap for better indexing

6. Local SEO (if applicable):

- Claim and optimize your Google My Business listing
- Ensure consistent Name, Address, and Phone Number (NAP) across the web
- Encourage client reviews on Google and other platforms

7. Image Optimization:

- Use descriptive file names and alt text for images
- Compress images to improve load times

8. User Experience:

- Design an intuitive, easy-to-navigate website
- Ensure your site is accessible to all users, including those with disabilities

Leveraging Digital Marketing for Brand Visibility

To increase your online visibility and strengthen your personal brand, consider these digital marketing strategies:

1. Content Marketing:

- Develop a content strategy aligned with your brand and audience needs
- Create diverse content types (blog posts, videos, infographics, podcasts)
- Establish a consistent publishing schedule

2. Social Media Marketing:

- Choose platforms most relevant to your industry and audience
- Share your content and engage with your followers regularly
- Use hashtags strategically to increase visibility

3. Email Marketing:

- Build an email list of interested followers
- Send regular newsletters with valuable content and updates
- Personalize your emails to increase engagement

4. Influencer Collaboration:

- Identify influencers in your industry
- Seek opportunities for collaboration or guest appearances

5. Paid Advertising:

- Use platforms like Google Ads or social media advertising to reach a wider audience
- Start with small budgets and test different ad formats and targeting options

6. Video Marketing:

- Create video content for platforms like YouTube or LinkedIn
- Use video to showcase your personality and expertise

7. Webinars and Online Events:

- Host or participate in webinars related to your field
- Use these events to demonstrate your expertise and connect with your audience

8. Personal Branding Consistency:

- Ensure your messaging and visual branding are consistent across all platforms
- Develop a unique voice and style that sets you apart

By implementing these SEO and digital marketing strategies, you can significantly enhance your online visibility and strengthen your personal brand. Remember, like Neil Patel, the key is to consistently provide value to your audience while strategically optimizing your online presence for maximum visibility and engagement.

3. Social Media and Blogging Success

In the digital age, social media and blogging have become powerful tools for personal branding. To understand how to leverage these platforms effectively, let's examine the case of Huda Kattan, who built a beauty empire through strategic use of social media.

Case Study: Huda Kattan - Building a Beauty Empire Through Social Media

Huda Kattan, founder of Huda Beauty, transformed her passion for makeup into a multi-million dollar beauty brand, largely through her savvy use of social media.

Key aspects of Kattan's approach:

1. Authenticity: Kattan shares personal stories and behind-the-scenes content, creating a genuine connection with her audience.

2. Consistent Content: She maintains a regular posting schedule across platforms, keeping her audience engaged.

3. Visual Appeal: Kattan's content is visually striking, showcasing makeup looks and product demonstrations.

4. Engagement: She actively interacts with her followers, responding to comments and messages.

5. Influencer Collaborations: Kattan collaborates with other influencers, expanding her reach.

6. Multi-Platform Presence: She maintains active profiles on Instagram, YouTube, Facebook, and her blog.

Impact of Kattan's strategy:

- Built a following of over 50 million across social platforms
- Launched a successful beauty brand based on her online influence
- Became a recognized authority in the beauty industry

Strategies for Effective Social Media Management

Drawing from Kattan's success and broader best practices, here are key strategies for managing your social media presence:

1. Choose the Right Platforms:

- Focus on platforms where your target audience is most active
- Align platform choice with your content type (e.g., visual content for Instagram, professional content for LinkedIn)

2. Develop a Content Strategy:

- Plan your content in advance
- Create a mix of promotional, educational, and engaging content
- Use a content calendar to maintain consistency

3. Engage Authentically:

- Respond to comments and messages promptly
- Initiate conversations with your followers
- Share personal insights and behind-the-scenes content

4. Leverage Visual Content:

- Use high-quality images and videos
- Maintain a consistent visual style that aligns with your brand

5. Use Hashtags Strategically:

- Research relevant hashtags in your industry
- Create branded hashtags for your content

6. Analyze and Adapt:

- Use platform analytics to understand what content resonates with your audience
- Adjust your strategy based on these insights

7. Collaborate and Network:

- Engage with other professionals in your field
- Seek collaboration opportunities to expand your reach

8. Stay Consistent:

- Maintain a regular posting schedule
- Ensure your messaging and visual style are consistent across platforms

Creating Engaging Blog Content

Blogging remains a powerful tool for establishing expertise and improving SEO. Here's how to create engaging blog content:

1. Know Your Audience:

- Understand your readers' needs, interests, and pain points
- Create content that addresses these specific areas

2. Choose Relevant Topics:

- Stay up-to-date with industry trends
- Address common questions or challenges in your field

3. Create Valuable Content:

- Provide actionable insights or in-depth analysis
- Use your unique expertise to offer fresh perspectives

4. Use an Engaging Writing Style:

- Write in a conversational tone
- Use short paragraphs and subheadings for readability

5. Incorporate Visuals:

- Include relevant images, infographics, or videos
- Use visuals to break up text and illustrate key points

6. Optimize for SEO:

- Use relevant keywords naturally throughout your content
- Create compelling meta descriptions and titles

7. Encourage Interaction:

- End posts with questions to encourage comments
- Respond to comments to foster engagement

8. Promote Your Content:

- Share blog posts across your social media platforms
- Consider email marketing to distribute your content

By implementing these strategies for social media and blogging, you can build a strong online presence that enhances your personal brand and connects you with your target audience.

4. Dominating Video Platforms

Video content has become increasingly important in personal branding, offering a dynamic way to showcase your personality and expertise. To understand how to leverage video platforms effectively, let's examine the case of PewDiePie, one of YouTube's most successful creators.

Case Study: PewDiePie (Felix Kjellberg) - YouTube Success and Brand Building

Felix Kjellberg, known online as PewDiePie, built one of the largest YouTube channels in the world, turning his gaming content into a personal brand empire.

Key aspects of PewDiePie's approach:

1. Consistency: Regular uploads keep his audience engaged and coming back for more.

2. Authenticity: PewDiePie's genuine reactions and personality shine through in his videos.

3. Audience Engagement: He actively involves his audience through comments, challenges, and inside jokes.

4. Adaptability: PewDiePie has evolved his content over time to stay relevant and interesting.

5. Cross-Platform Presence: While focusing on YouTube, he maintains a presence on other platforms to expand his reach.

6. Merchandise and Brand Extensions: He leveraged his popularity to create merchandise and other business ventures.

Impact of PewDiePie's strategy:

- Built the most-subscribed individual YouTube channel (over 110 million subscribers)
- Created a recognizable personal brand beyond gaming content
- Successfully monetized his brand through various revenue streams

Video Content Strategies for Personal Branding

Drawing from PewDiePie's success and broader video marketing best practices, here are key strategies for creating effective video content:

1. Define Your Niche:

- Identify your area of expertise and the type of content you want to create
- Ensure your content aligns with your overall personal brand

2. Develop a Consistent Style:

- Create a recognizable intro and outro for your videos
- Maintain a consistent tone and presentation style

3. Plan Your Content:

- Develop a content calendar for regular uploads
- Plan series or themed content to keep viewers coming back

4. Focus on Quality:

- Invest in good lighting and audio equipment
- Edit your videos for a professional look

5. Optimize for Search:

- Use relevant keywords in your titles, descriptions, and tags
- Create eye-catching thumbnails

6. Engage with Your Audience:

- Respond to comments and incorporate viewer feedback
- Create content that encourages interaction (Q&As, challenges, etc.)

7. Collaborate with Others:

- Partner with other content creators in your field
- Cross-promote to expand your reach

8. Analyze and Adapt:

- Use platform analytics to understand what content performs best
- Adjust your strategy based on viewer feedback and engagement metrics

Leveraging Multiple Video Platforms

While YouTube remains the dominant video platform, others offer unique opportunities for personal branding:

1. YouTube:

- Ideal for longer-form content and in-depth discussions
- Offers robust monetization options
- Focus on SEO and building a subscriber base

2. TikTok:

- Perfect for short, creative content
- Use trending sounds and hashtags to increase visibility
- Engage with challenges and duets to boost engagement

3. Instagram Reels:

- Great for reaching your existing Instagram audience
- Use to share quick tips or behind-the-scenes glimpses
- Leverage Instagram's broader features (Stories, IGTV) for a comprehensive strategy

4. LinkedIn Video:

- Ideal for professional content and thought leadership
- Share industry insights and career advice
- Engage with your professional network

5. Twitter Video:

- Good for sharing quick updates or reactions
- Use to drive traffic to longer content on other platforms

6. Facebook Live:

- Excellent for real-time engagement with your audience
- Host Q&A sessions or live events

Tips for Cross-Platform Video Strategy:

1. Repurpose Content: Adapt longer YouTube videos into shorter clips for TikTok or Instagram Reels.

2. Platform-Specific Optimization: Tailor your content format and style to each platform's unique features and audience expectations.

3. Consistent Branding: Maintain visual consistency across platforms to reinforce your personal brand.

4. Cross-Promotion: Use each platform to drive traffic to your content on other platforms.

5. Experiment and Analyze: Try different types of content on each platform and use analytics to refine your strategy.

By implementing these video content strategies across multiple platforms, you can significantly enhance your personal brand's visibility and engagement. Remember, like PewDiePie, the key is to consistently provide value to your audience while staying true to your authentic self and adapting to the evolving digital landscape.

5. Personal Website Development

A personal website serves as the central hub of your online presence, offering a platform you fully control to showcase your brand, expertise, and achievements. An effective personal website can significantly enhance your professional credibility and attract opportunities.

Essential Elements of an Effective Personal Website

1. Clear and Compelling Homepage:

- Immediately communicate who you are and what you offer
- Include a prominent call-to-action (CTA)
- Use a professional photo or brand logo

2. About Page:

- Share your professional story and brand narrative
- Highlight key achievements and skills
- Include a professional bio

3. Services or Expertise Section:

- Clearly outline your professional offerings or areas of expertise
- Use clear, benefit-focused language

4. Portfolio or Case Studies:

- Showcase your best work or notable projects
- Include testimonials or client feedback

5. Blog or Content Hub:

- Regularly updated with relevant, valuable content
- Demonstrates your expertise and improves SEO

6. Contact Information:

- Easy-to-find contact details or contact form

- Links to professional social media profiles

7. Testimonials or Endorsements:

- Feature positive feedback from clients or colleagues
- Include names and positions for credibility

8. Resume or Professional History:

- Provide an overview of your professional experience
- Consider offering a downloadable CV

9. Media or Press Section (if applicable):

- Showcase interviews, publications, or speaking engagements

User Experience (UX) and Design Considerations

1. Mobile Responsiveness:

- Ensure your site looks good and functions well on all devices

2. Fast Loading Speed:

- Optimize images and minimize unnecessary scripts
- Use a reliable hosting service

3. Intuitive Navigation:

- Create a clear, logical menu structure
- Use breadcrumbs for easy navigation on larger sites

4. Consistent Branding:

- Use colors, fonts, and imagery that align with your personal brand
- Maintain visual consistency across all pages

5. White Space:

- Use ample white space to create a clean, professional look

- Avoid cluttered layouts that can overwhelm visitors

6. Readable Typography:

- Choose fonts that are easy to read on screens
- Use appropriate font sizes and line spacing

7. High-Quality Imagery:

- Use professional photos and graphics
- Ensure images are relevant to your content and brand

8. Accessibility:

- Ensure your site is usable for people with disabilities
- Use alt text for images and ensure good color contrast

9. Clear Calls-to-Action (CTAs):

- Guide visitors towards desired actions (e.g., contact you, download a resource)
- Use prominent, clearly labeled buttons for CTAs

10. Security:

- Use SSL encryption (https) to protect user data
- Regularly update your website software and plugins

Remember, your personal website should evolve with your career. Regularly update your content and design to ensure it accurately represents your current professional status and goals.

6. Content Creation Strategies

Content creation is a powerful way to demonstrate your expertise, engage your audience, and improve your online visibility. A well-planned content strategy can significantly enhance your personal brand and professional opportunities.

Developing a Content Strategy Aligned with Your Brand

1. Define Your Goals:

- Identify what you want to achieve with your content (e.g., demonstrate expertise, generate leads, build community)
- Ensure these goals align with your overall brand objectives

2. Understand Your Audience:

- Create detailed personas of your target audience
- Identify their pain points, interests, and preferred content types

3. Choose Your Content Pillars:

- Identify 3-5 main topics that align with your expertise and audience interests
- Ensure these pillars support your brand positioning

4. Determine Content Types:

- Choose formats that suit your skills and audience preferences (e.g., blog posts, videos, podcasts, infographics)
- Aim for a mix of content types to cater to different learning styles

5. Create a Content Calendar:

- Plan your content topics and publication schedule in advance
- Ensure consistent publication to maintain audience engagement

6. Develop a Distribution Plan:

- Identify platforms where you'll share your content
- Plan for cross-promotion across different channels

7. Set Metrics for Success:

- Define KPIs to measure the effectiveness of your content (e.g., engagement rates, lead generation, website traffic)
- Regularly review these metrics and adjust your strategy accordingly

8. Plan for Repurposing:

- Identify ways to repurpose content across different formats and platforms
- This maximizes the value of each piece of content you create

Balancing Promotional Content with Value-Added Content

Striking the right balance between promotional and value-added content is crucial for maintaining audience interest and building trust. Here's how to achieve this balance:

1. Follow the 80/20 Rule:

- Aim for 80% value-added content and 20% promotional content
- This ratio helps build trust and keeps your audience engaged

2. Integrate Subtle Promotion:

- Incorporate your products or services naturally within value-added content
- Use case studies or success stories to demonstrate your expertise without hard selling

3. Create Educational Content:

- Share your knowledge and insights freely
- Establish yourself as a helpful resource, not just a service provider

4. Tell Stories:

- Use storytelling to make your content more engaging and relatable
- Share personal experiences or client stories that indirectly promote your brand

5. Solve Problems:

- Create content that addresses your audience's pain points
- Offer practical solutions that demonstrate your expertise

6. Use Varied Content Types:

- Use different content types for promotion vs. value-added content
- For example, use blog posts for in-depth value-added content and social media for more promotional messages

7. Time Your Promotional Content:

- Schedule promotional content strategically, perhaps around product launches or special offers
- Avoid overwhelming your audience with constant promotion

8. Make Promotional Content Valuable:

- Even when promoting, focus on the benefits to your audience
- Explain how your offerings solve specific problems or add value

9. Encourage Engagement:

- Ask for feedback and encourage discussions on your content
- This engagement can naturally lead to interest in your services

10. Monitor and Adjust:

- Pay attention to how your audience responds to different types of content

- Adjust your balance based on engagement metrics and feedback

By developing a thoughtful content strategy and maintaining a balance between promotional and value-added content, you can create a powerful content marketing approach that enhances your personal brand, engages your audience, and drives your professional goals.

7. Building an Email List and Newsletter Strategy

Email marketing remains one of the most effective tools for personal branding and direct communication with your audience. A well-crafted email strategy can help you nurture relationships, showcase your expertise, and drive engagement with your brand.

The Importance of Email Marketing in Personal Branding

1. Direct Communication: Email provides a direct line to your audience, unfiltered by social media algorithms.

2. Ownership: Unlike social media followers, your email list is an asset you own and control.

3. Personalization: Email allows for highly personalized content delivery.

4. Higher Engagement: Email often has higher engagement rates compared to social media posts.

5. Conversion Potential: Email marketing typically yields higher conversion rates for products or services.

6. Brand Reinforcement: Regular emails keep your brand top-of-mind for your audience.

7. Thought Leadership: Newsletters are an excellent platform for sharing insights and establishing expertise.

Crafting Engaging Newsletters and Growing Your List

1. Define Your Newsletter's Purpose:

- Determine the primary goal (e.g., sharing insights, promoting services, building community)
- Ensure alignment with your overall brand strategy

2. Create Valuable Content:

- Focus on providing information that your audience finds useful or interesting
- Mix educational content with personal insights and industry news

3. Establish a Consistent Schedule:

- Decide on a frequency that you can maintain (e.g., weekly, bi-weekly, monthly)
- Stick to your schedule to build audience expectation and trust

4. Craft Compelling Subject Lines:

- Use clear, intriguing subject lines to improve open rates
- Avoid clickbait tactics that can erode trust

5. Design for Readability:

- Use a clean, mobile-responsive design
- Break content into easily digestible sections
- Include visuals to enhance engagement

6. Personalize Your Emails:

- Use subscriber names and segment your list for targeted content
- Tailor content based on subscriber preferences or behaviors

7. Include Clear Calls-to-Action (CTAs):

- Guide readers towards desired actions (e.g., read a blog post, book a consultation)
- Use prominent, clearly labeled buttons for CTAs

8. Grow Your List Organically:

- Offer valuable lead magnets (e.g., ebooks, webinars) in exchange for email signups

- Include signup forms on your website and social media profiles
- Mention your newsletter in speaking engagements or networking events

9. Use Double Opt-in:

- Implement a double opt-in process to ensure subscriber intent and improve list quality

10. Analyze and Optimize:

- Monitor key metrics like open rates, click-through rates, and unsubscribes
- Use A/B testing to refine your email strategy over time

11. Comply with Regulations:

- Ensure compliance with email marketing laws (e.g., GDPR, CAN-SPAM Act)
- Always provide an easy unsubscribe option

Remember, building a quality email list and creating engaging newsletters takes time and consistent effort. Focus on providing value to your subscribers, and your email marketing efforts will significantly enhance your personal brand and professional relationships.

8. Online Reputation Management

In the digital age, your online reputation can significantly impact your personal brand and professional opportunities. Proactive management of your online presence is crucial for maintaining a positive image and addressing any potential issues.

Monitoring Your Online Presence

1. Set Up Google Alerts:

- Create alerts for your name, brand, and key terms related to your professional identity
- Receive notifications when you're mentioned online

2. Use Social Listening Tools:

- Utilize tools like Mention, Hootsuite, or Brand24 to track mentions across social media and the web
- Monitor conversations about you or your brand

3. Regularly Google Yourself:

- Conduct regular searches for your name and brand
- Use incognito mode to see unbiased search results

4. Monitor Review Sites:

- If applicable, keep track of reviews on platforms like LinkedIn, Glassdoor, or industry-specific review sites

5. Check Your Social Media Accounts:

- Regularly review comments, tags, and mentions on your social media profiles

6. Set Up Profiles on Key Platforms:

- Claim your name on major social media and professional networking sites, even if you don't plan to use them actively

Dealing with Negative Content or Reviews

1. Respond Promptly and Professionally:

- Address negative feedback quickly to show responsiveness
- Maintain a professional tone, even if the criticism is unfair

2. Take the Conversation Offline:

- For detailed issues, offer to continue the discussion privately via email or phone

3. Apologize When Appropriate:

- If a mistake was made, offer a sincere apology
- Explain how you plan to address the issue or prevent it in the future

4. Provide Context:

- If negative content is misleading, provide factual context without being defensive

5. Encourage Positive Reviews:

- Ask satisfied clients or colleagues to share their positive experiences online

6. Create Positive Content:

- Regularly publish high-quality content to push down negative results in search rankings

7. Legal Action (as a last resort):

- For defamatory or false content, consider legal options, but use this as a last resort

8. Learn from Feedback:

- Use negative feedback as an opportunity for improvement
- Implement changes based on valid criticisms

9. Leverage SEO:

- Optimize your owned content to rank higher in search results for your name

10. Be Consistent:

- Maintain a consistent, positive online presence across all platforms

Remember, the best defense against negative online content is a strong, positive online presence. By consistently sharing valuable content, engaging positively with your audience, and promptly addressing any issues, you can build and maintain a strong online reputation that supports your personal brand.

Chapter 7 Decision Tree: Establishing a Strong Online Presence

This decision tree guides you through building and optimizing your online presence to enhance your personal brand and connect with your target audience.

Start: Have you assessed your current online presence?

• **Yes** → Proceed to identifying key platforms

• **No** → Conduct an online presence audit:

- Google yourself and review the results.
- List all existing online profiles.
- Identify areas needing improvement.

Next: Have you identified the key platforms for your personal brand?

• **Yes** → Proceed to profile optimization.

• **No** → Select relevant platforms:

- Research where your target audience is most active.
- Consider industry-specific platforms.
- Choose platforms that align with your content strategy.

Next: Are your profiles optimized across all chosen platforms?

• **Yes** → Proceed to content strategy development.

• **No** → Optimize profiles:

- Ensure consistent branding across all profiles.
- Complete all sections of each profile.
- Use keywords relevant to your personal brand.

Next: Have you developed a content strategy for online engagement?

- **Yes** → Proceed to SEO implementation.
- **No** → Create a content strategy:
    - Define content themes aligned with your brand.
    - Determine posting frequency for each platform.
    - Plan a mix of content types (text, images, videos).

Next: Have you implemented SEO best practices?

- **Yes** → Proceed to online reputation management.
- **No** → Apply SEO strategies:
    - Research and use relevant keywords.
    - Optimize your website for search engines.
    - Create high-quality, shareable content.

Next: Are you actively managing your online reputation?

- **Yes** → Proceed to measuring effectiveness.
- **No** → Implement reputation management:
    - Set up Google Alerts for your name and brand.
    - Regularly monitor mentions and reviews.
    - Develop a strategy for responding to feedback.

Next: Are you measuring the effectiveness of your online presence?

- **Yes** → Analyze and refine your strategy.
- **No** → Implement measurement tools:
    - Set up analytics for your website and social profiles.
    - Track engagement metrics (likes, shares, comments).
    - Monitor growth in followers and website traffic.

Final: Regularly review and update your online presence strategy

Conclusion

Chapter 7 has addressed the challenges that professionals face in the current personal branding landscape, providing you with strategies to navigate and overcome these obstacles. As personal branding becomes increasingly essential in today's digital and interconnected world, understanding and addressing these challenges is critical to building a brand that is both resilient and impactful.

We explored the issue of oversaturation and the importance of standing out in a crowded marketplace. By identifying and emphasizing your unique value proposition, you can differentiate yourself from others and capture the attention of your target audience. Additionally, the chapter discussed the delicate balance between personal and professional personas, offering insights on how to maintain authenticity while strategically managing your public image.

Keeping up with rapidly changing digital trends was another key challenge highlighted in this chapter. As new platforms and technologies emerge, staying informed and adaptable is crucial to keeping your brand relevant and engaging. The chapter also emphasized the importance of maintaining authenticity while strategically building your brand, ensuring that your messaging remains true to your core identity and values.

The chapter further covered the complexities of measuring the return on investment (ROI) of personal branding efforts, providing practical tips on setting clear goals and using data-driven insights to assess the effectiveness of your branding strategies. Moreover, we discussed the importance of managing online reputation and being prepared for potential crises, offering guidance on how to respond to negative feedback and protect your brand's integrity.

Finally, we addressed the need for consistency across multiple platforms and the challenges of balancing privacy concerns with the need for online visibility. By establishing clear guidelines and regularly reviewing your brand's performance, you can ensure that your branding efforts remain cohesive and aligned with your long-term goals.

As you continue to navigate the personal branding landscape, remember that challenges are inevitable, but with the right strategies and mindset, they can be transformed into opportunities for growth and differentiation. By staying proactive, adaptable, and true to your brand's core values, you will build a personal brand that not only stands out but also withstands the test of time.

In conclusion, the challenges of personal branding in today's environment are real, but they are also surmountable. By understanding these challenges and applying the strategies discussed in this chapter, you will be better equipped to build a strong, authentic, and resilient personal brand that resonates with your audience and drives your professional success.

Chapter 8

Networking and Relationship Building

1. Introduction: The Power of Networking in Personal Branding

In the realm of personal branding, your network can be one of your most valuable assets. Networking is not just about collecting business cards or adding connections on LinkedIn; it's about building meaningful relationships that can support your professional growth, enhance your visibility, and open doors to new opportunities.

Effective networking can:

1. Expand your sphere of influence
2. Provide access to valuable resources and information
3. Create opportunities for collaboration and partnerships
4. Enhance your credibility and reputation
5. Offer support and mentorship
6. Generate referrals and new business leads

In today's interconnected world, networking takes place both online and offline. From professional networking platforms like LinkedIn to industry conferences and local meetups, there are numerous avenues to connect with peers, mentors, and potential clients or employers.

However, successful networking requires more than just making connections. It involves nurturing relationships, providing value to others, and strategically leveraging your network to support your personal brand and professional goals.

Throughout this chapter, we'll explore various strategies for effective networking and relationship building. We'll examine case studies of individuals who have masterfully used networking to enhance their personal brands, discuss key techniques for optimizing your professional network, and provide practical tips for building and maintaining valuable relationships.

By the end of this chapter, you'll have the knowledge and tools to create a powerful network that not only supports your personal brand but also contributes to your long-term professional success. Let's begin by diving into the world of LinkedIn and professional networking, starting with a case study of Reid Hoffman, the co-founder of LinkedIn and a master networker.

2. LinkedIn and Professional Networking

In the digital age, LinkedIn has become the cornerstone of professional networking. To understand how to leverage this platform effectively for personal branding, let's examine the case of Reid Hoffman, co-founder of LinkedIn and a pioneer in professional networking.

Case Study: Reid Hoffman - Leveraging LinkedIn for Personal Branding

Reid Hoffman, often referred to as "The Oracle of Silicon Valley," has not only created the world's largest professional networking platform but has also masterfully used it to build his personal brand.

Key aspects of Hoffman's approach:

1. Thought Leadership: Hoffman regularly shares insights on entrepreneurship, career development, and technology trends through LinkedIn articles and posts.

2. Network Cultivation: He strategically connects with influential figures across various industries, expanding his sphere of influence.

3. Engagement: Hoffman actively engages with his network, commenting on others' posts and participating in relevant discussions.

4. Authenticity: His LinkedIn presence reflects his genuine interests and expertise, creating an authentic personal brand.

5. Philanthropy and Social Impact: Hoffman uses his profile to highlight his philanthropic efforts and social initiatives, adding depth to his personal brand.

Impact of Hoffman's strategy:

- Established himself as a leading voice in entrepreneurship and technology
- Built a vast, high-quality network of industry leaders and innovators
- Created numerous business opportunities through his LinkedIn connections
- Enhanced his personal brand as a visionary and thought leader

Optimizing Your LinkedIn Profile

Drawing from Hoffman's approach and LinkedIn best practices, here are key strategies for optimizing your LinkedIn profile:

1. Professional Photo:

- Use a high-quality, professional headshot
- Ensure your photo aligns with your industry norms and personal brand

2. Compelling Headline:

- Craft a headline that goes beyond your job title
- Include keywords relevant to your expertise and industry

3. Engaging About Section:

- Write a compelling narrative about your professional journey and values
- Include key achievements and areas of expertise

4. Detailed Experience Section:

- Provide comprehensive details about your current and past roles
- Focus on achievements and results rather than just responsibilities

5. Skills and Endorsements:

- List relevant skills and seek endorsements from colleagues
- Regularly update your skills to reflect your current expertise

6. Recommendations:

- Request and provide recommendations to build credibility
- Aim for quality over quantity in recommendations

7. Accomplishments:

- Highlight publications, projects, awards, and other notable achievements
- Include volunteer experiences and causes you support

8. Custom URL:

- Create a custom LinkedIn URL with your name for easy sharing

9. Rich Media:

- Include relevant media such as presentations, videos, or articles in your profile

Strategies for Effective Networking on LinkedIn

To build and leverage your professional network on LinkedIn:

1. Expand Your Network Strategically:

- Connect with colleagues, industry peers, and thought leaders
- Personalize connection requests with a brief note

2. Engage Regularly:

- Share valuable content related to your industry and expertise
- Comment on and share others' posts to increase visibility

3. Join and Participate in Groups:

- Engage in relevant LinkedIn groups to expand your network
- Share insights and participate in discussions

4. Utilize LinkedIn Publishing:

- Write articles on LinkedIn to showcase your expertise
- Share your published articles with your network

5. Leverage LinkedIn Events:

- Attend virtual events and webinars to connect with peers
- Consider hosting your own LinkedIn events

6. Use Advanced Search:

- Utilize LinkedIn's advanced search features to find specific connections or opportunities

7. Maintain Regular Contact:

- Congratulate connections on new jobs or work anniversaries
- Share relevant articles or insights with specific connections

8. Seek and Offer Help:

- Be open to helping your connections when they need it
- Don't hesitate to reach out to your network for advice or introductions

9. Keep Your Profile Updated:

- Regularly update your profile to reflect new skills, experiences, or achievements

10. Be Authentic:

- Ensure your LinkedIn presence aligns with your overall personal brand
- Share content and engage in a way that feels genuine to you

By optimizing your LinkedIn profile and actively engaging on the platform, you can build a powerful professional network that enhances your personal brand and creates valuable opportunities. Remember, like Reid Hoffman, the key is to consistently provide value to your network while authentically representing your professional identity and expertise.

3. Building Relationships Within and Outside Your Industry

Effective relationship building, both within and outside your industry, is crucial for career growth and personal brand development. To understand this concept better, let's examine the case of Tim Cook, CEO of Apple.

Case Study: Tim Cook - Relationship Building at Apple and Beyond

Tim Cook's success at Apple and his influence in the tech industry and beyond can be largely attributed to his exceptional relationship-building skills.

Key aspects of Cook's approach:

1. Internal Relationships: Cook is known for his deep engagement with Apple employees at all levels, fostering a collaborative culture.

2. Supplier Relationships: He leverages his operations background to build strong relationships with suppliers, ensuring Apple's supply chain efficiency.

3. Industry Partnerships: Cook has expanded Apple's partnerships with other tech companies and traditional industries like finance and healthcare.

4. Government Relations: He actively engages with government officials on issues like privacy, environmental sustainability, and education.

5. Social Causes: Cook uses his position to advocate for social causes, building relationships with activists and organizations outside the tech industry.

Impact of Cook's relationship-building strategy:

- Created a more open and collaborative culture at Apple
- Strengthened Apple's supply chain and operational efficiency
- Expanded Apple's influence beyond consumer electronics
- Enhanced Apple's and his own reputation as a socially responsible leader

Cultivating Internal and External Professional Relationships

Drawing from Cook's approach, here are strategies for building relationships within and outside your industry:

Internal Relationships:

1. Foster Open Communication:

- Encourage dialogue across all levels of your organization
- Be approachable and receptive to ideas from colleagues

2. Collaborate Across Departments:

- Seek opportunities to work with different teams
- Understand and appreciate the roles of various departments

3. Mentor and Be Mentored:

- Offer guidance to junior colleagues
- Seek mentorship from more experienced professionals

4. Recognize and Appreciate Others:

- Acknowledge the contributions of your colleagues
- Celebrate team successes

External Relationships:

1. Attend Industry Events:

- Participate in conferences, seminars, and trade shows
- Engage in meaningful conversations, not just casual small talk

2. Join Professional Associations:

- Become an active member of relevant industry associations
- Consider taking on leadership roles within these organizations

3. Engage in Cross-Industry Networking:

- Attend events outside your primary industry
- Look for innovative ideas that could apply to your field

4. Utilize Social Media:

- Share insights and engage with professionals on platforms like Twitter or LinkedIn
- Join and contribute to industry-specific online forums or groups

5. Volunteer or Support Causes:

- Engage in community service or support causes aligned with your values
- Use these opportunities to connect with like-minded professionals

Balancing Networking with Job Responsibilities

While networking is crucial, it's important to balance it with your primary job responsibilities:

1. Set Clear Networking Goals:

- Define what you want to achieve through networking
- Prioritize networking activities that align with these goals

2. Schedule Networking Time:

- Allocate specific time for networking activities
- Treat networking as part of your professional development

3. Leverage Technology:

- Use tools like LinkedIn or scheduling apps to streamline networking efforts
- Engage in virtual networking events to save time

4. Integrate Networking into Daily Activities:

- Look for networking opportunities within your regular work tasks
- Turn meetings or work events into relationship-building opportunities

5. Quality Over Quantity:

- Focus on building meaningful relationships rather than collecting contacts
- Nurture key relationships that provide mutual value

6. Be Efficient:

- Prepare talking points before networking events
- Follow up promptly and efficiently after making new connections

7. Evaluate and Adjust:

- Regularly assess the impact of your networking efforts
- Adjust your approach based on what's most effective for you

By cultivating relationships both within and outside your industry, and balancing these efforts with your job responsibilities, you can create a robust network that supports your career growth and enhances your personal brand.

4. Networking Strategies for Entrepreneurship

For entrepreneurs, networking is not just beneficial—it's essential. A strong network can provide support, resources, and opportunities crucial for business growth. To understand effective networking in entrepreneurship, let's examine the case of Richard Branson.

Case Study: Richard Branson - The Power of Personal Connections in Business

Richard Branson, founder of the Virgin Group, is renowned for his networking prowess and how he leverages personal connections to drive business success.

Key aspects of Branson's approach:

1. Personal Touch: Branson is known for his charismatic and personable approach to networking, making genuine connections with people at all levels.

2. Diverse Network: He maintains relationships across various industries, from entertainment to space travel.

3. Publicity Leverage: Branson uses his high profile to create networking opportunities and promote his ventures.

4. Social Causes: He connects with people through shared interests in social and environmental causes.

5. Informal Networking: Branson often combines business with pleasure, networking in relaxed, social settings.

Impact of Branson's networking strategy:

- Built a diverse business empire spanning multiple industries
- Created numerous partnership opportunities for Virgin companies
- Enhanced his personal brand as an adventurous and socially conscious entrepreneur
- Attracted top talent and investors to his ventures

Building a Diverse Network as an Entrepreneur

Drawing from Branson's approach, here are strategies for building a diverse network as an entrepreneur:

1. Attend Industry Events:

- Participate in conferences, trade shows, and seminars relevant to your business
- Look for speaking opportunities to increase your visibility

2. Join Entrepreneurial Organizations:

- Become a member of local and national entrepreneurship groups
- Engage in startup incubators or accelerator programs

3. Utilize Social Media:

- Build a strong presence on platforms like LinkedIn and Twitter
- Share your entrepreneurial journey and insights to attract like-minded connections

4. Network Beyond Your Industry:

- Attend events in related or complementary industries
- Look for cross-industry collaboration opportunities

5. Engage in Community and Social Causes:

- Participate in local community events or charity functions
- Use these opportunities to connect with diverse groups of people

6. Create Your Own Networking Opportunities:

- Host events or meetups for fellow entrepreneurs
- Start a podcast or blog to connect with industry leaders and potential customers

7. Leverage Alumni Networks:

- Reconnect with former classmates and professors
- Attend alumni events to expand your network

Leveraging Relationships for Business Growth

To effectively use your network for business growth:

1. Provide Value First:

- Look for ways to help your connections before asking for favors
- Share knowledge, resources, or introductions that could benefit others

2. Seek Mentorship:

- Identify potential mentors in your network who can guide your business growth
- Be open to learning from both successes and failures of others

3. Form Strategic Partnerships:

- Look for complementary businesses in your network for potential collaborations
- Create win-win partnerships that can expand your market reach

4. Tap into Your Network for Funding:

- Build relationships with potential investors before you need funding
- Use your network for introductions to venture capitalists or angel investors

5. Leverage Connections for Talent Acquisition:

- Use your network to find and attract top talent for your business
- Seek referrals from trusted connections for key positions

6. Gain Customer Insights:

- Use your network to gather feedback on your products or services

- Leverage connections for introductions to potential customers

7. Create an Advisory Board:

- Invite experienced professionals from your network to form an advisory board
- Leverage their expertise and connections for business growth

8. Utilize Network for Problem-Solving:

- When facing challenges, reach out to your network for advice and solutions
- Participate in mastermind groups with fellow entrepreneurs

9. Share Your Journey:

- Be open about your entrepreneurial experiences, both successes and setbacks
- This transparency can attract support and opportunities from your network

10. Continuously Nurture Relationships:

- Regularly check in with key contacts, not just when you need something
- Show genuine interest in others' ventures and successes

By building a diverse network and effectively leveraging these relationships, entrepreneurs can create a supportive ecosystem that fuels business growth and personal brand development. Remember, like Richard Branson, the key is to approach networking with authenticity, always looking for ways to create mutual value and foster genuine connections.

5. Online Networking Strategies

In today's digital age, online networking has become an essential component of personal branding and professional growth. The ability to connect virtually has opened up new opportunities for building relationships across geographical boundaries.

Virtual Networking Events and Webinars

1. Choose Relevant Events:

- Select virtual events that align with your industry or interests
- Look for events hosted by reputable organizations or industry

leaders

2. Prepare in Advance:

- Research speakers and attendees
- Prepare questions or talking points

3. Engage Actively:

- Participate in Q&A sessions
- Use chat features to connect with other attendees

4. Follow Up:

- Connect with speakers and interesting attendees on LinkedIn after the event
- Send personalized messages referencing the event

5. Host Your Own Events:

- Organize webinars or virtual meetups in your area of expertise
- This positions you as a thought leader and expands your network

6. Utilize Breakout Rooms:

- In larger virtual events, take advantage of breakout sessions for more intimate networking

7. Be Visible:

- Turn on your video when possible to create a more personal connection
- Use a professional virtual background if needed

Building Relationships Through Content Engagement

1. Share Valuable Content:

- Regularly post insightful content on platforms like LinkedIn or Twitter
- Share articles, videos, or infographics relevant to your industry

2. Engage with Others' Content:

- Comment thoughtfully on posts by industry leaders and peers
- Share others' content with your own insights added

3. Join Online Communities:

- Participate in LinkedIn groups or Facebook groups relevant to your field
- Contribute to discussions and offer help when possible

4. Create a Content Series:

- Start a blog, podcast, or video series to showcase your expertise
- Invite guest contributors to expand your network

5. Utilize Hashtags:

- Use relevant hashtags to increase the visibility of your posts
- Follow industry-specific hashtags to discover new connections

6. Engage in Twitter Chats:

- Participate in scheduled Twitter chats related to your industry
- Use these opportunities to connect with like-minded professionals

7. Offer Online Office Hours:

- Set up virtual "office hours" where people can book short slots to connect with you
- This can help you build relationships while positioning yourself as an expert

8. Collaborate on Online Projects:

- Seek opportunities for online collaborations, such as co-authoring articles or co-hosting webinars
- This can help you tap into your collaborator's network

Remember, successful online networking requires consistency and authenticity. Regularly engage with your online community, provide value, and be genuine in your interactions to build meaningful professional relationships.

6. Offline Networking Strategies

While online networking has gained prominence, offline or in-person networking remains a powerful way to build strong, lasting professional relationships. Face-to-face interactions often lead to deeper connections and more memorable exchanges.

Attending Industry Events and Conferences

1. Choose the Right Events:

- Select events that align with your professional goals and interests
- Consider both large industry conferences and smaller, niche

events

2. Set Clear Objectives:

- Define what you want to achieve from each event (e.g., learn about trends, meet potential clients, find mentors)
- Research attendees and speakers in advance

3. Prepare Your Elevator Pitch:

- Craft a concise, engaging introduction of yourself and your work
- Practice your pitch to ensure it sounds natural

4. Bring Business Cards:

- Have plenty of professional business cards on hand
- Consider including a QR code linking to your online profile

5. Attend Workshops and Breakout Sessions:

- Participate in smaller group activities for more intimate networking opportunities
- Ask questions and contribute to discussions to increase visibility

6. Leverage Social Events:

- Attend conference social events, dinners, or mixers
- These informal settings often lead to more relaxed and genuine conversations

7. Follow Up After the Event:

- Send personalized follow-up messages to key contacts within 48 hours
- Reference specific conversations to jog their memory

Effective Strategies for In-Person Networking

1. Listen More Than You Speak:

- Show genuine interest in others by asking thoughtful questions
- Practice active listening to build stronger connections

2. Body Language Matters:

- Maintain open body language (avoid crossing arms)
- Make appropriate eye contact and offer a firm handshake

3. Be a Connector:

- Introduce people who might benefit from knowing each other
- This positions you as a valuable node in your network

4. Offer Help Before Asking for Favors:

- Look for ways to assist others in your network
- Building goodwill leads to stronger, more reciprocal relationships

5. Use the "Triangle" Technique:

- When joining a conversation, position yourself to form a triangle with the other participants
- This makes it easier to integrate into the group naturally

6. Practice Inclusive Networking:

- Make an effort to connect with diverse individuals
- Be welcoming to newcomers in group settings

7. Quality Over Quantity:

- Focus on making a few meaningful connections rather than collecting a stack of business cards
- Spend more time with fewer people for deeper conversations

8. Share Personal Interests:

- Don't be afraid to discuss hobbies or interests outside of work
- These personal touches can make you more memorable and relatable

9. Be Authentic:

- Stay true to yourself and your values
- Authenticity builds trust and leads to more genuine connections

10. Follow Through on Commitments:

- If you promise to make an introduction or send information, do it promptly
- Reliability enhances your professional reputation

Effective offline networking is about building genuine relationships, not just exchanging contact information. By approaching networking events with a mindset of curiosity and a willingness to help others, you can create valuable connections that support your personal brand and professional growth.

Remember, the most successful networkers seamlessly blend online and offline strategies, leveraging the strengths of each approach to build a robust and diverse professional network.

7. Building and Nurturing Professional Relationships

Building and maintaining strong professional relationships is a crucial skill that can significantly impact your career growth and personal brand. It's not just about making initial connections, but about fostering meaningful, long-lasting relationships.

Techniques for Meaningful Conversation and Active Listening

1. Ask Open-Ended Questions:

- Use questions that encourage detailed responses
- Example: "What challenges are you facing in your industry?" instead of "Do you like your job?"

2. Practice Active Listening:

- Give your full attention to the speaker
- Avoid interrupting or formulating your response while others are speaking

3. Use the FORD Technique:

- Discuss Family, Occupation, Recreation, and Dreams to build rapport
- This helps create a more personal connection beyond work-related topics

4. Demonstrate Empathy:

- Try to understand the other person's perspective
- Acknowledge their feelings and experiences

5. Provide Thoughtful Responses:

- Reflect on what's been said before responding
- Offer insights or share relevant experiences

6. Use Non-Verbal Cues:

- Maintain appropriate eye contact
- Use nodding and facial expressions to show engagement

7. Avoid Dominating the Conversation:

- Aim for a balanced exchange
- Be conscious of giving others space to contribute

8. Practice Mindfulness:

- Stay present in the conversation
- Avoid distractions like checking your phone

Maintaining Long-Term Connections

1. Regular Check-Ins:

- Schedule periodic check-ins with key contacts
- Use a mix of methods: emails, calls, or in-person meetings

2. Share Relevant Information:

- Send articles, resources, or opportunities that might interest your contacts
- This shows you're thinking of them and adds value to the relationship

3. Offer Support:

- Be there for your connections during challenges or transitions
- Offer help or advice when appropriate

4. Celebrate Successes:

- Acknowledge and celebrate your contacts' achievements
- A simple congratulatory message can go a long way

5. Be Consistent:

- Maintain consistent communication, not just when you need something
- Build trust through reliability and genuine interest

6. Utilize Social Media:

- Engage with your connections' posts on professional platforms
- Use social media to stay updated on their professional lives

7. Create Shared Experiences:

- Invite contacts to relevant events or webinars
- Collaborate on projects or initiatives when possible

8. Express Gratitude:

- Regularly thank people for their time, advice, or support
- Consider sending personalized thank-you notes for significant help

9. Be Patient:

- Understand that building strong relationships takes time
- Don't expect immediate returns from every interaction

10. Adapt to Changing Circumstances:

- Be flexible in how you maintain relationships as careers evolve
- Recognize that the nature of relationships may change over time

By focusing on meaningful conversations and consistently nurturing your professional relationships, you can build a strong, supportive network that enhances your personal brand and contributes to your long-term success.

8. Measuring Networking Success

Measuring the success of your networking efforts is crucial for understanding the effectiveness of your strategies and identifying areas for improvement. While networking outcomes can sometimes be intangible, there are several key performance indicators (KPIs) and tools you can use to evaluate your networking success.

Key Performance Indicators for Networking Efforts

1. Network Growth Rate:

- Track the number of new connections added over time
- Set goals for expanding your network in different sectors or industries

2. Engagement Level:

- Monitor the frequency and quality of interactions with your network
- Track responses to your outreach efforts

3. Referrals and Introductions:

- Count the number of referrals or introductions you receive from your network
- Also track the referrals you provide to others

4. Event Participation:

- Monitor the number of networking events you attend
- Track your level of engagement at these events (e.g., conversations initiated, business cards exchanged)

5. Online Engagement Metrics:

- Track likes, comments, and shares on your professional social media posts

- Monitor growth in followers or connections on platforms like LinkedIn

6. Collaboration Opportunities:

- Keep a record of joint projects, partnerships, or collaborations resulting from your network

7. Career Advancement:

- Note any job opportunities, promotions, or career advancements influenced by your network

8. Knowledge Acquisition:

- Track new skills or knowledge gained through your networking efforts

9. Brand Visibility:

- Monitor mentions of your name or brand in industry discussions or media

10. Return on Time Investment (ROTI):

- Assess the value gained from networking activities relative to the time invested

Tools for Managing and Evaluating Your Network

1. Customer Relationship Management (CRM) Systems:

- Use tools like Salesforce or HubSpot to manage contact information and interaction history
- These can help track the frequency and nature of your networking activities

2. LinkedIn Analytics:

- Utilize LinkedIn's built-in analytics to track profile views, post engagement, and network growth

3. Network Mapping Tools:

    - Use tools like Kumu or MindMeister to visualize your network and identify key connections or gaps

4. Time Tracking Apps:

    - Use apps like RescueTime or Toggl to monitor time spent on networking activities

5. Goal Setting and Tracking Tools:

    - Utilize tools like Asana or Trello to set and track networking goals

6. Social Media Analytics:

    - Use platform-specific or third-party analytics tools to measure engagement on professional social media accounts

7. Spreadsheets:

    - Create custom spreadsheets to log networking activities, outcomes, and follow-ups

8. Networking Apps:

    - Explore apps designed for professional networking, like Shapr or Meetup, which often include metrics on your networking activities

9. Feedback Surveys:

    - Periodically send surveys to your network to gather qualitative feedback on your networking efforts

10. Personal Journal:

    - Maintain a networking journal to record insights, lessons learned, and personal reflections on your networking journey

Remember, while metrics are important, they shouldn't be the sole focus of your networking efforts. The quality of relationships and the mutual value created are often more important than quantitative measures. Use these KPIs and tools as guides to refine your approach, but always prioritize building genuine, mutually beneficial relationships in your networking endeavors.

Chapter 8 Decision Tree: Mastering Networking and Relationship Building

This decision tree will guide you through the process of effective networking and relationship building for your personal brand. By using this tree, you'll:

1. Assess your current network
2. Identify networking goals aligned with your brand
3. Develop strategies for both online and offline networking
4. Learn to create meaningful connections
5. Maintain and nurture professional relationships
6. Leverage your network for mutual benefit
7. Measure the effectiveness of your networking efforts

Use this tree to build a strong, supportive network that enhances your personal brand and creates valuable opportunities.

Start: Have you assessed your current professional network?

• **Yes** → Proceed to **Setting Networking Goals**

• **No** → Conduct a **Network Audit**:

- List all professional contacts
- Categorize contacts (mentors, peers, potential clients, etc.)
- Identify gaps in your network

Next: Have you set clear networking goals aligned with your brand?

• **Yes** → Proceed to **Developing Networking Strategies**

• **No** → Define **Networking Objectives**:

- Identify types of connections you need

- Set specific, measurable networking targets
- Align goals with your overall brand strategy

Next: Have you developed strategies for both online and offline networking?

• **Yes** → Proceed to **Creating Meaningful Connections**

• **No** → Create a **Networking Strategy**:

- Plan for online networking (LinkedIn, professional forums, etc.)
- Identify relevant offline networking events
- Develop your elevator pitch

Next: Are you creating meaningful connections, not just collecting contacts?

• **Yes** → Proceed to **Maintaining Relationships**

• **No** → **Improve Connection Quality**:

- Focus on giving value before asking for favors
- Practice active listening in conversations
- Follow up after initial meetings

Next: Are you actively maintaining and nurturing professional relationships?

• **Yes** → Proceed to **Leveraging Your Network**

• **No** → Implement **Relationship Nurturing Tactics**:

- Schedule regular check-ins with key contacts
- Share relevant content or opportunities with your network
- Offer help or support when appropriate

Next: Are you effectively leveraging your network for mutual benefit?

• **Yes** → Proceed to **Measuring Networking Effectiveness**

• **No** → Develop **Network Leveraging Strategies**:

- Identify ways your network can support your goals
- Look for opportunities to connect others in your network
- Be prepared to reciprocate when others help you

Next: Are you measuring the effectiveness of your networking efforts?

• **Yes → Analyze and Refine Your Networking Strategy**

• **No** → Implement **Networking Metrics**:

- Track new connections made and their relevance
- Monitor opportunities arising from your network
- Assess the strength and reciprocity of your relationships

Final: Regularly review and adjust your networking strategy to align with your evolving brand and goals

CONCLUSION

Chapter 8 has provided you with industry-specific considerations for personal branding, emphasizing that while the core principles of branding are universal, each profession has its unique nuances that must be understood and respected. This chapter has underscored the importance of tailoring your personal branding efforts to align with the expectations and demands of your specific industry, whether you are a consultant, accountant, lawyer, mentor, coach, trainer, or solopreneur.

We explored how different industries require different approaches to building trust, credibility, and authority. For instance, consultants need to highlight their problem-solving skills and thought leadership, while lawyers must balance professionalism with approachability, all while adhering to strict ethical standards. Coaches and mentors, on the other hand, should focus on showcasing their personal growth journeys and their ability to foster development in others.

The chapter also delved into the importance of understanding the unique challenges and opportunities within your industry. Whether it's navigating regulatory requirements, addressing confidentiality concerns, or leveraging industry-specific platforms, understanding these nuances allows you to create a personal brand that resonates deeply with your target audience.

We also discussed the significance of continuous learning and adaptation, particularly in industries that are rapidly evolving. Staying informed about the latest trends, technologies, and best practices in your field not only enhances your expertise but also positions your brand as current and forward-thinking.

Moreover, the chapter highlighted the value of professional networks and associations in building your brand's credibility. Engaging with industry-specific communities, whether online or offline, provides opportunities for collaboration, visibility, and endorsement, all of which can significantly boost your personal brand.

As you continue to develop your personal brand, remember that industry-specific branding is not about conforming to norms, but rather about understanding them so you can effectively differentiate yourself within your field. By aligning your branding efforts with industry expectations while infusing your unique value proposition, you will create a brand that stands out and connects authentically with your audience.

In conclusion, personal branding within specific industries requires a nuanced approach that balances general branding principles with industry-specific insights. By understanding and addressing the unique considerations of your profession, you will be better positioned to build a personal brand that is both effective and sustainable, setting you apart as a leader and expert in your field.

Chapter 9

Establishing Thought Leadership

1. Introduction: The Power of Thought Leadership in Personal Branding

In the landscape of personal branding, thought leadership stands out as a powerful way to differentiate yourself and create lasting impact. Thought leadership goes beyond simply being an expert in your field; it involves shaping industry conversations, inspiring innovation, and influencing others through your ideas and insights.

Establishing yourself as a thought leader can:

1. Enhance your credibility and authority in your industry

2. Attract high-value opportunities and partnerships

3. Increase your visibility and expand your influence

4. Drive innovation and change within your field

5. Create a lasting legacy beyond your immediate work

Thought leadership is not about self-promotion, but about providing genuine value to your industry and society at large. It requires a deep understanding of your field, a unique perspective, and the ability to communicate complex ideas in an accessible and compelling manner.

Throughout this chapter, we'll explore various strategies for establishing and maintaining thought leadership. We'll examine case studies of individuals who have successfully transitioned into thought leadership roles, discuss key techniques for building your platform, and provide practical tips for creating and sharing thought leadership content.

By the end of this chapter, you'll have the knowledge and tools to begin your journey towards becoming a recognized thought leader in your field, enhancing your personal brand and creating meaningful impact. Let's begin by exploring how one of the world's most famous tech entrepreneurs transitioned into a global thought leader in philanthropy and social impact.

2. From Tech Pioneer to Global Thought Leader

Bill Gates' journey from co-founder of Microsoft to a global thought leader in philanthropy and social impact provides valuable insights into leveraging industry expertise for broader influence and building a platform for global impact.

Case Study: Bill Gates - Transitioning from Microsoft to Philanthropy

Bill Gates, co-founder of Microsoft, has successfully transformed his personal brand from a tech innovator to a global thought leader in philanthropy, health, and education.

Key aspects of Gates' transition:

1. Strategic Shift: In 2000, Gates stepped down as Microsoft CEO to focus on the Bill & Melinda Gates Foundation, signaling a clear shift in priorities.

2. Leveraging Tech Background: Gates applied his analytical, data-driven approach from tech to tackle global challenges in health and education.

3. Continuous Learning: He immersed himself in new fields, working closely with experts in global health and development.

4. Public Communication: Gates increased his public presence through speeches, books, and social media to share insights on global issues.

5. Collaborative Approach: He partnered with governments, NGOs, and other philanthropists to amplify his impact.

Impact of Gates' transition:

- Established himself as a leading voice in global health and development
- Influenced policy decisions and funding priorities in philanthropy and international aid
- Inspired other tech billionaires to engage in large-scale philanthropy
- Created a model for leveraging business success for social impact

Leveraging Industry Expertise for Broader Influence

Drawing from Gates' example, here are strategies for leveraging your industry expertise to build broader influence:

1. Identify Transferable Skills:

- Recognize how your industry-specific skills can apply to broader challenges
- For Gates, his analytical skills from tech applied well to complex global issues

2. Educate Yourself:

- Invest time in learning about new areas where you want to have an impact
- Engage with experts and immerse yourself in the field

3. Start with What You Know:

- Begin by addressing issues within or adjacent to your industry
- Gradually expand your focus as you build credibility

4. Collaborate Across Sectors:

- Partner with experts and organizations in your new area of focus
- These collaborations can provide credibility and expand your knowledge

5. Communicate Your Journey:

    - Share your learning process and insights as you explore new areas
    - This transparency can engage others and build trust

6. Apply Your Unique Perspective:

    - Use your industry background to bring fresh insights to new fields
    - Highlight how your experience offers a unique approach to challenges

Building a Platform for Global Impact

To create a platform for broader influence and impact:

1. Develop a Clear Mission:

    - Articulate a clear, compelling mission that drives your work
    - Ensure this mission aligns with your values and expertise

2. Create High-Quality Content:

    - Produce insightful articles, reports, or books that showcase your thinking
    - Ensure your content adds value and offers unique perspectives

3. Leverage Digital Platforms:

    - Use social media, blogs, and digital publications to share your ideas
    - Engage with your audience and participate in online discussions

4. Public Speaking:

    - Seek opportunities to speak at conferences, TED talks, or industry events
    - Use these platforms to share your vision and insights

5. Build Strategic Partnerships:

- Collaborate with organizations that align with your mission
- These partnerships can amplify your message and extend your

reach

6. Engage with Media:

- Develop relationships with journalists and media outlets
- Offer expert commentary on relevant issues

7. Establish a Think Tank or Foundation:

- Consider creating an organization to further your mission
- This can provide a structured platform for your work and ideas

8. Measure and Communicate Impact:

- Track the impact of your work and share results
- Use data and stories to demonstrate the effectiveness of your approach

9. Adapt and Evolve:

- Stay current with emerging trends and challenges in your focus areas
- Be willing to evolve your thinking and approach as you learn

10. Mentor and Inspire Others:

- Share your knowledge and experiences with the next generation
- Inspire others to leverage their expertise for broader impact

By following these strategies, you can begin to transition from an industry expert to a thought leader with broader influence. Remember, like Bill Gates, this transition requires patience, continuous learning, and a genuine commitment to creating positive change. Your unique background and expertise can offer valuable perspectives on global challenges, positioning you to make a significant impact beyond your original field.

3. Advocacy and Leadership in Corporate Settings

Thought leadership within corporate environments presents unique challenges and opportunities. To understand how to effectively balance corporate responsibilities with personal advocacy, let's examine the case of Sheryl Sandberg and her "Lean In" movement.

Case Study: Sheryl Sandberg - "Lean In" and Women's Leadership Advocacy

Sheryl Sandberg, COO of Facebook (now Meta), has successfully leveraged her corporate position to become a prominent advocate for women's leadership in the workplace.

Key aspects of Sandberg's approach:

1. Personal Experience: Sandberg drew from her own experiences as a woman in tech and leadership roles.

2. Research-Backed Insights: She combined personal anecdotes with data and research on gender inequality in the workplace.

3. Corporate Platform: Sandberg used her high-profile position at Facebook to amplify her message.

4. Book and Non-Profit: She published "Lean In" and founded the Lean In organization to further her advocacy work.

5. Organizational Change: Sandberg implemented policies at Facebook to support women and families.

Impact of Sandberg's advocacy:

- Sparked global conversations about women in leadership
- Inspired the creation of thousands of Lean In circles worldwide
- Influenced corporate policies on diversity and inclusion
- Established Sandberg as a thought leader beyond her corporate role

Balancing Corporate Responsibilities with Personal Advocacy

Drawing from Sandberg's example, here are strategies for balancing corporate duties with personal advocacy:

1. Align with Company Values:

- Ensure your advocacy aligns with your company's mission and values
- Look for ways your advocacy can benefit the company's culture and reputation

2. Set Clear Boundaries:

- Distinguish between personal views and official company positions
- Be transparent about when you're speaking in a personal capacity

3. Lead by Example:

- Implement changes within your own team or department
- Demonstrate how your advocacy principles can be applied in the workplace

4. Leverage Internal Platforms:

- Use company events, newsletters, or intranets to share your message
- Start employee resource groups or mentorship programs

5. Collaborate with HR and Leadership:

- Work with HR to develop policies that support your advocacy goals
- Engage leadership to gain support for initiatives

6. Balance Time and Energy:

- Ensure your advocacy doesn't interfere with your primary responsibilities

- Use personal time for external advocacy activities when necessary

7. Be Prepared for Scrutiny:

- Understand that your advocacy may invite additional scrutiny of your company
- Be prepared to address how your advocacy relates to your corporate role

Using Your Position to Drive Social Change

To effectively use your corporate position for social impact:

1. Identify Key Issues:

- Focus on issues where you can make a meaningful impact
- Choose causes that align with your expertise and company's domain

2. Build Coalitions:

- Collaborate with other leaders and companies on shared goals
- Join or form industry groups focused on social issues

3. Leverage Corporate Resources:

- Utilize company resources (with permission) to support your cause
- This could include funding, technology, or employee volunteer time

4. Influence Policy:

- Use your corporate standing to influence industry standards or public policy
- Participate in relevant industry boards or government advisory groups

5. Measure and Report Impact:

- Track the outcomes of your initiatives
- Share results to inspire others and demonstrate the business case for social responsibility

6. Develop Future Leaders:

- Mentor and support emerging leaders who share your values
- Create pathways for others to engage in social impact work

7. Continuous Learning:

- Stay informed about evolving social issues and best practices
- Be open to feedback and willing to adjust your approach

By thoughtfully balancing corporate responsibilities with personal advocacy, you can leverage your position to drive meaningful social change while enhancing your personal brand as a thought leader.

4. Thought Leadership Through Writing and Public Speaking

Writing and public speaking are powerful tools for establishing thought leadership. To understand how to effectively use these mediums, let's examine the case of Malcolm Gladwell, who has built a strong personal brand through his books and talks.

Case Study: Malcolm Gladwell - Building a Brand Through Books and Talks

Malcolm Gladwell has established himself as a preeminent thought leader through his bestselling books and engaging public speeches.

Key aspects of Gladwell's approach:

1. Unique Perspective: Gladwell is known for presenting counterintuitive ideas that challenge conventional wisdom.

2. Storytelling: He uses compelling narratives to illustrate complex concepts.

3. Interdisciplinary Approach: Gladwell draws insights from various fields, including psychology, sociology, and history.

4. Accessible Language: He explains complex ideas in clear, engaging prose.

5. Consistent Themes: His work often revolves around themes of success, decision-making, and social dynamics.

6. Media Presence: Gladwell maintains a strong presence across various media, including podcasts and documentaries.

Impact of Gladwell's work:

- Popularized concepts like the "10,000-hour rule" and "The Tipping Point"
- Influenced discussions in business, education, and public policy
- Established a recognizable brand associated with intellectual curiosity and insight

Developing a Unique Voiceand Perspective

To develop your own unique voice and perspective as a thought leader:

1. Identify Your Niche:

- Focus on areas where you have deep expertise or unique insights
- Look for unexplored angles or connections in your field

2. Cultivate Curiosity:

- Continuously explore new ideas and disciplines
- Look for patterns and connections across different fields

3. Challenge Assumptions:

- Question conventional wisdom in your industry
- Propose alternative viewpoints backed by evidence

4. Develop a Signature Style:

- Create a distinctive way of presenting ideas (e.g., Gladwell's use of anecdotes and research)
- Consistently use this style across your writing and speaking

5. Stay Current:

- Keep abreast of the latest developments in your field
- Engage with emerging trends and technologies

6. Engage with Your Audience:

- Understand your audience's needs and interests
- Tailor your content to address their most pressing questions

Strategies for Effective Public Speaking and Writing

For impactful public speaking:

1. Know Your Audience:

- Research your audience to tailor your message effectively
- Address their specific interests and pain points

2. Structure Your Talk:

- Use a clear, logical structure (e.g., problem-solution, chronological)
- Include a strong opening and memorable conclusion

3. Use Storytelling:

- Incorporate anecdotes and case studies to illustrate your points
- Use vivid language to create mental images

4. Practice Delivery:

- Rehearse your talk multiple times
- Work on pacing, tone, and body language

5. Engage Interactively:

- Incorporate audience participation when possible
- Use rhetorical questions to keep the audience engaged

6. Master Q&A Sessions:

- Anticipate potential questions and prepare responses
- Use questions as opportunities to reinforce key messages

For effective writing:

1. Develop a Writing Routine:

- Set aside regular time for writing
- Create a conducive environment for focused work

2. Start with an Outline:

- Organize your thoughts before diving into full-length pieces
- Ensure a logical flow of ideas

3. Use Clear, Concise Language:

- Avoid jargon and overly complex sentences
- Explain technical concepts in accessible terms

4. Incorporate Research:

- Back your ideas with credible data and studies
- Properly cite all sources

5. Edit Ruthlessly:

- Revise your work multiple times for clarity and impact
- Consider having others review your writing for feedback

6. Develop a Consistent Publishing Schedule:

- Regularly share your writing through blogs, articles, or social media
- Build an expectation of consistent, valuable content among your audience

7. Engage with Readers:

- Respond to comments and encourage discussion
- Use reader feedback to inform future topics

By developing a unique voice and mastering the arts of public speaking and writing, you can effectively share your ideas and establish yourself as a thought leader. Remember, like Malcolm Gladwell, the key is to consistently provide valuable, thought-provoking content that resonates with your audience and contributes meaningfully to your field.

5. Creating and Distributing Valuable Content

Creating and distributing high-quality content is crucial for establishing and maintaining thought leadership. Your content should not only demonstrate your expertise but also provide genuine value to your audience.

Developing a Content Strategy Aligned with Thought Leadership Goals

1. Define Your Objectives:

- Clarify what you want to achieve through your thought leadership (e.g., influence policy, drive innovation, educate)
- Set specific, measurable goals for your content efforts

2. Identify Your Target Audience:

- Determine who you want to reach and influence
- Understand their needs, challenges, and preferences

3. Choose Your Key Topics:

- Select 3-5 core topics that align with your expertise and audience interests
- Ensure these topics support your thought leadership positioning

4. Develop a Content Calendar:

- Plan your content creation and distribution schedule

- Balance timely topics with evergreen content

5. Diversify Content Formats:

- Include a mix of blog posts, articles, white papers, videos, and podcasts
- Tailor formats to your strengths and audience preferences

6. Maintain Consistency:

- Develop a consistent voice and style across all content
- Regularly produce content to maintain audience engagement

7. Incorporate Thought Leadership Elements:

- Present original ideas or unique perspectives
- Back claims with data, research, or real-world examples
- Offer actionable insights or solutions

8. Collaborate with Others:

- Consider co-creating content with other experts or influencers
- This can expand your reach and add diverse perspectives

Content Distribution Channels for Maximum Impact

1. Personal Website or Blog:

- Use your own platform as the primary hub for your content
- Optimize for search engines to increase visibility

2. LinkedIn Articles:

- Publish long-form content directly on LinkedIn to reach professional networks
- Engage with comments to foster discussion

3. Medium:

- Reach a broader audience interested in thought leadership content

- Take advantage of Medium's built-in distribution system

4. Guest Posting:

- Contribute articles to respected publications in your industry
- This can help reach new audiences and build credibility

5. Email Newsletter:

- Build a subscriber list to directly share your content
- Use newsletters to provide exclusive insights or early access to content

6. Social Media:

- Share snippets or key insights from your content on platforms like Twitter, LinkedIn, and Facebook
- Use relevant hashtags to increase discoverability

7. Podcasts:

- Start your own podcast or appear as a guest on others
- This format allows for in-depth exploration of topics

8. Video Platforms:

- Use YouTube or Vimeo to share video content
- Consider live streaming on platforms like LinkedIn Live or Facebook Live

9. SlideShare:

- Share presentation decks to reach professionals looking for quick, visual insights

10. Repurposing Content:

- Adapt content for different platforms (e.g., turn a blog post into an infographic or video)
- This maximizes the reach and impact of your ideas

The key to effective content distribution is to meet your audience where they are. Analyze which channels are most effective for reaching your target audience and focus your efforts there.

6. Speaking Engagements and Public Appearances

Public speaking is a powerful way to establish thought leadership, allowing you to directly engage with your audience and share your ideas.

Finding Speaking Opportunities

1. Industry Conferences:

- Research major conferences in your field
- Start with smaller sessions or panels before aiming for keynote spots

2. Professional Associations:

- Offer to speak at local chapter meetings
- Propose webinars or online sessions for national associations

3. Academic Institutions:

- Contact universities to guest lecture or participate in speaker series
- Engage with alumni associations for speaking opportunities

4. Corporate Events:

- Reach out to companies for internal training or motivational speaking
- Participate in corporate conferences or summits

5. TEDx Events:

- Apply to speak at local TEDx events
- Use these as a stepping stone to larger speaking platforms

6. Podcasts and Webinars:

- Offer to be a guest on relevant podcasts

- Host or participate in webinars related to your expertise

7. Community Organizations:

- Speak at local chambers of commerce or rotary clubs
- Engage with non-profits aligned with your area of expertise

8. Create Your Own Events:

- Organize workshops or seminars to showcase your expertise
- Use these self-created opportunities to build your speaking portfolio

Preparing for Different Types of Speaking Engagements

1. Keynote Speeches:

- Develop a strong central message or theme
- Use storytelling to illustrate key points
- Practice extensively to ensure smooth delivery
- Prepare for a longer format (usually 30-60 minutes)

2. Panel Discussions:

- Research other panelists and the moderator
- Prepare concise points to contribute
- Be ready to build on or respectfully disagree with others' points
- Practice active listening to engage effectively in the discussion

3. Workshop or Training Sessions:

- Develop interactive elements to engage participants
- Prepare handouts or digital resources
- Plan for audience participation and questions
- Structure content for the specific time allotted (could be hours or days)

4. Q&A Sessions:

- Anticipate potential questions and prepare responses

- Practice thinking on your feet for unexpected questions
- Prepare a few key messages to reinforce throughout

5. Virtual Presentations:

- Familiarize yourself with the technology platform
- Ensure good lighting, sound, and background for video presentations
- Prepare visual aids that work well in a virtual format
- Practice engaging with a virtual audience (e.g., using polls, chat features)

6. Short-Form Talks (e.g., TED-style):

- Craft a tightly focused message
- Use vivid examples or demonstrations
- Practice rigorously to fit within strict time limits (often 10-20 minutes)

General Preparation Tips:

1. Know Your Audience:

- Research attendee demographics and interests
- Tailor your content and examples to resonate with the specific audience

2. Customize Your Content:

- Adapt your core message to fit the specific event or organization
- Include relevant case studies or examples

3. Prepare Visual Aids:

- Create clear, engaging slides or props if appropriate
- Ensure visuals enhance rather than distract from your message

4. Practice, Practice, Practice:

- Rehearse your presentation multiple times

- If possible, practice in the actual venue or a similar setting

5. Prepare for Technical Issues:

- Have backup plans for potential technical problems
- Bring backup copies of your presentation on multiple devices

By carefully preparing for each speaking engagement and tailoring your approach to the specific format and audience, you can maximize the impact of your public appearances and strengthen your position as a thought leader.

7. Writing and Publishing to Boost Your Brand

Writing and publishing are powerful tools for establishing and reinforcing your thought leadership. They provide a platform to share your ideas in depth and reach a wider audience.

Writing Articles for Industry Publications

1. Identify Target Publications:

- Research journals, magazines, and online platforms in your industry
- Consider the audience and reach of each publication

2. Understand Submission Guidelines:

- Carefully review each publication's requirements
- Note word counts, formatting rules, and preferred topics

3. Develop Unique Angles:

- Offer fresh perspectives on industry trends or challenges
- Use your expertise to provide insights not found elsewhere

4. Write Compelling Pitches:

- Craft concise, engaging pitches for your article ideas
- Clearly explain why your article would be valuable to the publication's readers

5. Focus on Quality Content:

- Ensure your articles are well-researched and fact-checked
- Provide actionable insights or solutions to industry problems

6. Incorporate Data and Case Studies:

- Use relevant statistics and real-world examples to support your points
- Conduct original research if possible to offer unique data

7. Develop a Consistent Writing Style:

- Create a distinctive voice that aligns with your personal brand
- Maintain this style across different publications for brand consistency

8. Build Relationships with Editors:

- Network with editors at industry events
- Engage with publications on social media

9. Repurpose Content:

- Adapt your articles for your blog or other platforms
- Share key insights on social media to extend reach

Authoring Books or E-books

1. Choose a Relevant Topic:

- Select a subject that showcases your expertise
- Ensure the topic has broad appeal within your industry

2. Develop a Comprehensive Outline:

- Create a detailed structure for your book
- Ensure a logical flow of ideas and chapters

3. Consider Your Publishing Options:

- Weigh the pros and cons of traditional publishing vs. self-publishing
- Research potential publishers or self-publishing platforms

4. Write Consistently:

- Set a regular writing schedule
- Aim for a consistent word count or time commitment each day/week

5. Seek Feedback:

- Share drafts with trusted colleagues or mentors
- Consider hiring a professional editor

6. Include Supporting Materials:

- Add charts, graphs, or illustrations to enhance your content
- Consider including case studies or expert interviews

7. Plan Your Launch Strategy:

- Develop a marketing plan for your book
- Leverage your network and social media for promotion

8. Create Supplementary Content:

- Develop blog posts, articles, or videos that complement your book
- Use these to generate interest and provide additional value

9. Engage with Readers:

- Plan book signings or virtual Q&A sessions
- Encourage and respond to reader feedback

10. Use Your Book as a Business Card:

- Leverage your book to secure speaking engagements or consulting opportunities
- Offer your book as a high-value lead magnet

Remember, whether writing articles or books, the key is to provide valuable, insightful content that reinforces your position as a thought leader in your field.

8. Measuring Your Impact as a Thought Leader

To ensure your thought leadership efforts are effective, it's crucial to measure your impact and analyze the return on investment (ROI) of your activities.

Key Performance Indicators for Thought Leadership

1. Audience Growth:

- Track increases in social media followers, email subscribers, and website traffic
- Monitor growth in attendance at your speaking engagements or webinars

2. Engagement Metrics:

- Measure likes, shares, comments, and mentions across platforms
- Analyze time spent on your website or blog posts

3. Media Mentions:

- Track the number of times you're quoted or featured in industry publications
- Monitor the quality and relevance of media outlets mentioning you

4. Speaking Engagements:

- Record the number and prestige of speaking invitations received

- Track audience feedback and repeat invitations

5. Content Performance:

- Analyze views, downloads, and shares of your articles, videos, or podcasts
- Monitor the performance of your books or e-books (sales, reviews)

6. Influence on Industry Conversations:

- Track how often your ideas or frameworks are referenced by others
- Monitor the adoption of concepts or terminology you've introduced

7. Network Growth:

- Measure the expansion of your professional network
- Track the quality of new connections made through your thought leadership activities

8. Business Impact:

- Analyze increases in leads or business opportunities attributed to your thought leadership
- Track revenue growth related to your personal brand

Analyzing the ROI of Thought Leadership Activities

1. Set Clear Objectives:

- Define specific, measurable goals for your thought leadership efforts
- Align these objectives with your overall business or career goals

2. Track Time and Resources Invested:

- Monitor the time spent on content creation, speaking engagements, etc.
- Track financial investments in marketing, travel, or publishing

3. Quantify Benefits:

    - Assign monetary value to outcomes where possible (e.g., new client acquisitions, speaking fees)
    - Consider intangible benefits like improved brand perception or industry influence

4. Use Attribution Models:

    - Implement systems to track how leads or opportunities are generated from your thought leadership activities
    - Use tools like UTM parameters or custom landing pages to track online conversions

5. Conduct Regular Reviews:

    - Perform quarterly or annual assessments of your thought leadership impact
    - Compare results against your set objectives and industry benchmarks

6. Gather Qualitative Feedback:

    - Conduct surveys or interviews with your audience to gauge the impact of your thought leadership
    - Collect testimonials or case studies demonstrating your influence

7. Adjust Strategy Based on Results:

    - Use your analysis to refine your thought leadership approach
    - Double down on activities showing the highest ROI

8. Consider Long-Term Impact:

    - Recognize that some benefits of thought leadership may take time to materialize
    - Balance short-term metrics with long-term brand building

By consistently measuring and analyzing your impact as a thought leader, you can refine your strategy, focus on the most effective activities, and demonstrate the value of your thought leadership efforts to stakeholders or clients. Remember, thought leadership is often about building long-term influence and credibility, so balance immediate metrics with a view towards sustained impact in your industry.

Chapter 9 Decision Tree: Becoming a Thought Leader in Your Field

Purpose: This decision tree guides you through the essential steps to establish yourself as a thought leader, enhancing your personal brand and opening up new opportunities.

Start: Have you identified your specific area of expertise?

• **Yes** → Proceed to **Developing a Unique Perspective**

• **No** → Define Your Niche:

- Assess your skills, experience, and passions
- Research gaps in your industry's knowledge
- Choose a focus area that aligns with your brand

Next: Have you developed a unique perspective or methodology in your field?

• **Yes** → Proceed to **Content Creation Strategy**

• **No** → Cultivate Your Unique Approach:

- Analyze current trends and challenges in your field
- Develop innovative solutions or viewpoints
- Test and refine your ideas

Next: Do you have a strategy for creating and sharing valuable content?

• **Yes** → Proceed to **Building Your Platform**

• **No** → Develop Content Strategy:

- Choose appropriate content formats (articles, videos, podcasts)
- Create a content calendar

- Ensure content aligns with your expertise and audience needs

Next: Have you built a platform for sharing your insights?

• **Yes** → Proceed to **Industry Engagement**

• **No** → Establish Your Platform:

- Develop a professional website or blog
- Optimize your social media profiles for thought leadership
- Seek opportunities for guest posting or speaking engagements

Next: Are you actively engaging with your industry and audience?

• **Yes** → Proceed to **Measuring Impact**

• **No** → Implement Engagement Strategies:

- Participate in industry events and discussions
- Collaborate with other thought leaders
- Respond to comments and questions from your audience

Next: Are you measuring the impact of your thought leadership efforts?

• **Yes** → Analyze and Refine Your Approach

• **No** → Establish Measurement Metrics:

- Track content engagement and reach
- Monitor growth in followers and subscribers
- Assess speaking invitations and media mentions

Final: Continuously evolve your thought leadership to stay relevant and impactful

Conclusion

Chapter 9 has taken you on a forward-looking journey into the future of personal branding, highlighting the emerging trends and technological advancements that are set to shape the branding landscape in the coming years. As the world becomes increasingly digital and interconnected, staying ahead of these trends will be crucial to maintaining a relevant and impactful personal brand.

We explored the growing integration of Artificial Intelligence (AI) and machine learning in personal branding, emphasizing how these technologies can help you optimize your online presence, create personalized content, and analyze audience engagement with unprecedented precision. The chapter also touched on the potential for virtual and augmented reality experiences to extend your brand into immersive digital spaces, offering new ways to engage and connect with your audience.

The trend towards hyper-personalization was another key focus, with advanced data analytics enabling more tailored and targeted branding efforts. However, this also brings the challenge of balancing personalization with privacy, underscoring the need for transparency and ethical data management in your branding strategy.

We discussed the increasing importance of digital ethics and privacy, recognizing that as personal brands become more data-driven, they must also be more vigilant about protecting their audience's information and respecting their digital rights. The chapter also highlighted the rise of micro and nano influencers, indicating a shift towards valuing niche expertise and highly engaged followings over broad but less connected audiences.

Sustainability and social responsibility emerged as critical components of future branding, with audiences expecting brands to stand for more than just business success. This trend suggests that aligning your brand with social causes and demonstrating a commitment to ethical practices will be essential in building a brand that resonates with the conscious consumer of the future.

The chapter also forecasted the increasing importance of continuous learning and adaptability, as professionals will need to stay updated on evolving technologies and trends to keep their brands relevant. Finally, we explored the potential for global and cross-cultural branding as remote work and digital platforms continue to blur geographical boundaries, making cultural intelligence a valuable asset in personal branding.

As you look to the future, remember that personal branding is not a static endeavor—it is an ongoing process of evolution and adaptation. By staying informed about emerging trends and integrating them thoughtfully into your branding strategy, you can ensure that your personal brand remains dynamic, relevant, and impactful in an ever-changing world.

In conclusion, the future of personal branding is filled with exciting opportunities and challenges. By embracing technological advancements, prioritizing ethical practices, and remaining adaptable, you will be well-positioned to build a personal brand that not only thrives in the present but also leads the way into the future. Keep your focus on the horizon, and let your brand evolve in response to the changing landscape, ensuring that it continues to inspire, engage, and connect with your audience for years to come.

Chapter 10

Personal Branding Across Different Industries

1. Introduction: The Importance of Industry-Specific Branding

While the core principles of personal branding remain constant across industries, the nuances of how to effectively present yourself can vary significantly depending on your professional field. Understanding and adapting to these industry-specific expectations is crucial for building a personal brand that resonates with your target audience and stands out in your chosen sector.

Each industry has its own culture, values, and norms that influence how professionals are perceived and what attributes are most valued. For instance, the creativity and cutting-edge style prized in the fashion industry might be less appropriate in the more conservative world of finance. Similarly, the technical prowess that's paramount in the tech sector might need to be balanced with different skills in fields like health-care or education.

Effective industry-specific branding requires:

1. A deep understanding of your industry's culture and expectations

2. Awareness of the specific challenges and opportunities in your field

3. The ability to highlight industry-relevant skills and experiences

4. An understanding of how to communicate effectively with your industry peers and target audience

Throughout this chapter, we'll explore how personal branding manifests in various industries, examining case studies of successful individuals who have mastered the art of industry-specific branding. We'll discuss strategies for adapting your personal brand to different professional contexts and provide practical tips for standing out in your chosen field.

By the end of this chapter, you'll have the insights and tools needed to craft a personal brand that not only reflects your unique value proposition but also aligns perfectly with the expectations and opportunities of your specific industry. Let's begin by examining personal branding in one of the most dynamic and influential sectors: the tech industry.

2. Personal Branding in the Tech Industry

The tech industry, known for its rapid pace of innovation and disruptive thinking, presents unique opportunities and challenges for personal branding. To understand how to effectively brand oneself in this dynamic field, let's examine the case of Mark Zuckerberg, one of the most recognizable figures in Silicon Valley.

Case Study: Mark Zuckerberg - Building a Personal Brand in Silicon Valley

Mark Zuckerberg, co-founder and CEO of Facebook (now Meta), has crafted a personal brand that embodies many of the values prized in the tech industry.

Key aspects of Zuckerberg's brand:

1. Innovation Focus: Zuckerberg consistently positions himself and his company at the forefront of technological innovation.

2. Casual Authenticity: His infamous hoodie-and-jeans style reflects Silicon Valley's casual work culture and emphasis on substance over appearance.

3. Mission-Driven: Zuckerberg frequently articulates a vision of connecting the world, aligning his personal brand with a larger purpose.

4. Technical Expertise: While leading a major corporation, he maintains an image of being deeply involved in the technical aspects of his products.

5. Continuous Learning: He publicly shares his personal challenges and

learning journeys, reinforcing the tech industry's value of constant self-improvement.

Impact of Zuckerberg's branding:

- Established himself as a thought leader in social media and emerging technologies
- Created a relatable image for a tech CEO, especially appealing to younger audiences
- Successfully navigated the transition from startup founder to leader of a global corporation

Balancing Innovation with Reliability in Tech Branding

In the tech industry, personal branding often requires striking a balance between showcasing innovative thinking and demonstrating reliability. Here's how to achieve this balance:

1. Highlight Forward-Thinking Ideas:

- Share your vision for future technologies or industry trends
- Engage in discussions about emerging tech and its potential impacts

2. Demonstrate Practical Application:

- Show how your innovative ideas translate into real-world solutions
- Share case studies or examples of successful implementations

3. Maintain a Learning Mindset:

- Openly discuss your continuous learning journey
- Share insights from courses, conferences, or personal experiments

4. Showcase Problem-Solving Skills:

- Highlight your ability to tackle complex technical challenges
- Share your approach to troubleshooting and problem-solving

5. Build a Track Record:

- Document and share your successes and lessons learned
- Use data and metrics to back up your achievements

6. Engage with the Tech Community:

    - Participate in open-source projects or hackathons
    - Contribute to tech forums or write for industry publications

7. Stay Current with Industry Standards:

    - Maintain relevant certifications or qualifications
    - Demonstrate knowledge of best practices and industry standards

Leveraging Technical Expertise in Personal Branding

To effectively leverage your technical skills in personal branding:

1. Develop a Niche:

    - Focus on a specific area of technology where you excel
    - Become known as the go-to expert in your chosen niche

2. Create Technical Content:

    - Write blog posts, articles, or whitepapers on technical topics
    - Develop tutorials or how-to guides for complex technical processes

3. Speak at Tech Conferences:

    - Present your insights and innovations at industry events
    - Offer workshops or training sessions in your area of expertise

4. Engage in Online Tech Communities:

    - Actively participate in platforms like GitHub, Stack Overflow, or specialized forums
    - Share your knowledge and help others solve technical problems

5. Showcase Your Projects:

- Maintain a portfolio of your technical projects
- Use platforms like GitHub to share your code and contributions

6. Leverage Data Visualization:

- Use infographics or interactive visualizations to explain complex technical concepts
- Demonstrate your ability to make technical information accessible

7. Collaborate on Innovative Projects:

- Engage in cutting-edge projects or research
- Share updates and insights from these collaborations

8. Mentor Others:

- Offer mentorship to junior developers or tech enthusiasts
- This reinforces your expertise and contributes to the tech community

Remember, in the tech industry, your personal brand should reflect not only your current skills but also your capacity to adapt and grow with the rapidly changing technological landscape. By balancing innovation with reliability and effectively showcasing your technical expertise, you can build a personal brand that stands out in the competitive world of technology.

3. Branding in the Fashion Industry

The fashion industry is inherently visual and trend-driven, making personal branding particularly crucial and challenging. To understand effective personal branding in this field, let's examine the case of Sara Blakely, founder of Spanx.

Case Study: Sara Blakely - Personal Branding with Spanx

Sara Blakely has successfully intertwined her personal brand with her product line, creating a powerful presence in the fashion and entrepreneurship worlds.

Key aspects of Blakely's brand:

1. Authenticity: Blakely often shares her entrepreneurial journey, including initial struggles and failures.

2. Empowerment: Her brand focuses on empowering women, both through her products and her personal story.

3. Innovation: Blakely positions herself as a problem-solver and innovator in the fashion industry.

4. Accessibility: Despite her success, she maintains a relatable and approachable image.

5. Humor: Blakely often uses humor in her branding, making her and her products more memorable.

Impact of Blakely's branding:

- Established Spanx as a household name in shapewear
- Positioned herself as a role model for female entrepreneurs
- Created a brand that resonates with women beyond just product features

Creating a Personal Brand that Complements a Product Line

To create a personal brand that enhances your fashion product line:

1. Embody Your Brand's Values:

- Ensure your personal image aligns with your product's ethos
- Live the lifestyle that your brand promotes

2. Be the Face of Your Brand:

- Actively represent your products in marketing and media
- Share personal stories of how and why you created your products

3. Showcase Your Expertise:

- Demonstrate your knowledge of fashion trends and industry insights
- Offer styling tips and advice related to your products

4. Build a Consistent Visual Identity:

- Develop a personal style that complements your brand aesthetic
- Maintain consistency across personal and brand imagery

5. Engage with Your Community:

- Interact directly with customers through social media and events
- Create a sense of community around your brand and personal values

6. Collaborate Strategically:

- Partner with other brands or influencers that align with your values
- Use collaborations to expand your reach and reinforce your brand identity

Navigating the Visual-Centric Nature of Fashion Branding

In the highly visual world of fashion, consider these strategies:

1. Develop a Signature Look:

- Create a personal style that becomes part of your brand identity
- Ensure this look aligns with your brand's aesthetic

2. Master Visual Storytelling:

- Use platforms like Instagram and Pinterest to tell your brand's story visually
- Create compelling, on-brand content consistently

3. Behind-the-Scenes Content:

- Share the process behind your designs or brand decisions
- This adds depth to your brand and engages audiences

4. Leverage Fashion Events:

- Attend and participate in fashion weeks and industry events
- Use these platforms to showcase your personal and brand style

5. Collaborate with Photographers and Stylists:

- Work with professionals to create high-quality, on-brand imagery
- Develop a consistent visual language for your personal brand

6. Embrace Video Content:

- Use video platforms to showcase your personality and expertise
- Create tutorials, behind-the-scenes footage, or trend forecasts

7. Adaptive Branding:

- Stay current with fashion trends while maintaining your core brand identity
- Show how your personal style evolves while staying true to your brand

By creating a personal brand that complements your product line and effectively navigating the visual nature of the fashion industry, you can build a powerful presence that resonates with your target audience and stands out in a crowded market.

4. Personal Branding in the Culinary World

The culinary industry offers unique opportunities for personal branding, blending creativity, skill, and often, social consciousness. To understand effective personal branding in this field, let's examine the case of Jamie Oliver, who has created a multi-faceted brand that extends far beyond the kitchen.

Case Study: Jamie Oliver - Combining Cooking Expertise with Social Causes

Jamie Oliver has built a personal brand that combines his culinary skills with a strong focus on social issues, particularly in food education and nutrition.

Key aspects of Oliver's brand:

1. Accessibility: Oliver is known for making cooking approachable and fun for the average person.

2. Social Activism: He's campaigned for better school lunches and overall improvement in public nutrition.

3. Multi-Platform Presence: Oliver leverages TV shows, cookbooks, social media, and restaurants to build his brand.

4. Authenticity: He maintains a down-to-earth, genuine persona across all his endeavors.

5. Educational Focus: Oliver's brand emphasizes teaching cooking skills and nutritional knowledge.

Impact of Oliver's branding:

- Established himself as more than just a chef, but a food educator and activist
- Created a global brand that spans media, retail, and restaurants
- Influenced public policy on food and nutrition in several countries

Building a Multi-Faceted Brand in the Food Industry

To create a multi-faceted culinary brand:

1. Develop a Unique Culinary Point of View:

- Define your cooking style or culinary philosophy
- Ensure this POV is consistent across all your brand expressions

2. Expand Beyond Cooking:

- Identify causes or issues in the food world that you're passionate about
- Integrate these causes into your brand messaging and activities

3. Create Diverse Content:

- Develop cookbooks, cooking shows, online tutorials, and social media content
- Ensure each platform showcases a different aspect of your expertise

4. Build a Strong Online Presence:

- Use social media to share recipes, cooking tips, and behind-the-scenes content
- Engage with your audience through Q&As, live cooking sessions, etc.

5. Collaborate with Others in the Industry:

- Partner with other chefs, food producers, or relevant brands
- Use these collaborations to broaden your expertise and reach

6. Develop Products or Services:

- Create product lines (e.g., cookware, food products) that align with your brand
- Offer services like cooking classes or consultations

Leveraging Media Platforms for Culinary Personal Branding

To effectively use media for culinary branding:

1. Television and Streaming:

- Develop cooking shows that showcase your personality and skills
- Use these platforms to reach a broad audience and build brand recognition

2. YouTube and Video Content:

- Create regular cooking videos, from quick tips to full recipes
- Use video to show your personality and connect with viewers

3. Instagram and Visual Platforms:

- Share beautifully styled food photos and short video recipes
- Use Stories and Reels for behind-the-scenes content and quick tips

4. Podcasts:

- Start a food-related podcast discussing trends, interviewing guests, or sharing stories
- Use audio to delve deeper into food topics and showcase your expertise

5. Blogging:

- Maintain a blog with recipes, food stories, and industry insights
- Use this platform for longer-form content and SEO benefits

6. Cookbooks:

- Publish cookbooks that reflect your culinary style and philosophy
- Use book tours and signings as opportunities for face-to-face brand building

7. Food Photography:

- Develop strong food photography skills or work with talented photographers
- Create a consistent visual style that becomes part of your brand identity

8. Live Demonstrations and Events:

- Participate in food festivals, cooking demonstrations, and live events
- Use these opportunities to connect directly with your audience

By building a multi-faceted brand and effectively leveraging various media platforms, you can create a strong personal brand in the culinary world. Remember, the key is to remain authentic to your culinary vision while adapting to the diverse opportunities the food industry offers for brand expression and growth.

5. Personal Branding for Consultants and Coaches

In the consulting and coaching industries, your personal brand is often your most valuable asset. It's what sets you apart from competitors and attracts clients. Effective personal branding in these fields requires a strategic approach to establishing credibility and differentiating yourself in a crowded market.

Establishing Credibility and Expertise

1. Showcase Your Experience:

- Highlight your professional journey and key achievements
- Share case studies and success stories from your work with clients

2. Develop Thought Leadership:

- Regularly publish articles, blog posts, or whitepapers in your area of expertise
- Speak at industry conferences or webinars to demonstrate your knowledge

3. Obtain Relevant Certifications:

- Pursue and maintain industry-specific certifications
- Display these credentials prominently in your marketing materials

4. Leverage Client Testimonials:

- Collect and showcase testimonials from satisfied clients
- Use video testimonials for added authenticity and impact

5. Create Valuable Content:

- Develop free resources like e-books, templates, or tools that showcase your expertise
- Use these as lead magnets to grow your audience and demonstrate value

6. Engage in Continuous Learning:

- Stay updated with the latest trends and methodologies in your field
- Share your learning journey to show your commitment to growth

Differentiating Yourself in a Crowded Market

1. Define Your Niche:

- Specialize in a specific industry, methodology, or type of client
- Become the go-to expert in your chosen niche

2. Develop a Unique Methodology:

- Create a proprietary process or framework for your work
- Brand this methodology and use it as a key differentiator

3. Cultivate a Distinct Personal Style:

- Develop a unique communication style or coaching approach
- Ensure this style is consistent across all your brand touchpoints

4. Leverage Your Background:

- Use your unique experiences or unconventional career path to stand out
- Show how your diverse background adds value to your consulting or coaching

5. Focus on Results:

- Emphasize the specific outcomes and ROI you deliver for clients
- Use data and metrics to quantify your impact

6. Build Strategic Partnerships:

- Collaborate with complementary professionals or brands
- Use these partnerships to offer unique value propositions

7. Utilize Technology:

- Incorporate innovative tools or platforms in your practice
- Position yourself as a forward-thinking consultant or coach

8. Personalize Your Approach:

- Highlight your ability to tailor your services to each client's needs
- Share examples of how you've customized solutions for different clients

By focusing on establishing credibility and differentiating yourself, you can create a powerful personal brand that attracts clients and establishes you as a leader in the consulting or coaching field.

6. Personal Branding for Lawyers and Accountants

For lawyers and accountants, personal branding presents unique challenges due to professional regulations and the need for client confidentiality. However, effective personal branding can significantly enhance your professional reputation and attract clients.

Balancing Professional Ethics with Personal Branding

1. Understand Regulatory Guidelines:

- Familiarize yourself with your profession's rules regarding marketing and advertising
- Ensure all branding efforts comply with these regulations

2. Focus on Education Over Promotion:

- Position yourself as an educator in your field rather than a promoter
- Share insights and explanations of complex legal or financial concepts

3. Maintain Professional Tone:

- Keep your branding efforts professional and aligned with industry expectations
- Avoid overly casual or sensationalist approaches

4. Emphasize Integrity:

- Make ethical practice a key part of your brand message
- Highlight your commitment to professional standards and client welfare

5. Use Disclaimers When Necessary:

- Include appropriate disclaimers in your content or marketing materials
- Clarify that your general insights do not constitute specific legal or financial advice

6. Seek Approval When Required:

- Have your marketing materials reviewed by your firm or professional association if necessary
- Implement a process for content approval to ensure compliance

Showcasing Expertise While Maintaining Client Confidentiality

1. Discuss General Concepts:

- Write about general legal or financial principles without referencing specific clients
- Use hypothetical scenarios to illustrate your points

2. Leverage Public Information:

- Comment on public cases or financial reports to demonstrate your expertise
- Analyze trends or changes in legislation relevant to your field

3. Obtain Proper Permissions:

- If sharing client success stories, always obtain explicit permission
- Consider anonymizing case studies to protect client privacy

4. Focus on Your Process:

- Highlight your approach to problem-solving without discussing specific cases
- Share your methodology for tackling common challenges in your field

5. Develop Thought Leadership:

- Write articles or whitepapers on emerging trends in your industry
- Participate in panel discussions or webinars on general topics in your field

6. Showcase Credentials and Awards:

- Highlight your educational background, certifications, and industry recognition
- Share any awards or rankings you've received from reputable sources

7. Utilize Client Testimonials Carefully:

- Use testimonials that speak to your skills and character without revealing sensitive information
- Ensure you have written permission to use any client testimonials

8. Engage in Community and Pro Bono Work:

- Highlight your involvement in community service or pro bono activities
- This showcases your expertise and commitment to social responsibility

9. Leverage Professional Associations:

- Take leadership roles in professional associations
- Share insights from industry events or conferences you attend

By carefully balancing professional ethics with personal branding efforts, lawyers and accountants can build strong personal brands that enhance their credibility and attract clients while maintaining the highest standards of professional conduct.

7. Personal Branding in Academia and Research

In the world of academia and research, personal branding plays a crucial role in establishing credibility, attracting funding, and disseminating knowledge. Effective personal branding in this field requires a balance between scholarly rigor and accessible communication.

Building a Brand Around Scholarly Work

1. Develop a Clear Research Focus:

- Define your area of expertise and stick to it consistently
- Ensure your research agenda is coherent and builds upon itself

2. Publish Regularly:

- Aim for publications in reputable, peer-reviewed journals
- Balance between quantity and quality of publications

3. Present at Conferences:

- Regularly present your work at relevant academic conferences
- Use these opportunities to network and build collaborations

4. Secure Research Grants:

- Successfully obtaining grants adds to your credibility
- Highlight your grant success in your professional profile

5. Collaborate Strategically:

- Partner with other respected researchers in your field
- Engage in interdisciplinary collaborations to broaden your impact

6. Develop a Strong Online Presence:

- Maintain profiles on academic platforms like ResearchGate or Google Scholar
- Create a professional website showcasing your research and publications

7. Engage in Peer Review:

- Participate in peer review processes for journals in your field
- This demonstrates your standing in the academic community

8. Mentor Students and Junior Researchers:

- Building a strong academic lineage enhances your reputation
- Highlight your role in developing new talent in your field

Translating Complex Ideas for Broader Audiences

1. Develop Clear Communication Skills:

- Practice explaining your research in simple, jargon-free language
- Use analogies and real-world examples to illustrate complex concepts

2. Engage with Media:

- Make yourself available for media interviews on your area of expertise

- Prepare concise, impactful statements about your research for media use

3. Write for Non-Academic Publications:

- Contribute articles to popular science magazines or respected online platforms
- Adapt your writing style to suit a general audience while maintaining accuracy

4. Use Social Media Effectively:

- Share insights and research findings on platforms like Twitter or LinkedIn
- Engage in discussions with both academic and non-academic audiences

5. Create Multimedia Content:

- Develop videos, podcasts, or infographics explaining your research
- Use visual aids to make complex data more accessible

6. Participate in Public Lectures or TED-style Talks:

- Seek opportunities to present your work to general audiences
- Craft compelling narratives around your research findings

7. Engage in Science Communication Workshops:

- Improve your skills in communicating complex ideas to lay audiences
- Learn techniques for effective public speaking and writing for non-specialists

8. Collaborate with Science Communicators:

- Partner with professional science communicators or journalists
- This can help translate your work for wider dissemination

By building a strong brand around your scholarly work and effectively translating complex ideas for broader audiences, you can enhance your impact both within academia and in the wider world. This approach not only boosts your personal brand but also contributes to the broader goal of public engagement with science and research.

8. Cross-Industry Personal Branding

In today's dynamic job market, professionals often transition between industries. Developing a versatile personal brand that can adapt to different sectors is crucial for career flexibility and growth.

Strategies for Professionals Transitioning Between Industries

1. Identify Transferable Skills:

- Analyze your skill set to identify abilities that are valuable across industries
- Highlight these transferable skills in your personal brand messaging

2. Focus on Core Competencies:

- Build your brand around fundamental competencies like leadership, innovation, or problem-solving
- These core skills are often applicable across various sectors

3. Emphasize Adaptability:

- Showcase instances where you've successfully adapted to new environments
- Highlight your ability to quickly learn and apply new knowledge

4. Leverage Diverse Experiences:

- Frame your cross-industry experience as an asset, bringing fresh perspectives
- Show how your varied background contributes to innovative thinking

5. Network Across Industries:

- Build connections in your target industry before making the transition
- Attend cross-industry events and join relevant professional associations

6. Continual Learning:

- Invest in learning about your new industry through courses, certifications, or self-study
- Share your learning journey as part of your personal brand narrative

7. Reframe Your Narrative:

- Craft a compelling story that logically connects your past experience to your new direction
- Emphasize how your unique journey adds value in your new field

Building a Versatile Personal Brand

1. Develop a Broad Professional Mission:

- Create a personal brand statement that's not tied to a specific industry
- Focus on the impact you aim to make, rather than industry-specific goals

2. Cultivate a Diverse Skill Set:

- Continuously develop a range of skills that are valuable across multiple industries
- Highlight your ability to bring diverse skill sets together

3. Build a Flexible Online Presence:

- Design your personal website and social media profiles to accommodate different professional directions

- Use language and imagery that's not limited to one specific industry

4. Create Industry-Agnostic Content:

- Produce content that demonstrates your expertise in ways applicable to multiple fields
- Focus on universal themes like innovation, leadership, or strategic thinking

5. Emphasize Results and Achievements:

- Highlight outcomes and impacts rather than industry-specific processes
- Quantify your achievements in ways that translate across sectors

6. Develop a Personal Brand Toolkit:

- Create versions of your resume, bio, and elevator pitch tailored for different industries
- Be prepared to quickly adapt your brand messaging for various opportunities

7. Seek Cross-Functional Roles:

- Look for positions that span multiple areas or require diverse skill sets
- These roles can serve as bridges between industries

By developing a versatile personal brand and employing strategies for smooth industry transitions, professionals can position themselves for diverse opportunities and long-term career success. This approach not only facilitates easier movement between sectors but also builds resilience in an ever-changing job market.

7. Personal Branding in Academia and Research

In the world of academia and research, personal branding plays a crucial role in establishing credibility, attracting funding, and disseminating knowledge. Effective personal branding in this field requires a balance between scholarly rigor and accessible communication.

Building a Brand Around Scholarly Work

1. Develop a Clear Research Focus:

- Define your area of expertise and stick to it consistently
- Ensure your research agenda is coherent and builds upon itself

2. Publish Regularly:

- Aim for publications in reputable, peer-reviewed journals
- Balance between quantity and quality of publications

3. Present at Conferences:

- Regularly present your work at relevant academic conferences
- Use these opportunities to network and build collaborations

4. Secure Research Grants:

- Successfully obtaining grants adds to your credibility
- Highlight your grant success in your professional profile

5. Collaborate Strategically:

- Partner with other respected researchers in your field
- Engage in interdisciplinary collaborations to broaden your impact

6. Develop a Strong Online Presence:

- Maintain profiles on academic platforms like ResearchGate or Google Scholar
- Create a professional website showcasing your research and publications

7. Engage in Peer Review:

- Participate in peer review processes for journals in your field

- This demonstrates your standing in the academic community

8. Mentor Students and Junior Researchers:

- Building a strong academic lineage enhances your reputation
- Highlight your role in developing new talent in your field

Translating Complex Ideas for Broader Audiences

1. Develop Clear Communication Skills:

- Practice explaining your research in simple, jargon-free language
- Use analogies and real-world examples to illustrate complex concepts

2. Engage with Media:

- Make yourself available for media interviews on your area of expertise
- Prepare concise, impactful statements about your research for media use

3. Write for Non-Academic Publications:

- Contribute articles to popular science magazines or respected online platforms
- Adapt your writing style to suit a general audience while maintaining accuracy

4. Use Social Media Effectively:

- Share insights and research findings on platforms like Twitter or LinkedIn
- Engage in discussions with both academic and non-academic audiences

5. Create Multimedia Content:

- Develop videos, podcasts, or infographics explaining your research

- Use visual aids to make complex data more accessible

6. Participate in Public Lectures or TED-style Talks:

- Seek opportunities to present your work to general audiences
- Craft compelling narratives around your research findings

7. Engage in Science Communication Workshops:

- Improve your skills in communicating complex ideas to lay audiences
- Learn techniques for effective public speaking and writing for non-specialists

8. Collaborate with Science Communicators:

- Partner with professional science communicators or journalists
- This can help translate your work for wider dissemination

By building a strong brand around your scholarly work and effectively translating complex ideas for broader audiences, you can enhance your impact both within academia and in the wider world. This approach not only boosts your personal brand but also contributes to the broader goal of public engagement with science and research.

8. Cross-Industry Personal Branding

In today's dynamic job market, professionals often transition between industries. Developing a versatile personal brand that can adapt to different sectors is crucial for career flexibility and growth.

Strategies for Professionals Transitioning Between Industries

1. Identify Transferable Skills:

- Analyze your skill set to identify abilities that are valuable across industries
- Highlight these transferable skills in your personal brand messaging

2. Focus on Core Competencies:

- Build your brand around fundamental competencies like leadership, innovation, or problem-solving
- These core skills are often applicable across various sectors

3. Emphasize Adaptability:

- Showcase instances where you've successfully adapted to new environments
- Highlight your ability to quickly learn and apply new knowledge

4. Leverage Diverse Experiences:

- Frame your cross-industry experience as an asset, bringing fresh perspectives
- Show how your varied background contributes to innovative thinking

5. Network Across Industries:

- Build connections in your target industry before making the transition
- Attend cross-industry events and join relevant professional associations

6. Continual Learning:

- Invest in learning about your new industry through courses, certifications, or self-study
- Share your learning journey as part of your personal brand narrative

7. Reframe Your Narrative:

- Craft a compelling story that logically connects your past experience to your new direction
- Emphasize how your unique journey adds value in your new field

Building a Versatile Personal Brand

1. Develop a Broad Professional Mission:

- Create a personal brand statement that's not tied to a specific industry
- Focus on the impact you aim to make, rather than industry-specific goals

2. Cultivate a Diverse Skill Set:

- Continuously develop a range of skills that are valuable across multiple industries
- Highlight your ability to bring diverse skill sets together

3. Build a Flexible Online Presence:

- Design your personal website and social media profiles to accommodate different professional directions
- Use language and imagery that's not limited to one specific industry

4. Create Industry-Agnostic Content:

- Produce content that demonstrates your expertise in ways applicable to multiple fields
- Focus on universal themes like innovation, leadership, or strategic thinking

5. Emphasize Results and Achievements:

- Highlight outcomes and impacts rather than industry-specific processes
- Quantify your achievements in ways that translate across sectors

6. Develop a Personal Brand Toolkit:

- Create versions of your resume, bio, and elevator pitch tailored for different industries

- Be prepared to quickly adapt your brand messaging for various opportunities

7. Seek Cross-Functional Roles:

- Look for positions that span multiple areas or require diverse skill sets
- These roles can serve as bridges between industries

By developing a versatile personal brand and employing strategies for smooth industry transitions, professionals can position themselves for diverse opportunities and long-term career success. This approach not only facilitates easier movement between sectors but also builds resilience in an ever-changing job market.

Chapter 10 Decision Tree: Tailoring Your Personal Brand to Your Industry

Purpose: This decision tree helps you adapt your personal brand to the specific needs and expectations of your industry. Follow the steps to ensure your brand resonates within your field while setting you apart from competitors.

Start: Have you identified the unique characteristics and expectations of your industry?

• **Yes:** Proceed to **Step 2: Aligning Brand with Industry Norms**

• **No:** Research industry specifics:

- Analyze successful personal brands in your field
- Identify industry-specific values and priorities
- Understand communication norms in your sector

Step 2: Is your personal brand aligned with industry norms while maintaining authenticity?

• **Yes:** Proceed to **Step 3: Developing Industry-Specific Strategies**

• **No:** Adjust brand alignment:

- Identify areas where your brand can conform to industry expectations

- Determine aspects of your brand that should remain unique
- Develop a strategy to balance conformity and differentiation

Step 3: Have you developed industry-specific branding strategies?

• **Yes:** Proceed to **Step 4: Navigating Industry Challenges**

• **No:** Create tailored strategies:

- Identify key platforms and channels in your industry
- Develop content that addresses industry-specific pain points
- Tailor your messaging to resonate with industry stakeholders

Step 4: Are you effectively navigating challenges unique to your field?

• **Yes:** Proceed to **Step 5: Leveraging Industry-Specific Platforms**

• **No:** Address industry challenges:

- Identify common obstacles in your field
- Develop strategies to overcome these challenges
- Showcase how you've addressed industry-specific issues

Step 5: Are you leveraging industry-specific platforms and networks?

• **Yes:** Proceed to **Step 6: Measuring Brand Effectiveness**

• **No:** Utilize industry platforms:

- Join industry-specific professional associations
- Participate in sector-focused online forums or social networks
- Attend industry conferences and events

Step 6: Are you measuring your brand's effectiveness within your industry context?

• **Yes:** Analyze and refine your industry-specific brand

• **No:** Implement industry-specific metrics:

- Track industry-relevant engagement metrics
- Monitor your reputation among industry peers
- Assess how well your brand addresses industry-specific needs

Final: Continuously evolve your personal brand to stay relevant in your changing industry

CONCLUSION

Chapter 10 has provided you with a practical roadmap for implementing and sustaining your personal brand, emphasizing the importance of a strategic approach to ensure long-term success. As we have journeyed through the previous chapters, you have gained a comprehensive understanding of what it takes to build a compelling personal brand. This final chapter has brought it all together, guiding you on how to put your knowledge into action and maintain your brand's momentum.

We explored the significance of setting clear, measurable goals for your personal branding efforts. By defining what success looks like for your brand, whether it's increased visibility, client acquisition, or thought leadership, you can tailor your strategies to achieve these outcomes effectively. The chapter also discussed the importance of creating a detailed action plan that outlines the specific steps you will take to reach your branding goals, from content creation to networking and beyond.

Sustaining your personal brand requires ongoing effort and adaptability. This chapter emphasized the need for continuous learning and regular reassessment of your branding strategies. The branding landscape is ever-evolving, with new platforms, tools, and trends emerging regularly. By staying informed and being willing to pivot when necessary, you can keep your brand fresh and relevant.

We also covered the importance of consistency in your branding efforts, both in the way you present yourself across different platforms and in the frequency of your engagement with your audience. Consistency builds trust and reinforces your brand message, making it easier for your audience to recognize and connect with you.

Moreover, the chapter highlighted the value of feedback and analytics in refining your brand. Regularly seeking feedback from your audience, peers, and mentors, as well as analyzing the performance of your branding activities, allows you to identify areas for improvement and adjust your strategies accordingly.

Finally, we addressed the importance of resilience and patience in the branding process. Building a strong personal brand is not an overnight endeavor; it requires dedication, perseverance, and the ability to learn from setbacks. By staying committed to your brand vision and continually refining your approach, you will gradually build a brand that is not only successful but also enduring.

As you move forward, remember that personal branding is a dynamic, lifelong process. The knowledge and tools you have gained throughout this book are just the beginning. By implementing the strategies outlined in this chapter and remaining proactive in your branding efforts, you will create a personal brand that stands the test of time and continues to grow with you.

In conclusion, Chapter 10 has equipped you with the final pieces of the personal branding puzzle, helping you to implement your brand strategy effectively and sustain it over the long term. With a clear plan, consistent efforts, and a commitment to continuous improvement, you are well on your way to building a personal brand that not only achieves your professional goals but also leaves a lasting impact on your industry and audience.

Chapter 11

Personal Branding for Career Advancement

1. Introduction: The Role of Personal Branding in Career Growth

In today's competitive professional landscape, personal branding has become an essential tool for career advancement. Your personal brand is not just about self-promotion; it's a strategic approach to showcasing your unique value proposition, skills, and experiences in a way that aligns with your career aspirations.

A well-crafted personal brand can:

1. Differentiate you from other professionals in your field
2. Increase your visibility to potential employers or clients
3. Position you as an expert or thought leader in your industry
4. Create opportunities for career advancement and professional growth
5. Build a network of valuable connections and supporters

Personal branding for career advancement goes beyond simply maintaining a polished LinkedIn profile or having a professional website. It involves consistently demonstrating your expertise, building meaningful relationships, and strategically positioning yourself for the career moves you aspire to make.

Throughout this chapter, we'll explore various strategies for leveraging your personal brand to advance your career. We'll examine case studies of individuals who have successfully used personal branding to climb the career ladder, discuss key techniques for aligning your brand with your career goals, and provide practical tips for using your brand to create new opportunities.

By the end of this chapter, you'll have the knowledge and tools to strategically use your personal brand as a powerful asset in your career advancement toolkit. Let's begin by exploring how to leverage your personal brand for career progression, starting with a case study of Sheryl Sandberg, who has masterfully used her personal brand to propel her career to new heights.

2. Personal Brand and Career Progression

To understand how personal branding can drive career progression, let's examine the case of Sheryl Sandberg, whose strategic use of personal branding has been instrumental in her remarkable career trajectory.

Case Study: Sheryl Sandberg - Leveraging Personal Brand for Career Growth

Sheryl Sandberg, COO of Facebook (now Meta), has built a powerful personal brand that has both supported and accelerated her career advancement.

Key aspects of Sandberg's personal branding strategy:

1. Thought Leadership: Sandberg positioned herself as a thought leader on women in the workplace, most notably through her book "Lean In."

2. Authentic Storytelling: She openly shares personal experiences and challenges, making her relatable and authentic.

3. Advocacy: Sandberg's brand is closely tied to her advocacy for women's empowerment in the workplace.

4. Cross-Industry Influence: Her brand extends beyond tech, influencing discussions in business, leadership, and social issues.

5. Consistency: Sandberg maintains a consistent message across various platforms, from social media to public speaking engagements.

Impact of Sandberg's personal branding on her career:

- Elevated her profile beyond her role at Facebook
- Created opportunities for high-profile speaking engagements and media appearances
- Positioned her as a leader in discussions about workplace diversity and women's empowerment
- Enhanced her influence both within and outside the tech industry

Aligning Personal Brand with Career Goals

To effectively use your personal brand for career advancement:

1. Define Your Career Objectives:

- Clearly articulate your short-term and long-term career goals
- Identify the key positions or achievements you're aiming for

2. Assess Your Current Brand:

- Evaluate how you're currently perceived in your industry
- Identify any gaps between your current brand and your career aspirations

3. Develop a Brand Strategy:

- Create a personal brand statement that aligns with your career goals
- Identify the key attributes and skills you need to highlight

4. Curate Your Online Presence:

- Ensure your LinkedIn profile, personal website, and other online platforms reflect your career aspirations
- Share content and engage in discussions that reinforce your desired professional image

5. Seek Relevant Experiences:

- Pursue projects, roles, or volunteer opportunities that align with your career goals
- Highlight these experiences in your brand narrative

6. Build a Relevant Network:

- Connect with professionals in positions you aspire to
- Engage with industry leaders and influencers in your desired field

7. Develop Necessary Skills:

- Identify and acquire the skills needed for your target roles
- Showcase your commitment to continuous learning and growth

Using Your Brand to Create Opportunities

Your personal brand can be a powerful tool for creating career opportunities:

1. Become a Thought Leader:

- Share insights and expertise through articles, blog posts, or speaking engagements
- Position yourself as a go-to expert in your field

2. Leverage Social Media:

- Use platforms like LinkedIn and Twitter to share valuable content and engage with industry leaders
- Participate in relevant online discussions and Twitter chats

3. Speak at Events:

- Seek opportunities to present at industry conferences or webinars
- Use these platforms to showcase your expertise and expand your network

4. Write for Industry Publications:

- Contribute articles to respected publications in your field
- This enhances your credibility and visibility to potential employers or clients

5. Engage in Networking:

- Attend industry events and actively network with professionals in your desired field
- Use your personal brand as a conversation starter and point of connection

6. Seek Mentorship Relationships:

- Approach potential mentors who can guide your career progression
- Offer value in return, perhaps through reverse mentoring

7. Create Your Own Opportunities:

- Start a podcast, blog, or YouTube channel related to your expertise
- These platforms can attract attention from potential employers or clients

8. Volunteer for High-Visibility Projects:

- Seek out projects within your organization that align with your career goals
- Use these opportunities to demonstrate your capabilities to decision-makers

By strategically aligning your personal brand with your career goals and actively using it to create opportunities, you can significantly accelerate your career progression. Remember, like Sheryl Sandberg, the key is to consistently reinforce your brand message and leverage it to position yourself for the career advancements you desire.

3. Personal Branding for Leadership Roles

As professionals aspire to leadership positions, personal branding becomes increasingly crucial. A strong leadership brand can set you apart from other candidates and inspire confidence in your ability to guide an organization. Let's examine the case of Indra Nooyi to understand how to build a brand as a global business leader.

Case Study: Indra Nooyi - Building a Brand as a Global Business Leader

Indra Nooyi, former CEO of PepsiCo, has cultivated a powerful personal brand that exemplifies visionary leadership and global business acumen.

Key aspects of Nooyi's leadership brand:

1. Visionary Thinking: Nooyi is known for her forward-thinking approach, particularly her "Performance with Purpose" strategy at PepsiCo.

2. Cultural Ambassador: She often speaks about her Indian heritage and how it influences her leadership style.

3. Advocate for Diversity: Nooyi is a vocal proponent of diversity in corporate leadership.

4. Emphasis on Work-Life Integration: She openly discusses the challenges of balancing career and family.

5. Focus on Sustainability: Nooyi positioned herself as a leader in corporate sustainability efforts.

Impact of Nooyi's leadership brand:

- Established her as one of the most influential business leaders globally
- Positioned PepsiCo as a forward-thinking, socially responsible corporation
- Inspired other women and minorities to pursue leadership roles
- Created a lasting legacy beyond her tenure as CEO

Developing an Executive Presence

To build a strong leadership brand:

1. Cultivate Self-Awareness:

- Understand your strengths, weaknesses, and unique leadership style
- Seek feedback from colleagues, mentors, and subordinates

2. Develop a Compelling Leadership Philosophy:

- Articulate your vision of leadership
- Connect your leadership style to tangible business outcomes

3. Enhance Your Communication Skills:

- Practice articulating complex ideas clearly and concisely
- Develop storytelling skills to make your messages more impactful

4. Build Credibility Through Expertise:

- Stay informed about industry trends and global business issues
- Share insights through thought leadership content

5. Project Confidence:

- Work on your body language and vocal tone
- Dress appropriately for leadership roles in your industry

6. Network Strategically:

- Build relationships with other leaders in your industry
- Seek mentorship from experienced executives

7. Demonstrate Emotional Intelligence:

- Show empathy and understanding in your interactions
- Manage your emotions effectively, especially in high-stress situations

Communicating Vision and Inspiring Others Through Your Brand

1. Craft a Compelling Vision:

- Develop and articulate a clear vision for your organization or team
- Connect this vision to broader societal or industry trends

2. Use Storytelling:

- Share personal anecdotes that illustrate your leadership journey
- Use stories to make your vision more relatable and inspiring

3. Lead by Example:

- Ensure your actions align with your stated values and vision
- Be visible in championing key initiatives

4. Engage in Two-Way Communication:

- Create opportunities for dialogue with team members at all levels
- Show that you value and act on input from others

5. Leverage Multiple Platforms:

- Use a mix of internal communications, social media, and public speaking to share your message
- Tailor your communication style to each platform while maintaining consistency in your core message

6. Show Vulnerability:

- Share challenges you've faced and lessons learned
- This authenticity can make you more relatable and inspirational

7. Celebrate Team Successes:

- Use your platform to highlight the achievements of your team
- This reinforces your brand as a leader who empowers others

By developing a strong leadership brand, you can position yourself effectively for executive roles and inspire confidence in your ability to lead. Remember, like Indra Nooyi, your leadership brand should reflect your authentic self while also embodying the qualities that make a great leader in your industry.

4. Personal Branding During Career Transitions

Career transitions, whether within the same industry or to a completely new field, require careful management of your personal brand. Let's examine how Satya Nadella navigated his personal brand during his ascent to the CEO position at Microsoft.

Case Study: Satya Nadella - Rebranding for a CEO Position

Satya Nadella's transition from a long-time Microsoft executive to CEO involved a strategic shift in his personal brand.

Key aspects of Nadella's rebranding:

1. Emphasis on Innovation: Nadella positioned himself as a champion of innovation and cloud computing.

2. Cultural Transformation: He branded himself as an agent of change, promoting a growth mindset culture.

3. Collaborative Leadership: Nadella emphasized a more open and collaborative leadership style compared to his predecessors.

4. Technical Expertise with Business Acumen: He balanced his deep technical knowledge with strategic business thinking.

5. Personal Story: Nadella shared his personal journey, including his immigrant background and family life.

Impact of Nadella's rebranding:

- Successfully transitioned Microsoft's image from a PC-centric company to a cloud and mobile-first organization
- Revitalized Microsoft's corporate culture
- Positioned himself as a visionary tech leader on the global stage

Adapting Your Personal Brand for New Roles

To effectively adapt your personal brand during career transitions:

1. Assess Your Current Brand:

- Evaluate how you're currently perceived in your industry
- Identify elements of your brand that are transferable to your new role

2. Research Your New Role/Industry:

- Understand the key competencies and qualities valued in your target position
- Identify any gaps between your current brand and what's needed in the new role

3. Reframe Your Experience:

- Highlight aspects of your background that are most relevant to your new role
- Show how your diverse experience brings unique value to the position

4. Develop New Skills:

- Acquire and showcase skills specific to your new role
- Demonstrate your ability to learn and adapt quickly

5. Update Your Brand Messaging:

- Revise your elevator pitch, bio, and online profiles to align with your new direction
- Ensure your language resonates with your new target audience

6. Build a New Network:

- Connect with professionals in your new field
- Seek mentors who can guide you in your transition

7. Create Relevant Content:

- Share insights and thought leadership pieces related to your new role or industry
- This establishes credibility in your new field

Managing Your Brand During Career Pivots

1. Communicate Your Transition:

- Be transparent about your career change with your network

- Share your motivations and the value you bring to your new role

2. Maintain Consistency:

- Ensure your brand message is consistent across all platforms
- Gradually transition your content focus to align with your new direction

3. Leverage Transferable Skills:

- Emphasize skills and experiences that are valuable in both your old and new roles
- Show how your unique background provides fresh perspectives

4. Address Potential Concerns:

- Anticipate and proactively address any doubts about your transition
- Showcase your commitment to succeeding in your new role

5. Seek Visibility Opportunities:

- Look for speaking engagements or writing opportunities in your new field
- Participate in industry events to increase your visibility

6. Be Patient:

- Understand that building credibility in a new field takes time
- Consistently reinforce your new brand message over time

7. Stay Connected to Your Past:

- Don't completely disconnect from your previous network
- Your diverse background can be a unique selling point

8. Continuous Learning:

- Publicly share your learning journey in your new field
- This demonstrates your commitment and adaptability

By strategically adapting your personal brand during career transitions, you can successfully navigate new roles and industries. Remember, like Satya Nadella, the key is to build on your existing strengths while clearly communicating your ability to bring value in your new position. Your personal brand should evolve to reflect your growth and new direction while maintaining the core attributes that define your professional identity.

5. Leveraging Your Brand in Job Searches

In today's competitive job market, a strong personal brand can significantly enhance your chances of landing your dream job. Your personal brand should be consistently reflected across all touchpoints of your job search, from your resume to your interview performance.

Optimizing Your Resume and Online Profiles

1. Craft a Brand-Aligned Resume:

- Begin with a powerful personal statement that encapsulates your brand
- Tailor your experience descriptions to highlight brand-relevant achievements
- Use language that reflects your personal brand voice

2. LinkedIn Optimization:

- Ensure your LinkedIn headline is compelling and brand-aligned
- Write a summary that tells your professional story and highlights your unique value proposition
- Use the Featured section to showcase brand-relevant projects or content

3. Personal Website:

- If applicable, create a personal website that serves as a comprehensive brand showcase
- Include a portfolio, testimonials, and examples of your work
- Ensure the design and content align with your personal brand

4. Other Social Media Platforms:

- Audit and update all professional social media profiles to ensure brand consistency
- Share content that reinforces your expertise and aligns with your brand

5. Digital Portfolio:

- Create a digital portfolio that highlights your best work
- Ensure it's easily accessible to potential employers

Using Your Personal Brand in Interviews and Networking

1. Prepare Brand-Aligned Stories:

- Develop a repertoire of stories that illustrate your brand attributes
- Practice delivering these stories concisely and engagingly

2. Dress the Part:

- Ensure your appearance in interviews aligns with your personal brand
- This includes both in-person and video interviews

3. Consistent Communication:

- Use language and communication style that reflects your brand during interviews
- Ensure your verbal and non-verbal communication align with your brand attributes

4. Ask Brand-Reinforcing Questions:

- Prepare questions for interviewers that subtly reinforce your brand
- For example, if innovation is part of your brand, ask about the company's approach to innovation

5. Follow-Up Communication:

- Send follow-up emails or letters that reinforce your brand message
- Reference specific points from the interview that align with your brand

6. Networking Strategy:

- Develop a networking pitch that succinctly communicates your brand
- Attend industry events or join professional groups that align with your brand

7. Provide Value:

- In networking situations, focus on how you can provide value to others
- This approach reinforces a brand of generosity and expertise

8. Online Engagement:

- Engage in online discussions or forums related to your industry
- Share insights that reinforce your brand and expertise

By consistently leveraging your personal brand throughout the job search process, you create a compelling narrative for potential employers. This coherent presentation of your professional self can set you apart from other candidates and increase your chances of securing the positions you desire.

6. Personal Branding for Freelancers and Consultants

For freelancers and consultants, a strong personal brand is not just an asset—it's a necessity. Your brand is often the primary factor that attracts clients and sets you apart in a crowded marketplace.

Building Credibility and Attracting Clients

1. Establish Expertise:

- Create and share content that demonstrates your knowledge
- Publish articles, blog posts, or whitepapers in your area of expertise
- Speak at industry events or webinars to increase visibility

2. Showcase Your Work:

- Develop a compelling portfolio that highlights your best projects
- Include case studies that detail the problems you solved for clients
- Use visual storytelling to make your achievements more impactful

3. Gather and Display Testimonials:

- Collect testimonials from satisfied clients
- Feature these prominently on your website and marketing materials
- Use video testimonials for added authenticity

4. Develop a Signature Methodology:

- Create a unique approach or framework for your work
- Brand this methodology and use it as a key differentiator

5. Leverage Social Proof:

- Highlight any awards, certifications, or notable clients
- Showcase media mentions or features

6. Networking and Partnerships:

- Build relationships with complementary service providers
- Seek referral partnerships to expand your client base

7. Consistent Brand Presence:

- Ensure all your online and offline materials reflect a consistent brand image
- This includes your website, social media, business cards, and pitch decks

Differentiating Yourself in a Gig Economy

1. Niche Specialization:

- Focus on a specific industry or type of client
- Become the go-to expert in a particular niche

2. Unique Value Proposition:

- Clearly articulate what sets you apart from competitors
- Emphasize the unique benefits clients gain from working with you

3. Personal Brand Storytelling:

- Share your professional journey and what drives you
- Use storytelling to create an emotional connection with potential clients

4. Innovative Service Offerings:

- Develop unique service packages or delivery methods
- Consider productizing some of your services for scalability

5. Thought Leadership:

- Position yourself as a thought leader through content creation and speaking engagements

- Offer fresh perspectives or innovative solutions to industry challenges

6. Client Experience:

- Design a unique and memorable client experience
- This could include your onboarding process, communication style, or deliverables format

7. Continuous Learning and Adaptation:

- Regularly update your skills and knowledge
- Share your learning journey to demonstrate your commitment to growth

8. Personal Touch:

- In a world of automation, emphasize the personal attention clients receive
- Showcase your personality and values in your brand communications

By focusing on building credibility and differentiating yourself, you can create a powerful personal brand that attracts clients and sets you apart in the competitive freelance and consulting marketplace. Remember, your personal brand should clearly communicate the unique value you offer and why clients should choose you over other options in the gig economy.

7. Building a Personal Brand as an Intrapreneur

Intrapreneurship—the act of behaving like an entrepreneur while working within a large organization—has become increasingly valuable in today's fast-paced business environment. Building a personal brand as an intrapreneur can set you apart within your company and drive significant organizational change.

Showcasing Innovation Within Corporate Structures

1. Develop an Innovation Mindset:

   - Cultivate and communicate a forward-thinking approach to problem-solving
   - Stay informed about industry trends and emerging technologies

2. Create and Lead Cross-Functional Projects:

   - Initiate projects that span different departments or units
   - Use these opportunities to demonstrate your ability to drive innovation

3. Champion New Ideas:

   - Regularly propose new ideas or improvements to existing processes
   - Be known as the go-to person for creative solutions

4. Build an Internal Network:

   - Connect with colleagues across different departments
   - Cultivate relationships with senior leaders who can support your initiatives

5. Share Knowledge:

   - Organize internal workshops or lunch-and-learn sessions
   - Create a blog or newsletter to share insights with colleagues

6. Embrace Calculated Risks:

   - Be willing to take on projects with some level of risk
   - Demonstrate how to manage and learn from both successes and failures

Using Your Brand to Drive Change in Your Organization

1. Develop a Change Vision:

- Articulate a clear vision for positive change within your organization
- Align this vision with the company's overall goals and values

2. Build a Coalition:

- Identify and collaborate with like-minded colleagues
- Create a network of change agents within the organization

3. Communicate Effectively:

- Develop compelling presentations and proposals for your ideas
- Use storytelling to illustrate the potential impact of your

initiatives

4. Lead by Example:

- Embody the change you want to see in the organization
- Be known for your proactive and positive approach to challenges

5. Measure and Showcase Results:

- Track the impact of your initiatives
- Share success stories and lessons learned with leadership and colleagues

6. Mentor Others:

- Guide and support colleagues in developing their intrapreneurial skills
- This reinforces your brand as a leader and change-maker

7. Leverage External Insights:

- Bring external perspectives into the organization

- Attend industry events and share learnings with your team

8. Persistence and Adaptability:

- Be persistent in pursuing your vision, but flexible in your approach
- Demonstrate resilience in the face of setbacks

By building a strong personal brand as an intrapreneur, you position yourself as a valuable asset to your organization. This brand can lead to increased responsibilities, leadership opportunities, and the chance to make a significant impact within your company.

8. Measuring the Impact of Your Personal Brand on Career Advancement

To ensure your personal branding efforts are effectively supporting your career goals, it's crucial to measure their impact and adjust your strategy accordingly.

Key Performance Indicators for Career-Focused Personal Branding

1. Professional Advancement:

- Track promotions, salary increases, or expanded responsibilities
- Monitor the quality and quantity of new opportunities presented to you

2. Network Growth:

- Measure the expansion of your professional network
- Track the number of meaningful connections made, especially with industry leaders

3. Thought Leadership Metrics:

- Monitor engagement with your content (articles, posts, presentations)
- Track invitations to speak at events or contribute to publications

4. Online Presence:

- Analyze growth in followers and engagement on professional social media platforms
- Monitor your personal website traffic and engagement metrics

5. Media Exposure:

- Track mentions in industry publications or media
- Monitor requests for interviews or expert commentary

6. Client or Project Acquisition:

- For consultants or freelancers, track new client acquisitions or project opportunities
- Measure the quality and desirability of incoming opportunities

7. Internal Recognition:

- Monitor acknowledgments or awards received within your organization
- Track instances where your work is cited or showcased internally

8. Industry Recognition:

- Keep track of industry awards or recognitions received
- Monitor invitations to join professional boards or committees

Adjusting Your Strategy Based on Career Outcomes

1. Regular Self-Assessment:

- Conduct quarterly reviews of your personal brand performance
- Compare results against your career goals and adjust as necessary

2. Seek Feedback:

- Regularly ask for feedback from colleagues, mentors, and industry peers
- Use this feedback to identify areas for improvement in your personal brand

3. Analyze Successful Outcomes:

- When you achieve a career milestone, analyze which aspects of your personal brand contributed to this success
- Double down on strategies that are proving effective

4. Identify Gaps:

- If you're not seeing desired outcomes, identify gaps in your personal brand strategy
- This might include skills you need to develop or platforms you need to leverage

5. Stay Current:

- Regularly update your skills and knowledge to stay relevant in your field
- Adjust your brand messaging to reflect your evolving expertise

6. Experiment and Iterate:

- Try new personal branding tactics and measure their effectiveness
- Be willing to pivot your strategy if certain approaches aren't yielding results

7. Long-Term Vision:

- Ensure your personal branding efforts align with your long-term career goals
- Make adjustments as your career aspirations evolve

8. Industry Trends:

- Stay aware of changes in your industry that might affect personal branding strategies
- Be prepared to adapt your approach to stay relevant

By consistently measuring the impact of your personal brand and adjusting your strategy based on outcomes, you can ensure that your branding efforts are effectively supporting your career advancement. Remember, personal branding is an ongoing process that requires regular attention and refinement to yield the best results for your career.

Chapter 11 Decision Tree: Leveraging Your Personal Brand for Career Growth

This decision tree will help you strategically use your personal brand to advance your career by aligning your brand with your goals, identifying opportunities, positioning yourself effectively, and continuously evolving your brand.

Start: Is your personal brand aligned with your current career goals?

• **Yes** → Proceed to **Identifying Advancement Opportunities**

• **No → Realign your brand with career goals**

- Clearly define your short-term and long-term career objectives
- Identify gaps between your current brand and career goals
- Adjust your brand messaging to support your career aspirations

Next: Have you identified specific opportunities for career advancement?

• **Yes** → Proceed to **Positioning Your Brand**

• **No → Research advancement opportunities**

- Analyze job market trends in your field
- Identify skills and experiences required for desired positions
- Look for growth opportunities within your current organization

Next: Is your brand positioned effectively for your desired role or promotion?

• **Yes** → Proceed to **Leveraging Your Brand in Applications/Interviews**

• **No → Reposition your brand**

- Highlight skills and experiences relevant to target position
- Develop thought leadership content aligned with desired role
- Adjust your online presence to reflect your career aspirations

Next: Are you effectively using your brand in job applications and interviews?

• **Yes** → Proceed to **Leveraging Your Network**

• **No → Enhance brand application**

- Tailor your resume and cover letter to reflect your personal brand
- Prepare brand-aligned stories and examples for interviews
- Ensure your online presence supports your application materials

Next: Are you leveraging your network for career opportunities?

• **Yes** → Proceed to **Brand Evolution Planning**

• **No → Activate your network**

- Inform your network about your career goals
- Seek introductions to key people in target organizations
- Offer value to your network to encourage reciprocal support

Next: Do you have a plan for evolving your brand as your career progresses?

• **Yes** → Implement and monitor your career branding strategy

• **No → Develop brand evolution plan**

- Anticipate how your brand needs to change for future roles
- Plan for acquiring and showcasing new skills and experiences

- Set regular intervals to review and update your brand

Final: Continuously align your personal brand with your evolving career path and industry trends

CONCLUSION

Chapter 11 has provided valuable insights into leveraging the power of content to amplify your personal brand. Content is the lifeblood of modern branding, serving as the primary vehicle through which you communicate your expertise, values, and personality to your audience. This chapter has emphasized that creating and sharing high-quality content is not just a strategy for visibility—it is a key component of establishing authority and building lasting relationships with your audience.

We explored the different types of content that can effectively showcase your brand, including blogs, videos, podcasts, social media posts, and more. Each format offers unique opportunities to engage with your audience, and selecting the right mix of content types that align with your brand goals and audience preferences is crucial. The chapter also highlighted the importance of consistency in content creation, noting that regular, value-driven content keeps your audience engaged and positions you as a reliable source of information and insight in your field.

The chapter delved into the art of storytelling, emphasizing that your content should not only inform but also connect emotionally with your audience. By sharing your personal experiences, challenges, and triumphs, you humanize your brand and create a narrative that resonates with your audience on a deeper level. This storytelling approach makes your content more relatable and memorable, helping you to stand out in a crowded digital landscape.

We also discussed the importance of optimizing your content for different platforms, recognizing that each platform has its own audience, style, and algorithm. Understanding these nuances allows you to tailor your content for maximum impact, whether you're posting on LinkedIn, Instagram, or your own blog. Additionally, the chapter covered the value of repurposing content, enabling you to maximize your reach and efficiency by adapting your content across multiple platforms and formats.

Analytics and feedback were another key focus, with the chapter emphasizing the need to track the performance of your content to understand what resonates with your audience and where there is room for improvement. By using data-driven insights to refine your content strategy, you can continuously enhance the effectiveness of your branding efforts.

As you continue to build and share content, remember that it's not just about quantity—it's about creating content that aligns with your brand's mission and delivers real value to your audience. High-quality content that educates, inspires, and engages will not only elevate your brand but also foster a loyal community of followers and clients.

In conclusion, Chapter 11 has equipped you with the knowledge and tools to harness the power of content in building a strong, influential personal brand. By consistently creating and sharing content that is authentic, valuable, and strategically optimized, you will amplify your brand's presence, connect meaningfully with your audience, and position yourself as a thought leader in your field. As you move forward, let your content be a true reflection of your brand's essence, driving long-term success and impact.

Chapter 12

Personal Branding for Entrepreneurs

1. Introduction: The Unique Challenges of Entrepreneur Personal Branding

For entrepreneurs, personal branding takes on a unique significance. Unlike traditional employees, entrepreneurs often find their personal brand inextricably linked with their business ventures. This symbiotic relationship between personal and business branding presents both opportunities and challenges.

Key challenges for entrepreneur personal branding include:

1. Balancing personal and business identities

2. Maintaining brand consistency across multiple ventures

3. Leveraging personal reputation to build business credibility

4. Adapting the brand as the business evolves

5. Managing public perception during business ups and downs

6. Standing out in a crowded marketplace of entrepreneur personalities

However, when done effectively, a strong personal brand can be a powerful asset for an entrepreneur. It can attract investors, customers, and talent to your ventures. It can open doors to new opportunities and partnerships. Most importantly, it can create a lasting legacy that extends beyond any single business venture.

Throughout this chapter, we'll explore strategies for building and leveraging a personal brand as an entrepreneur. We'll examine case studies of successful entrepreneur personal brands, discuss techniques for maintaining brand consistency across diverse business interests, and provide practical tips for using your personal brand to drive business success.

By the end of this chapter, you'll have the knowledge and tools to create a powerful personal brand that supports your entrepreneurial journey and helps you achieve your business goals. Let's begin by exploring how to develop branding strategies that work across multiple businesses, starting with a case study of Elon Musk, a master of personal branding across diverse ventures.

2. Branding Strategies for Multiple Businesses

For entrepreneurs involved in multiple ventures, creating a cohesive personal brand that supports all business interests can be challenging. Let's examine how Elon Musk has successfully navigated this challenge.

Case Study: Elon Musk - Personal Branding Across Diverse Ventures

Elon Musk has built a powerful personal brand that spans multiple industries, from electric vehicles (Tesla) to space exploration (SpaceX) to neural technology (Neuralink).

Key aspects of Musk's personal branding strategy:

1. Visionary Identity: Musk positions himself as a forward-thinking innovator tackling humanity's biggest challenges.

2. Technological Focus: Across all ventures, Musk emphasizes cutting-edge technology and innovation.

3. Direct Communication: He uses social media, particularly Twitter, to communicate directly with the public about all his ventures.

4. Controversial Persona: Musk's sometimes controversial statements keep him in the public eye and reinforce his maverick image.

5. Interconnected Vision: He presents his various ventures as part of a larger, interconnected vision for the future.

Impact of Musk's personal branding:

- Created a strong association between his name and innovative technology
- Attracted talent and investment to his various ventures
- Generated significant media attention for his businesses
- Established himself as a thought leader in multiple industries

Unifying Personal Brand Across Different Business Interests

To create a cohesive personal brand across multiple ventures:

1. Identify Core Values and Themes:

- Define the fundamental principles that drive all your endeavors
- Use these as the foundation for your personal brand messaging

2. Develop an Overarching Narrative:

- Create a story that connects your various business interests
- Show how each venture contributes to your overall vision or mission

3. Maintain Consistent Messaging:

- Use consistent language and tone across all platforms and ventures
- Ensure your core message remains steady, even as you discuss different businesses

4. Create a Strong Personal Platform:

- Develop a personal website or blog that showcases all your ventures
- Use this as a hub to demonstrate how your various interests interconnect

5. Leverage Cross-Promotion:

- Use success in one venture to boost credibility in others
- Share how learnings from one business apply to others

6. Develop a Distinctive Personal Style:

- Create a recognizable personal brand image (like Musk's casual attire)
- Use this consistent image across all your business appearances

7. Balance Individual and Company Brands:

- Clearly delineate your personal brand from your company brands
- Show how your personal brand adds value to each business without overshadowing it

Leveraging Personal Brand for New Ventures

Your established personal brand can be a powerful asset when launching new ventures:

1. Use Your Reputation as a Launchpad:

- Leverage your existing audience and credibility to generate interest in new projects
- Use your personal network to secure initial funding or partnerships

2. Apply Known Strengths to New Areas:

- Highlight how your proven skills in one area translate to the new venture
- This builds confidence in your ability to succeed in a new field

3. Tell a Compelling Story:

- Frame the new venture as a natural evolution of your entrepreneurial journey
- Show how it aligns with your overall vision and values

4. Engage Your Existing Audience:

- Bring your current followers along on your new venture journey
- Use their support to create initial momentum for the new

business

5. Address Potential Skepticism:

- Proactively address questions about venturing into a new area
- Demonstrate your commitment and preparation for the new challenge

6. Collaborate with Established Experts:

- Partner with industry experts in your new field
- This adds credibility to your new venture

7. Maintain Authenticity:

- Be open about your learning process in the new industry
- Share both successes and challenges to maintain trust with your audience

By creating a unified personal brand across multiple ventures and leveraging this brand for new opportunities, entrepreneurs can build a powerful platform for ongoing success. Remember, like Elon Musk, the key is to create a consistent core message that ties all your endeavors together while allowing flexibility to explore diverse business interests.

3. From Media to Wellness Branding

Transitioning a personal brand to a new industry can be challenging, but when done effectively, it can open up new opportunities and reinvigorate an entrepreneur's career. Let's examine how Arianna Huffington successfully pivoted her personal brand from media to wellness.

Case Study: Arianna Huffington - Transitioning Personal Brand to New Industries

Arianna Huffington, co-founder of The Huffington Post, made a significant shift in her personal brand when she transitioned from media to wellness with the launch of Thrive Global.

Key aspects of Huffington's brand transition:

1. Personal Experience: Huffington used her own burnout experience as the foundation for her new brand focus.

2. Gradual Transition: She began incorporating wellness themes into her media work before fully pivoting.

3. Leveraging Existing Platform: Huffington used her media presence to build credibility in the wellness space.

4. Consistent Core Values: While the industry focus changed, her core values of empowerment and success remained constant.

5. Thought Leadership: She positioned herself as a thought leader in the new space through books, speaking engagements, and articles.

Impact of Huffington's brand transition:

- Successfully established Thrive Global as a leading wellness and productivity platform
- Maintained her influence and relevance in a new industry
- Expanded her audience to include both media and wellness enthusiasts

Evolving Your Brand as Your Business Focus Changes

To effectively evolve your personal brand alongside your changing business interests:

1. Identify Transferable Skills and Values:

- Highlight skills and values that apply to both your old and new focus areas
- Use these as a bridge to maintain brand consistency

2. Craft a Transition Narrative:

- Create a compelling story that explains your shift in focus
- Show how your new direction is a natural evolution of your journey

3. Gradually Introduce New Themes:

    - Begin incorporating elements of your new focus into your existing brand content
    - This helps prepare your audience for the upcoming shift

4. Educate Your Audience:

    - Share your learning process as you enter the new industry
    - This transparency can help maintain trust with your existing audience

5. Leverage Existing Networks:

    - Use your current professional network to gain introductions in your new industry
    - Collaborate with experts in the new field to build credibility

6. Rebrand Strategically:

    - Update your visual branding and messaging to reflect your new focus
    - Ensure the new branding still feels authentic to your established persona

7. Maintain Consistency in Core Values:

    - While your focus may change, ensure your fundamental values remain consistent
    - This helps maintain brand authenticity through the transition

Maintaining Credibility During Brand Pivots

1. Be Transparent About Your Journey:

    - Openly discuss your reasons for the pivot and your vision for the future
    - Share both successes and challenges in your new venture

2. Demonstrate Commitment to Learning:

- Show your dedication to understanding your new industry thoroughly
- Share insights and lessons learned to establish expertise

3. Seek Relevant Certifications or Education:

- Pursue formal education or certifications in your new field if applicable
- This demonstrates your serious commitment to the new direction

4. Collaborate with Established Experts:

- Partner with respected figures in your new industry
- This can help transfer their credibility to your evolving brand

5. Maintain Connections in Your Previous Industry:

- Don't completely abandon your old network
- Show how your new focus can still provide value to your previous connections

6. Produce High-Quality Content:

- Create valuable, well-researched content in your new area of focus
- This helps establish your authority in the new space

7. Address Skepticism Proactively:

- Anticipate and address potential doubts about your transition
- Be prepared to explain how your past experiences inform your new direction

By carefully managing your brand evolution and maintaining credibility throughout the transition, you can successfully pivot your personal brand to new industries or focus areas. Remember, like Arianna Huffington, the key is to create a coherent narrative that ties your past experiences to your new direction while consistently delivering value to your audience.

4. Social Entrepreneurship and Personal Branding

Social entrepreneurship presents unique opportunities and challenges for personal branding. Entrepreneurs in this space must balance business goals with social impact, creating a personal brand that reflects both aspects. Let's examine how Blake Mycoskie has successfully navigated this terrain with TOMS.

Case Study: Blake Mycoskie - TOMS and Purpose-Driven Branding

Blake Mycoskie, founder of TOMS, has built a powerful personal brand deeply intertwined with his company's social mission.

Key aspects of Mycoskie's purpose-driven branding:

1. Story-Centric Approach: Mycoskie's personal story of inspiration in Argentina is central to the TOMS brand narrative.

2. Visual Branding: His casual, adventurous style aligns with TOMS' brand image.

3. Hands-On Leadership: Mycoskie is often seen participating in TOMS' giving trips, reinforcing his commitment to the mission.

4. Thought Leadership: He positioned himself as a pioneer of the "One for One" business model.

5. Multi-Platform Presence: Mycoskie shares TOMS' mission through books, speaking engagements, and media appearances.

Impact of Mycoskie's personal branding:

- Created a strong association between his personal brand and social entrepreneurship
- Attracted customers who align with TOMS' values and mission
- Inspired other entrepreneurs to adopt socially responsible business models

Aligning Personal Values with Business Mission

To create a strong personal brand in social entrepreneurship:

1. Identify Core Values:

- Clearly define the personal values that drive your social mission
- Ensure these values are authentically reflected in your business practices

2. Develop a Compelling Origin Story:

- Create a narrative that explains how you came to your social mission
- Use this story consistently in your brand communications

3. Live Your Values:

- Demonstrate your commitment to your mission through your actions
- Be visibly involved in the social impact aspects of your business

4. Create a Unified Visual Identity:

- Develop a personal style that aligns with your brand's aesthetic
- Ensure your personal appearance reinforces your brand's values

5. Communicate Transparently:

- Be open about both the successes and challenges of your social mission
- Share impact reports and stories to demonstrate your commitment

6. Balance Profit and Purpose:

- Clearly articulate how your business model supports your social mission
- Address potential criticism about profiting from social causes proactively

7. Continuous Learning and Adaptation:

- Stay informed about developments in social entrepreneurship
- Be willing to adapt your approach as you learn more about effective social impact

Leveraging Personal Brand for Social Impact

To maximize the impact of your personal brand on your social mission:

1. Use Your Platform for Advocacy:

- Speak out on issues related to your social mission
- Use your personal brand to raise awareness about your cause

2. Collaborate with Other Change-Makers:

- Partner with other social entrepreneurs or non-profits
- These collaborations can amplify your impact and expand your reach

3. Engage in Storytelling:

- Share stories of individuals impacted by your social mission
- Use these narratives to create emotional connections with your audience

4. Leverage Media Opportunities:

- Seek out media appearances to discuss your social mission
- Use these opportunities to educate a wider audience about your cause

5. Create Educational Content:

- Develop content that informs your audience about the issues you're addressing
- Position yourself as a thought leader in your area of social impact

6. Involve Your Community:

- Create opportunities for your audience to participate in your social mission
- This can include volunteer opportunities, social media campaigns, or customer engagement programs

7. Measure and Communicate Impact:

- Regularly assess the impact of your social initiatives
- Share these results to reinforce the effectiveness of your approach

8. Inspire Others:

- Use your personal brand to inspire other entrepreneurs to pursue social impact
- Share your learnings and best practices with aspiring social entrepreneurs

By aligning your personal brand closely with your social mission and leveraging it effectively, you can create a powerful platform for driving social change. Remember, like Blake Mycoskie, the key is to create authentic connections between your personal story, your business model, and your social impact goals. This alignment can not only drive business success but also contribute to meaningful social change.

5. Balancing Personal and Business Branding

For entrepreneurs, the line between personal and business branding can often blur. While this can be advantageous, it also presents challenges in maintaining distinct identities when necessary. Striking the right balance is crucial for long-term success.

Strategies for Cohesive Messaging Across Personal and Business Platforms

1. Develop a Unified Core Message:

- Create an overarching narrative that encompasses both your personal journey and business mission

- Ensure this core message is consistently reflected across all platforms

2. Align Visual Branding:

- Use complementary color schemes and design elements for personal and business branding
- This creates visual cohesion while maintaining distinct identities

3. Cross-Promote Strategically:

- Share business updates on personal platforms and vice versa
- Ensure the content is relevant and adds value to the respective audiences

4. Maintain Consistent Voice:

- Develop a brand voice that works for both personal and business communications
- This helps create a seamless experience for your audience across platforms

5. Leverage Personal Stories for Business Impact:

- Use personal anecdotes to illustrate business principles or values
- This adds authenticity to your business brand while reinforcing your personal brand

6. Create Content that Serves Both Brands:

- Develop thought leadership content that enhances both your personal credibility and business authority
- This could include articles, videos, or podcasts that showcase your expertise

7. Engage Authentically:

- Respond to comments and messages in a way that reflects both your personal style and business values
- This builds stronger connections with your audience on both fronts

When to Separate Personal and Business Brands

While integration can be powerful, there are times when separation is necessary:

1. Different Target Audiences:

- If your personal and business brands cater to significantly different audiences, consider maintaining separate identities
- This allows for more targeted messaging and content

2. Multiple Business Ventures:

- If you're involved in diverse businesses, a separate personal brand can serve as an umbrella for all ventures
- This allows flexibility to pivot or launch new businesses without major brand disruption

3. Controversial Personal Views:

- If you hold personal views that might negatively impact your business, consider separating the brands
- This protects your business from potential backlash over personal opinions

4. Future Exit Strategies:

- If you plan to sell your business in the future, a separate business brand makes the transition easier
- It allows the business to have its own identity independent of you

5. Team Recognition:

- To highlight the contributions of your team, consider emphasizing the business brand over your personal brand
- This can be crucial for scaling and attracting top talent

6. Industry Norms:

- In some industries, a more corporate, less personalized brand might be expected
- Research your industry norms and adjust your branding strategy accordingly

7. Personal Privacy:

- If you value personal privacy, maintaining separate brands allows you to control how much of your personal life is associated with your business

By thoughtfully balancing personal and business branding, entrepreneurs can leverage the strengths of both while mitigating potential risks. The key is to maintain consistency in core values and messaging, while being strategic about when and how to separate the two brands.

6. Using Personal Branding to Attract Investors and Partners

A strong personal brand can be a powerful asset when seeking investment or partnerships for your business. It can build trust, demonstrate your expertise, and showcase your vision and leadership abilities.

Crafting a Compelling Founder's Story

Your founder's story is a crucial element of your personal brand that can significantly impact investors and potential partners. Here's how to craft an effective one:

1. Identify Your Unique Journey:

- Highlight the experiences that led you to start your business
- Focus on moments of insight, challenge, or inspiration

2. Showcase Problem-Solving Skills:

- Emphasize how you identified a market need or problem
- Explain your innovative approach to addressing this challenge

3. Demonstrate Passion and Commitment:

- Convey your deep passion for your business and its mission
- Show your long-term commitment to the venture

4. Highlight Relevant Expertise:

- Showcase your background, skills, and experiences that make you uniquely qualified to lead your business
- Include both successes and lessons learned from failures

5. Include a Vision for the Future:

- Articulate your long-term vision for the company
- Show how your personal goals align with the business objectives

6. Make it Relatable:

- Use anecdotes and personal details to make your story more engaging and memorable
- Ensure your story resonates with your target audience (investors, partners)

7. Practice Storytelling Techniques:

- Use a clear narrative structure with a beginning, middle, and end
- Incorporate elements of tension and resolution to make your story compelling

Leveraging Your Personal Brand in Pitch Meetings

Once you've crafted your founder's story, here's how to effectively leverage your personal brand in pitch meetings:

1. Align Personal and Business Brands:

- Ensure your personal presentation (appearance, communication style) aligns with your business brand
- This creates a cohesive and professional impression

2. Demonstrate Thought Leadership:

- Share insights about your industry that showcase your expertise
- Reference any published articles, speaking engagements, or media appearances

3. Use Your Network:

- Leverage your personal connections for warm introductions to investors or partners
- Mention relevant endorsements or support from respected figures in your industry

4. Show Traction Through Personal Brand:

- Highlight how your personal brand has contributed to business growth (e.g., attracted customers, media attention)
- Use metrics to demonstrate the impact of your personal brand on the business

5. Address Potential Concerns:

- Use your personal brand to instill confidence in areas where your business might be perceived as risky
- Share personal experiences that demonstrate your ability to overcome challenges

6. Be Authentic:

- Let your genuine passion and personality shine through
- Authenticity can create a stronger connection with potential investors or partners

7. Follow Up Effectively:

- Use your personal brand to stand out in post-meeting communications
- Share additional insights or relevant content that reinforces your expertise

8. Prepare for Due Diligence:

- Ensure your online presence aligns with the personal brand you present in meetings
- Be prepared to explain any discrepancies or potential red flags in your public persona

By effectively crafting your founder's story and leveraging your personal brand in pitch meetings, you can create a powerful impression on potential investors and partners. Remember, your personal brand should complement and enhance your business proposition, demonstrating why you and your venture are worthy of investment and partnership.

7. Scaling Your Personal Brand as Your Business Grows

As your business expands, your personal brand must evolve to support and reflect this growth. This evolution involves maintaining the core elements that made your brand successful while adapting to new responsibilities and a potentially larger audience.

Evolving Your Personal Brand Alongside Your Company

1. Expand Your Expertise:

- Broaden your knowledge to cover all aspects of your growing business
- Share insights on industry trends, leadership, and scaling challenges

2. Shift Focus from Details to Vision:

- As your company grows, transition from highlighting day-to-day operations to discussing long-term strategy and industry impact

- Position yourself as a visionary leader in your field

3. Increase Thought Leadership:

   - Engage in more high-profile speaking engagements and media appearances
   - Publish articles or books that showcase your broader business acumen

4. Build a Personal Platform:

   - Develop a strong personal website and social media presence separate from your company's
   - Use these platforms to share your personal insights and vision

5. Delegate Brand Ambassadorship:

   - Empower other team members to represent the company
   - This allows you to focus on high-level branding while building a strong company culture

6. Maintain Authenticity:

   - As your profile grows, stay true to the core values that defined your initial brand
   - Continue to share personal stories and insights, even as your business becomes more complex

7. Address a Wider Audience:

   - Adapt your communication style to resonate with a broader audience, including investors, partners, and industry leaders
   - Develop messaging that appeals to both your original supporters and new stakeholders

Transitioning from Founder to CEO in Your Branding

1. Emphasize Leadership Skills:

   - Highlight your ability to lead a larger organization
   - Share stories of how you've built and motivated your team

2. Showcase Strategic Thinking:

- Demonstrate your capacity for high-level decision-making and long-term planning
- Discuss how you're positioning your company for future growth and challenges

3. Build a Professional Network:

- Cultivate relationships with other CEOs and industry leaders
- Participate in CEO forums and leadership events

4. Maintain Founder Credibility:

- While embracing your CEO role, don't lose touch with your founder's passion and vision
- Continue to share the story of why you started the company

5. Develop a More Polished Image:

- Refine your personal appearance and communication style to reflect your CEO status
- This might involve updating your wardrobe, improving public speaking skills, or enhancing your media presence

6. Balance Accessibility with Authority:

- While maintaining approachability, establish yourself as the authoritative voice of your company
- Strike a balance between being relatable and being a respected industry leader

7. Address Broader Business Issues:

- Engage with topics beyond your specific industry, such as economic trends or social issues
- This positions you as a well-rounded business leader

By carefully evolving your personal brand as your business grows, you can continue to leverage your personal reputation to support your company's success. Remember, the transition from founder to CEO is not just about a change in title, but a shift in how you present yourself and your vision to the world.

8. Measuring the ROI of Personal Branding for Entrepreneurs

For entrepreneurs, measuring the return on investment (ROI) of personal branding efforts is crucial to ensure that time and resources are being used effectively. While some benefits of personal branding may be intangible, there are several key performance indicators (KPIs) that can help quantify its impact.

Key Performance Indicators for Entrepreneurial Personal Branding

1. Brand Awareness Metrics:

- Social media follower growth
- Website traffic to your personal site
- Mentions in media and industry publications

2. Engagement Metrics:

- Social media engagement rates (likes, comments, shares)
- Email newsletter open and click-through rates
- Attendance at speaking engagements or webinars you host

3. Lead Generation:

- Number of inbound inquiries for partnerships or business opportunities
- Quality and quantity of networking connections made
- Conversion rates from personal brand touchpoints to business leads

4. Thought Leadership Indicators:

- Invitations to speak at industry events
- Requests for interviews or expert commentary
- Citations of your work or ideas in industry publications

5. Business Growth Metrics:

- Increase in company revenue or valuation
- Growth in customer base or market share
- Improvement in talent acquisition and retention

6. Investor Relations:

- Number and quality of investor meetings secured
- Success rate in fundraising efforts
- Positive feedback from investors about your personal brand

7. Brand Sentiment:

- Positive mentions and reviews online
- Sentiment analysis of social media conversations about you
- Net Promoter Score (NPS) if applicable to your business

Analyzing the Connection Between Personal Brand Activities and Business Outcomes

1. Set Clear Objectives:

- Define specific goals for your personal branding efforts that align with business objectives
- This allows for more accurate measurement of impact

2. Use Attribution Models:

- Implement systems to track how leads or opportunities are generated from your personal brand activities
- This might include using unique URLs or referral codes

3. Conduct Regular Audits:

- Perform quarterly or annual assessments of your personal brand's impact on business metrics
- Look for correlations between personal branding activities and business outcomes

4. Gather Qualitative Feedback:

- Survey customers, partners, or investors about the impact of your personal brand on their decision to work with your company
- Collect testimonials that specifically mention your personal brand as a factor in business decisions

5. Monitor Time Investment:

- Track the time spent on personal branding activities
- Assess the opportunity cost and compare it to the benefits gained

6. Analyze Long-Term Trends:

- Look at how your personal brand activities correlate with business growth over time
- Consider both immediate impacts and long-term benefits

7. Adjust Strategy Based on ROI:

- Use your analysis to refine your personal branding approach
- Invest more in high-ROI activities and reduce or eliminate low-impact efforts

By consistently measuring and analyzing the ROI of your personal branding efforts, you can ensure that your activities are contributing meaningfully to your business goals. Remember, some benefits of personal branding may take time to materialize, so it's important to consider both short-term metrics and long-term impact in your analysis.

Chapter 12 Decision Tree: Building a Personal Brand as an Entrepreneur

Purpose:

This decision tree will guide you through the key steps to develop and leverage your personal brand as an entrepreneur.

Key Outcomes:

1. Align personal brand with business vision

2. Differentiate in a competitive market
3. Build credibility and trust
4. Balance personal and company brands
5. Leverage brand for growth
6. Adapt brand as business evolves

Start: Is your personal brand aligned with your business vision?

• Yes → Proceed to Market Differentiation

• No → Align Brand with Business

- Clearly define your business vision and values
- Identify overlaps between personal strengths and business needs
- Adjust personal brand to complement business goals

Next: Does your personal brand differentiate you in the market?

• Yes → Proceed to Building Credibility

• No → Enhance Brand Differentiation

- Identify your unique value proposition
- Highlight experiences or skills that set you apart
- Develop a distinctive brand voice and style

Next: Are you effectively using your brand to build credibility and trust?

• Yes → Proceed to Balancing Personal and Company Brands

• No → Boost Brand Credibility

- Share your entrepreneurial journey and lessons learned
- Develop and share valuable content in your expertise area
- Seek speaking engagements or media opportunities

Next: Have you found the right balance between your personal and company brands?

• Yes → Proceed to Leveraging Brand for Growth

• No → Adjust Brand Balance

- Clearly define the roles of personal and company brands
- Ensure your personal brand supports but doesn't overshadow the company
- Create guidelines for when to use personal vs. company brand

Next: Are you effectively leveraging your personal brand for business growth?

• Yes → Proceed to Brand Evolution Planning

• No → Enhance Brand Leverage

- Use your personal brand to open doors for business opportunities
- Leverage your personal network for business development
- Align personal thought leadership with business offerings

Next: Do you have a plan for evolving your brand as your business grows?

• Yes → Implement and Monitor Your Entrepreneurial Branding Strategy

• No → Develop a Brand Evolution Plan

- Anticipate how your role and brand may change as the business grows
- Plan for transitioning from founder to CEO brand if applicable
- Set regular intervals to review and update your brand

Final: Continuously align your personal brand with your evolving business needs and market trends

CONCLUSION

Chapter 12 has focused on the importance of networking and relationship-building as integral components of a successful personal brand. In today's interconnected world, the ability to cultivate meaningful relationships within your industry is not just an advantage—it's a necessity for sustained professional growth and brand development.

Throughout this chapter, we explored the different strategies for building a strong and supportive professional network. Whether through attending industry events, engaging in online communities, or leveraging social media platforms like LinkedIn, the emphasis was on the importance of being proactive and intentional in your networking efforts. Networking is more than just exchanging business cards; it's about building genuine connections that can lead to long-term collaborations, mentorships, and opportunities.

The chapter highlighted the value of giving as much as you receive in your professional relationships. By offering support, sharing knowledge, and providing value to others, you not only strengthen your network but also enhance your reputation as a trusted and respected figure in your field. This reciprocal approach to networking fosters a sense of community and mutual respect, which are essential for building a sustainable and influential personal brand.

We also discussed the role of strategic alliances and partnerships in expanding your brand's reach and impact. Collaborating with like-minded professionals and organizations can open doors to new audiences, increase your visibility, and add credibility to your brand. The chapter provided insights on how to identify and approach potential partners, ensuring that any collaboration aligns with your brand values and goals.

In addition, the chapter covered the importance of maintaining and nurturing relationships over time. Networking is not a one-time event but an ongoing process that requires consistent effort and engagement. Regularly checking in with your contacts, offering assistance when needed, and staying active in your professional communities are key to keeping your network strong and supportive.

As you continue to build your personal brand, remember that your network is one of your most valuable assets. The relationships you cultivate can provide you with opportunities, insights, and support that are critical to your success. By investing time and energy into building and maintaining a robust network, you will create a powerful foundation for your personal brand that extends beyond your individual efforts.

In conclusion, Chapter 12 has emphasized that networking and relationship-building are not just supplemental activities—they are central to the success of your personal brand. By approaching networking with a spirit of generosity, authenticity, and strategic intent, you will build a network that supports your brand's growth and sustains your professional journey. As you move forward, let your relationships be a source of strength and inspiration, driving your brand towards new heights and broader horizons.

Chapter 13

Measuring and Evolving Your Personal Brand

1. Introduction: The Importance of Brand Measurement and Evolution

In the dynamic landscape of personal branding, the ability to measure your brand's impact and evolve accordingly is crucial for long-term success. Your personal brand is not a static entity; it should grow and adapt as you progress in your career, as your industry changes, and as your goals evolve.

Measuring your personal brand allows you to:

1. Understand your current brand perception

2. Identify areas of strength and opportunities for improvement

3. Gauge the effectiveness of your branding efforts

4. Make data-driven decisions about your brand strategy

Meanwhile, evolving your brand is essential for:

1. Staying relevant in a changing market

2. Aligning your brand with your current goals and values

3. Capitalizing on new opportunities

4. Maintaining authenticity as you grow and change

Throughout this chapter, we'll explore various strategies for measuring the impact of your personal brand and techniques for evolving your brand effectively. We'll examine case studies of individuals who have successfully adapted their personal brands over time, discuss key metrics for brand measurement, and provide practical tips for managing brand evolution.

By the end of this chapter, you'll have the knowledge and tools to continually assess and refine your personal brand, ensuring it remains a powerful asset throughout your career journey. Let's begin by exploring the concept of constant evolution and adaptation, starting with a case study of Tim Ferriss, a master of personal brand evolution across multiple domains.

2. Constant Evolution and Adaptation

In the realm of personal branding, few individuals exemplify constant evolution and adaptation as well as Tim Ferriss. His ability to pivot his brand across multiple domains while maintaining a core identity offers valuable lessons in brand evolution.

Case Study: Tim Ferriss - Adapting Personal Brand Across Multiple Domains

Tim Ferriss has successfully transitioned his personal brand from productivity guru to lifestyle design expert to podcast host and investor.

Key aspects of Ferriss's brand evolution:

1. Consistent Core Message: Despite changing focus areas, Ferriss maintained a core brand message of optimization and self-improvement.

2. Experimentation: Ferriss often uses himself as a guinea pig for new ideas, making his evolution part of his brand.

3. Transparency: He's open about his transitions, bringing his audience along on his journey of exploration and growth.

4. Multi-Platform Presence: Ferriss adapts his content for various platforms, from books to podcasts to social media.

5. Collaborative Approach: He leverages relationships with experts in various fields to expand his brand's reach and credibility.

Impact of Ferriss's brand evolution:

- Maintained relevance across changing market trends
- Expanded his audience base to include diverse interest groups
- Established credibility in multiple domains
- Created multiple revenue streams through various brand extensions

Strategies for Staying Relevant in Changing Markets

1. Continuous Learning:

- Stay informed about industry trends and emerging technologies
- Regularly update your skills and knowledge base

2. Engage with Your Audience:

- Frequently interact with your audience to understand their evolving needs
- Use surveys, social media polls, and direct engagement to gather insights

3. Monitor Industry Changes:

- Keep a close eye on shifts in your industry or profession
- Attend conferences, read industry publications, and network with thought leaders

4. Embrace New Platforms:

- Be willing to adopt new communication platforms as they emerge
- Experiment with different content formats to reach diverse audience segments

5. Collaborate and Cross-Pollinate:

- Partner with professionals in adjacent fields
- This can help you tap into new markets and gain fresh perspectives

6. Refresh Your Visual Brand:

- Periodically update your visual elements (logo, website, etc.) to keep your brand looking current
- Ensure these updates align with your evolving brand message

7. Share Your Evolution:

- Document and share your learning and growth journey
- This transparency can strengthen your connection with your audience

Balancing Consistency with Necessary Evolution

While evolution is crucial, maintaining some level of consistency is important for brand recognition and trust. Here's how to strike that balance:

1. Identify Core Brand Elements:

- Determine the fundamental aspects of your brand that should remain constant
- These might include core values, overall mission, or key personality traits

2. Gradual Transitions:

- Instead of abrupt changes, evolve your brand gradually
- This allows your audience to adapt and maintains brand recognition

3. Explain Your Evolution:

- Communicate the reasons behind significant brand changes to your audience
- Frame evolution as a positive step in your ongoing journey

4. Maintain Consistent Quality:

- While your focus may change, maintain a consistent level of quality in your work

- This helps retain audience trust through transitions

5. Use Brand Storytelling:

- Craft a narrative that ties together different phases of your brand evolution
- Show how each transition is a logical progression of your overall journey

6. Retain Signature Elements:

- Keep some recognizable elements of your brand (e.g., a particular phrase, visual style, or content format)
- This provides continuity for your audience

7. Align Evolution with Audience Needs:

- Ensure your brand evolution addresses the changing needs of your core audience
- This helps maintain relevance while preserving your existing fan base

By embracing constant evolution and adaptation while maintaining core brand elements, you can keep your personal brand relevant and impactful over time. Remember, like Tim Ferriss, the key is to view your brand as a journey of growth and exploration, bringing your audience along with you as you evolve.

3. Measuring Impact and Evolving Brand Strategy

To effectively evolve your personal brand, it's crucial to measure its impact and adjust your strategy accordingly. Let's examine how Oprah Winfrey has masterfully tracked and adapted her brand influence over the years.

Case Study: Oprah Winfrey - Tracking and Adapting Brand Influence

Oprah Winfrey has successfully maintained and evolved her personal brand from talk show host to media mogul and cultural influencer.

Key aspects of Winfrey's brand measurement and evolution:

1. Audience Engagement: Winfrey consistently monitors audience response across various platforms.

2. Diverse Metrics: She uses a combination of traditional media ratings, social media engagement, and product sales to gauge brand impact.

3. Brand Extensions: Winfrey strategically launches new ventures based on audience interest and market trends.

4. Adaptability: She has successfully transitioned her brand from traditional media to digital platforms.

5. Social Impact Measurement: Winfrey tracks the influence of her philanthropic efforts as part of her overall brand impact.

Impact of Winfrey's approach:

- Maintained relevance across changing media landscapes
- Successfully launched multiple brand extensions (e.g., O Magazine, OWN Network)
- Established herself as a trusted voice in various domains, from entertainment to wellness

Key Performance Indicators for Personal Branding

To effectively measure your personal brand's impact, consider these key performance indicators (KPIs):

1. Audience Growth:

- Social media follower count
- Email subscriber list growth
- Website traffic

2. Engagement Metrics:

- Social media engagement rates (likes, comments, shares)
- Email open and click-through rates
- Time spent on website

3. Media Mentions:

- Frequency and quality of mentions in press and industry publications
- Sentiment analysis of media coverage

4. Speaking Engagements:

- Number and prestige of speaking invitations
- Audience feedback from events

5. Professional Opportunities:

- Job offers or promotions
- Partnership or collaboration requests
- Client acquisition (for entrepreneurs or freelancers)

6. Thought Leadership Indicators:

- Frequency of being quoted as an expert
- Invitations to contribute to industry publications
- Requests for interviews or podcast appearances

7. Financial Impact:

- Income growth related to personal brand
- Sales of brand-related products or services

8. Network Growth:

- Quality and quantity of new professional connections
- Invitations to exclusive professional groups or events

Tools and Techniques for Brand Monitoring

To effectively track these KPIs and monitor your brand, consider using:

1. Social Media Analytics:

- Platform-specific tools (e.g., Facebook Insights, Twitter Analytics)

- Third-party tools like Hootsuite or Sprout Social for comprehensive social media monitoring

2. Google Analytics:

- Track website traffic, user behavior, and conversion rates

3. Brand Monitoring Tools:

- Use tools like Google Alerts, Mention, or Brand24 to track online mentions of your name or brand

4. Surveys and Feedback:

- Regularly solicit feedback from your audience, clients, or colleagues
- Use tools like SurveyMonkey or Google Forms to create and distribute surveys

5. Sentiment Analysis Tools:

- Utilize AI-powered tools to analyze the sentiment of mentions and comments about your brand

6. Email Marketing Platforms:

- Use platforms like Mailchimp or ConvertKit to track email engagement metrics

7. Personal CRM:

- Tools like Contacts+ or Cloze can help track networking efforts and relationship growth

8. Professional Platforms:

- LinkedIn provides analytics for profile views and post engagement

By consistently monitoring these metrics and using these tools, you can gain valuable insights into your brand's performance and impact. This data will inform your strategy as you evolve your personal brand, allowing you to make informed decisions about where to focus your efforts and how to adapt to changing circumstances.

Remember, the key is not just to collect data, but to analyze it in the context of your goals and use it to drive meaningful improvements in your personal branding strategy. Like Oprah Winfrey, your ability to track, understand, and adapt to your brand's impact will be crucial in maintaining long-term relevance and influence.

4. Data-Driven Personal Brand Growth

In the digital age, leveraging data analytics for personal brand optimization has become increasingly important. Gary Vaynerchuk stands out as a prime example of using data to drive personal brand growth and evolution.

Case Study: Gary Vaynerchuk - Using Analytics for Brand Optimization

Gary Vaynerchuk, entrepreneur and internet personality, has built a powerful personal brand by meticulously analyzing data and adjusting his strategy accordingly.

Key aspects of Vaynerchuk's data-driven approach:

1. Platform Experimentation: He consistently tests content on new and emerging platforms, using data to determine where to focus his efforts.

2. Content Optimization: Vaynerchuk analyzes engagement metrics to refine his content strategy across platforms.

3. Audience Segmentation: He uses data to understand different audience segments and tailor his messaging accordingly.

4. Real-time Adaptation: Vaynerchuk is known for quickly pivoting his strategy based on performance data.

5. Transparency: He often shares his data-driven insights with his audience, making it part of his brand.

Impact of Vaynerchuk's approach:

- Rapid growth across multiple social media platforms

- Ability to stay ahead of platform and content trends
- Development of a highly engaged and loyal audience base

Leveraging Data Analytics in Personal Branding

To apply data analytics to your personal branding efforts:

1. Set Clear Objectives:

- Define specific, measurable goals for your personal brand
- Ensure these align with your overall career or business objectives

2. Identify Relevant Metrics:

- Determine which data points are most relevant to your goals
- Focus on metrics that provide actionable insights

3. Use Analytics Tools:

- Leverage platform-specific analytics (e.g., Instagram Insights, Twitter Analytics)
- Utilize third-party tools for more comprehensive data analysis

4. Track Audience Demographics:

- Understand who your content is reaching and engaging
- Use this data to refine your target audience

5. Analyze Content Performance:

- Monitor which types of content perform best on each platform
- Look for patterns in high-performing content

6. Monitor Engagement Patterns:

- Analyze when your audience is most active
- Identify which topics generate the most engagement

7. Conduct Competitive Analysis:

- Use tools to analyze competitors' performance
- Identify gaps and opportunities in your market

8. Implement A/B Testing:

- Test different approaches to content, visuals, or messaging
- Use data to determine which variations perform best

Making Data-Informed Decisions for Brand Evolution

To effectively use data for personal brand evolution:

1. Regular Data Review:

- Set up a routine for reviewing your analytics
- Look for trends and changes over time

2. Align Data with Goals:

- Consistently compare your data against your defined objectives
- Adjust your goals if necessary based on insights

3. Identify Growth Opportunities:

- Use data to spot emerging trends or untapped audience segments
- Experiment with new content or platforms based on these insights

4. Refine Your Message:

- Analyze which aspects of your brand resonate most with your audience
- Adjust your messaging to emphasize these elements

5. Optimize Resource Allocation:

- Focus your time and resources on platforms and content types that data shows are most effective

6. Personalize Your Approach:

- Use audience data to create more personalized content and interactions
- Tailor your brand voice to what data shows resonates with your audience

7. Predict Future Trends:

- Use historical data to forecast future performance
- Stay ahead of the curve by anticipating changes in your industry or audience preferences

8. Balance Data with Intuition:

- While data is crucial, don't lose sight of your authentic voice and vision
- Use data to inform, not dictate, your brand evolution

By adopting a data-driven approach to personal branding, you can make more informed decisions about your brand's direction and evolution. Remember, like Gary Vaynerchuk, the key is to consistently analyze your performance data and be willing to adapt quickly based on the insights you gain.

However, it's also important to balance data-driven decision-making with maintaining authenticity and staying true to your core brand values. Use data as a tool to refine and optimize your brand, not to fundamentally change who you are or what you stand for.

5. Conducting a Comprehensive Personal Brand Audit

A personal brand audit is a crucial step in understanding your current brand position and identifying areas for improvement. This process involves a thorough examination of all aspects of your personal brand, from your online presence to your professional reputation.

Step-by-Step Guide to Auditing Your Brand Presence

1. Define Your Brand Goals:

- Clearly articulate what you want your personal brand to achieve

- Identify your target audience and desired perception

2. Analyze Your Online Presence:

- Review all your social media profiles for consistency and alignment with your brand goals
- Examine your website or blog for brand messaging and user experience
- Google yourself and analyze the first page of search results

3. Evaluate Your Content:

- Assess the quality and consistency of your content across all platforms
- Determine if your content aligns with your brand message and resonates with your target audience

4. Review Your Visual Brand:

- Examine your profile pictures, logos, and other visual elements for consistency
- Ensure your visual brand aligns with your brand personality and goals

5. Assess Your Network:

- Review your professional connections and their alignment with your brand goals
- Evaluate the quality and relevance of your network

6. Gather Feedback:

- Conduct surveys or interviews with colleagues, clients, or mentors
- Seek honest feedback about how others perceive your brand

7. Analyze Your Offline Brand:

- Review your in-person networking efforts and speaking engagements

- Assess how well your offline presence aligns with your online brand

8. Examine Your Thought Leadership:

- Evaluate the impact and reach of your articles, presentations, or other thought leadership content
- Assess how well your expertise is recognized in your industry

Identifying Gaps and Areas for Improvement

After conducting your audit, analyze the results to identify:

1. Consistency Gaps:

- Look for discrepancies in messaging or visuals across different platforms
- Identify any misalignments between your online and offline presence

2. Content Gaps:

- Determine if your content fully represents your expertise and brand message
- Identify topics or formats that you should be leveraging more

3. Audience Misalignment:

- Assess if your current brand resonates with your target audience
- Identify any disconnects between your brand and audience needs

4. Visibility Issues:

- Determine if your brand has sufficient visibility in your industry
- Identify platforms or channels where you need to increase your presence

5. Reputation Gaps:

- Analyze if your desired brand perception matches the actual perception
- Identify any negative associations that need to be addressed

6. Skill Gaps:

- Determine if there are any skills you need to develop to support your brand goals
- Identify areas where additional training or experience could enhance your brand

7. Network Gaps:

- Identify key connections or partnerships that could strengthen your brand
- Determine if your network sufficiently supports your brand goals

By conducting a thorough brand audit and identifying these gaps, you can create a targeted plan for improving and evolving your personal brand. Remember, this should be an ongoing process, not a one-time event, to ensure your brand remains relevant and effective.

6. Interpreting Brand Data and Insights

Once you've collected data about your personal brand, the next crucial step is interpreting this information to derive meaningful insights. This process involves analyzing both quantitative and qualitative data to understand your brand's performance and impact.

Making Sense of Quantitative and Qualitative Data

Quantitative Data Analysis:

1. Trend Identification:

- Look for patterns in your metrics over time
- Identify upward or downward trends in key performance indicators

2. Benchmark Comparison:

- Compare your metrics to industry benchmarks or your past performance
- Understand how you're performing relative to your goals and competitors

3. Correlation Analysis:

- Look for relationships between different metrics
- For example, how does increased content posting correlate with engagement rates?

4. Segmentation:

- Break down your data by audience segments, platforms, or content types
- Understand which aspects of your brand resonate with different groups

Qualitative Data Analysis:

1. Thematic Analysis:

- Identify common themes in feedback, comments, or reviews
- Look for recurring words or sentiments associated with your brand

2. Sentiment Analysis:

- Assess the overall tone of comments and feedback
- Determine if the sentiment towards your brand is primarily positive, negative, or neutral

3. Context Consideration:

- Analyze feedback within the context it was given
- Consider factors that might influence opinions, such as current events or industry trends

4. Narrative Analysis:

- Look at the stories people tell about their interactions with your brand
- Understand how these narratives align with your intended brand perception

Correlating Brand Activities with Outcomes

To understand the effectiveness of your branding efforts:

1. Activity-Outcome Mapping:

- Create a timeline of your branding activities
- Align these activities with changes in your brand metrics

2. Content Performance Analysis:

- Analyze which types of content generate the most engagement or leads
- Understand how different content strategies impact your brand perception

3. Channel Effectiveness:

- Evaluate which platforms or channels are most effective for your brand
- Determine where you're getting the best return on your branding efforts

4. Audience Response Tracking:

- Monitor how different audience segments respond to your brand activities
- Identify which strategies are most effective for each segment

5. Long-term Impact Assessment:

- Look beyond immediate metrics to understand the long-term impact of your activities

- Consider how sustained efforts in certain areas have shaped your overall brand perception

6. ROI Calculation:

- Where possible, calculate the return on investment for your branding activities
- This might include financial returns, but also non-financial outcomes like improved reputation or increased opportunities

7. Feedback Loop Creation:

- Use insights from your analysis to inform future branding strategies
- Continuously test and refine your approach based on the data

When interpreting your brand data and insights, remember to:

- Look for actionable insights: Focus on findings that can inform concrete actions or strategies.
- Consider multiple data points: Don't rely on a single metric or piece of feedback. Look for corroborating evidence across different data sources.
- Account for external factors: Consider how external events or industry trends might be influencing your brand metrics.
- Think critically: Question your assumptions and be open to insights that might challenge your current brand strategy.

By effectively interpreting your brand data and insights, you can make informed decisions about how to evolve and improve your personal brand. This data-driven approach allows you to focus your efforts where they'll have the most impact, ensuring your personal brand continues to grow and resonate with your target audience.

7. Strategies for Brand Evolution and Pivoting

Personal brand evolution is a natural and necessary process as your career progresses, your industry changes, or your goals shift. The key is to recognize when it's time to evolve and to manage this evolution strategically.

Recognizing When It's Time to Evolve Your Brand

1. Market Changes:

- Monitor industry trends and shifts in your professional landscape
- If your current brand positioning becomes less relevant, it may be time to evolve

2. Career Progression:

- As you advance in your career, your brand should reflect your new roles and responsibilities
- Consider evolution when transitioning to leadership positions or new career paths

3. Audience Feedback:

- Pay attention to how your audience engages with your brand
- Declining engagement or relevance may signal the need for evolution

4. Personal Growth:

- As your skills, knowledge, and interests develop, your brand should reflect this growth
- Ensure your brand aligns with your current expertise and passions

5. Goal Misalignment:

- If your current brand no longer supports your professional or personal goals, evolution is necessary
- Regularly assess if your brand aligns with where you want to be in the future

6. Competitive Landscape:

- If competitors are outpacing you or your brand feels stagnant, it may be time for a refresh
- Stay ahead by evolving before your brand becomes outdated

Managing Potential Risks in Brand Evolution

1. Gradual Transition:

- Implement changes incrementally to maintain brand recognition
- Communicate changes clearly to your audience to bring them along on your journey

2. Core Value Retention:

- Identify the core elements of your brand that resonate most with your audience
- Maintain these elements while evolving other aspects of your brand

3. Audience Research:

- Conduct thorough research to understand how your audience might react to changes
- Use surveys, focus groups, or one-on-one conversations to gather insights

4. Soft Launch:

- Test brand changes with a smaller segment of your audience before full implementation
- Use feedback from this soft launch to refine your evolution strategy

5. Clear Communication:

- Clearly explain the reasons behind your brand evolution to your audience
- Frame changes positively, focusing on the enhanced value you'll provide

6. Consistency Across Platforms:

- Ensure all aspects of your brand evolve cohesively across different platforms

- Update all touchpoints simultaneously to avoid confusion

7. Monitor and Adjust:

- Closely monitor metrics and feedback after implementing changes
- Be prepared to make quick adjustments if the evolution isn't well-received

8. Professional Guidance:

- Consider working with a branding professional for significant evolutions
- Their expertise can help mitigate risks and ensure a smooth transition

Remember, brand evolution should be a thoughtful, strategic process. While it's important to stay relevant and adapt to changes, it's equally crucial to maintain the core essence of your brand that your audience trusts and values.

8. Setting and Adjusting Brand Goals

Setting clear, measurable goals for your personal brand is crucial for focused growth and evolution. These goals should align with your overall career objectives and be regularly reviewed and adjusted.

Establishing SMART Goals for Your Personal Brand

Use the SMART criteria to set effective personal brand goals:

1. Specific:

- Clearly define what you want to achieve with your brand
- Example: "Increase my industry thought leadership presence"

2. Measurable:

- Attach concrete metrics to your goals
- Example: "Publish two industry-related articles per month on reputable platforms"

3. Achievable:

- Ensure your goals are realistic given your resources and constraints
- Set challenging but attainable targets

4. Relevant:

- Align your brand goals with your broader career or business objectives
- Ensure each goal contributes to your overall brand strategy

5. Time-bound:

- Set specific timeframes for achieving your goals
- Example: "Increase LinkedIn followers by 25% within the next six months"

Examples of SMART Personal Brand Goals:

- Secure three speaking engagements at industry conferences within the next year
- Grow email newsletter subscribers from 1,000 to 5,000 in 12 months
- Achieve a 30% increase in media mentions by the end of the quarter

Regular Review and Adjustment of Brand Objectives

1. Schedule Regular Reviews:

- Set quarterly and annual review dates for your brand goals
- Use these reviews to assess progress and make necessary adjustments

2. Analyze Performance Data:

- Review metrics related to your goals during each assessment
- Identify areas of success and those needing improvement

3. Gather Feedback:

- Collect input from mentors, colleagues, or your audience
- Use this feedback to inform goal adjustments

4. Reassess Relevance:

- Ensure your goals still align with your current career trajectory and industry trends
- Be willing to discard or modify goals that no longer serve your overall strategy

5. Adjust Metrics and Timelines:

- Based on your performance, adjust your targets up or down as needed
- Extend or shorten timelines to keep goals challenging yet achievable

6. Add New Goals:

- As you achieve objectives, set new goals to continue your brand's growth
- Look for emerging opportunities or areas for improvement

7. Document Changes:

- Keep a record of goal adjustments and the reasons behind them
- This helps in understanding your brand's evolution over time

8. Celebrate Achievements:

- Acknowledge when you meet or exceed your goals
- Use these successes to motivate further growth and set more ambitious targets

By setting SMART goals and regularly reviewing and adjusting them, you create a dynamic framework for your personal brand's growth. This approach ensures that your branding efforts remain focused, measurable, and aligned with your evolving career aspirations. Remember, the process of setting and adjusting goals is ongoing – your personal brand, like your career, is a journey of continuous improvement and adaptation.

CHAPTER 13 DECISION TREE: EVALUATING AND ADAPTING YOUR PERSONAL BRAND

This decision tree will guide you through the process of measuring the impact of your personal brand and evolving it over time. By using this tree, you'll:

1. Establish key performance indicators (KPIs) for your personal brand.
2. Implement tools and strategies to track brand performance.
3. Analyze brand data and derive meaningful insights.
4. Identify areas for brand improvement and evolution.
5. Adapt your brand to changing market conditions and career goals.
6. Continuously refine your personal branding strategy.

Use this tree to ensure your personal brand remains effective, relevant, and aligned with your professional objectives as your career progresses.

Start: Have you established clear KPIs for your personal brand?

• **Yes:**→ Proceed to implementing tracking tools.

• **No:**→ Define brand KPIs:

- Identify metrics aligned with your brand goals (e.g., engagement rates, network growth).
- Set benchmarks for each KPI.
- Ensure KPIs are measurable and time-bound.

Next: Are you using tools to track your brand performance?

• **Yes:**→ Proceed to data analysis.

• **No:**→ Implement tracking methods:

- Set up Google Analytics for your personal website.
- Use social media analytics tools.

- Implement surveys or feedback mechanisms for qualitative data.

Next: Are you regularly analyzing your brand data?

• **Yes:**→ Proceed to identifying improvement areas.

• **No:**→ Establish analysis routine:

- Set a regular schedule for data review (e.g., monthly, quarterly).
- Look for trends and patterns in your data.
- Compare performance against your KPI benchmarks.

Next: Have you identified areas for brand improvement based on your analysis?

• **Yes:**→ Proceed to adapting to market changes.

• **No:**→ Conduct a brand audit:

- Identify underperforming aspects of your brand.
- Gather feedback from your network or audience.
- Compare your brand performance to industry standards or competitors.

Next: Is your brand adapting to changing market conditions and career goals?

• **Yes:**→ Proceed to continuous refinement.

• **No:**→ Implement adaptation strategies:

- Stay informed about industry trends and changes.
- Regularly reassess your career goals and adjust your brand accordingly.
- Be prepared to pivot your brand strategy if necessary.

Next: Do you have a system for continuously refining your personal brand?

• **Yes:**→ Implement your evolving brand strategy.

• **No:**→ Establish refinement process:

- Set regular intervals for comprehensive brand reviews.
- Create a feedback loop to continuously gather insights.
- Develop a process for testing and implementing brand adjustments.

Final: Consistently monitor, evaluate, and evolve your personal brand to ensure ongoing relevance and effectiveness

This decision tree guides readers through the key steps of measuring and evolving their personal brand, as discussed in Chapter 13. It provides a structured approach to setting up measurement systems, analyzing brand performance, identifying areas for improvement, and continuously refining the brand strategy to maintain relevance and effectiveness over time.

CONCLUSION

Chapter 13 has brought to light the importance of monitoring, evaluating, and refining your personal brand. In an ever-changing professional landscape, the ability to adapt and evolve your brand is essential to maintaining its relevance and effectiveness. This chapter has provided you with the tools and strategies necessary to assess your brand's performance and make informed adjustments that ensure continued growth and impact.

We began by exploring the key metrics and indicators that can help you measure the success of your personal branding efforts. From social media engagement and website analytics to client feedback and professional recognition, understanding how to track and interpret these metrics is crucial for identifying what's working and where there's room for improvement. By regularly reviewing these indicators, you can gain valuable insights into how your brand is perceived and how effectively it's resonating with your target audience.

The chapter also emphasized the importance of seeking feedback from your network, clients, and peers. Constructive feedback is a powerful tool for growth, providing you with an outside perspective on your brand's strengths and areas that may need adjustment. By being open to feedback and actively seeking it out, you demonstrate a commitment to continuous improvement, which not only enhances your brand but also builds trust and credibility with your audience.

We also discussed the value of staying attuned to industry trends and shifts in the marketplace. The professional environment is constantly evolving, and staying informed about these changes allows you to proactively adapt your brand strategy to remain relevant. Whether it's incorporating new technologies, responding to changes in audience preferences, or adjusting your messaging to align with current industry trends, flexibility and responsiveness are key to a successful personal brand.

Additionally, the chapter highlighted the importance of self-reflection in the branding process. Regularly taking the time to assess your own goals, values, and motivations ensures that your brand remains authentic and aligned with your personal and professional aspirations. This introspective approach allows you to make deliberate and meaningful adjustments to your brand as you grow and evolve.

As you continue to refine your personal brand, remember that branding is not a one-time task but an ongoing journey. The strategies and tools provided in this chapter are designed to help you stay on course, ensuring that your brand remains dynamic, impactful, and true to who you are. By consistently monitoring and refining your brand, you will not only achieve greater professional success but also create a brand that reflects your growth and evolution over time.

In conclusion, Chapter 13 has equipped you with the knowledge and strategies needed to maintain and enhance your personal brand through regular evaluation and adaptation. By embracing a mindset of continuous improvement, staying informed about industry trends, and remaining open to feedback, you will build a brand that not only stands the test of time but also evolves with you, driving long-term success and fulfillment.

Final Conclusion for the book: Building a Lasting Personal Brand

As we come to the end of this journey through *Branding You Mastery*, it's clear that personal branding is not just a strategy—it's an ongoing process that requires dedication, authenticity, and adaptability. This book has guided you through each essential aspect of creating, maintaining, and growing a personal brand that is both impactful and enduring.

We began by understanding the foundational principles of personal branding, exploring how it has evolved from a tool used by high-profile individuals to a necessity for professionals across all industries. As we progressed through the chapters, we delved into the specific strategies for defining your unique value proposition, understanding your target audience, crafting your brand story, and navigating the ethical considerations that come with representing yourself authentically and transparently.

You've learned the importance of content creation and storytelling in amplifying your brand's presence, the critical role of networking and relationship-building in expanding your influence, and the need for continuous evaluation and refinement to keep your brand relevant and effective. Each chapter has equipped you with practical tools and actionable insights to not only build a strong personal brand but also to sustain and grow it in an ever-changing professional landscape.

Throughout this book, a recurring theme has been the importance of staying true to yourself—your values, your goals, and your unique qualities. A personal brand that resonates with your audience is one that is built on authenticity and a deep understanding of both who you are and who you want to serve. As you move forward, let these principles guide your branding efforts, ensuring that your brand is a true reflection of your professional identity and aspirations.

Remember that personal branding is a journey, not a destination. The strategies and concepts you've learned are meant to be revisited and refined as you grow both personally and professionally. The world around us is constantly evolving, and your brand should evolve with it, adapting to new trends, technologies, and opportunities that come your way.

As you continue to build and nurture your personal brand, keep in mind that the most successful brands are those that not only stand out but also stand the test of time. They are brands that are built on trust, credibility, and a commitment to continuous improvement. By embracing these qualities and applying the insights from this book, you will create a personal brand that not only achieves your professional goals but also leaves a lasting impact on your industry and the world.

Thank you for taking this journey through *Branding You Mastery*. Your personal brand is your most valuable asset—cherish it, cultivate it, and let it be the beacon that guides you to your greatest success.

References

Sources, Inspirations, and Credited Works: Acknowledged Literature and Resources

1. **Peters, Tom.** "The Brand Called You." *Fast Company*, August 31, 1997. Link to article.
2. **Gladwell, Malcolm.** *The Tipping Point: How Little Things Can Make a Big Difference.* Little, Brown, and Company, 2000.
3. **Gladwell, Malcolm.** *Outliers: The Story of Success.* Little, Brown, and Company, 2008.
4. **Vaynerchuk, Gary.** *Crush It!: Why NOW Is the Time to Cash In on Your Passion.* Harper Studio, 2009.
5. **Vaynerchuk, Gary.** *Jab, Jab, Jab, Right Hook: How to Tell Your Story in a Noisy Social World.* Harper Business, 2013.
6. **Kelly, Kevin.** "1,000 True Fans." *The Technium*, 4 March 2008,
7. **Ferriss, Tim.** *The 4-Hour Work Week: Escape 9-5, Live Anywhere, and Join the New Rich.* Crown, 2007.
8. **Brown, Brené.** *Daring Greatly: How the Courage to Be Vulnerable Transforms the Way We Live, Love, Parent, and Lead.* Gotham Books, 2012.
9. **Brown, Brené.** *Rising Strong: The Reckoning, the Rumble, the Revolution.* Spiegel & Grau, 2015.
10. **Winfrey, Oprah.** *What I Know for Sure.* Flatiron Books, 2014.
11. **Carnegie, Dale.** *How to Win Friends and Influence People.* Simon & Schuster, 1936.
12. **Ries, Al, and Jack Trout.** *Positioning: The Battle for Your Mind.* McGraw-Hill, 1981.
13. **Hollis, Rachel.** *Girl, Wash Your Face: Stop Believing the Lies About Who You Are so You Can Become Who You Were Meant to Be.* Thomas Nelson, 2018.
14. **Huffington, Arianna.** *Thrive: The Third Metric to Redefining Success and Creating a Life of Well-Being, Wisdom, and Wonder.* Harmony Books, 2014.
15. **Mycoskie, Blake.** *Start Something That Matters.* Spiegel & Grau, 2011.
16. **Carroll, Lewis.** *Alice's Adventures in Wonderland.* Macmillan, 1865.

THE END